The Complete Idiot's Reference Card

Timeline of Ancient Egyptian

- **Early Dynastic or Archaic Period:** Dynasties
  The formative early dynasties of Egypt's develo...

- **Old Kingdom:** Dynasties 3–6, 2686–2181 B.C.
  The great age of pyramid-building, including those at Giza and Sakkara.

- **First Intermediate Period:** Dynasties 7–11, 2181–2055 B.C.
  A time of political disunity in Egypt with rival claims to royal authority.

- **Middle Kingdom:** Dynasties 11–13, 2055–1650 B.C.
  The greatness of Egypt is restored under a single ruler!

- **Second Intermediate Period:** Dynasties 14–17, 1650–1550 B.C.
  Foreign domination by the Hyksos.

- **New Kingdom:** Dynasties 18–20, 1550–1069 B.C.
  The expulsion of the Hyksos led to a rich age of empire and warrior pharaohs.

- **Third Intermediate Period:** Dynasties 21–25, 1069–644 B.C.
  Egypt is again disunited. Nubians rule at the end of this period.

- **Late Period:** Dynasties 26–31, 664–332 B.C.
  Egypt is dominated by the Assyrians and then the Persians.

- **Graeco-Roman Period:** 332 B.C.–A.D. 395 (Ptolemaic Period, 332–30 B.C.; Roman Period, 30 B.C.–A.D. 395)
  Alexander the Great conquers Egypt, and Greeks rule the land until the Romans take charge.

Note: Many of the earlier dates are approximate, and exact calendar years are debatable well into the first millennium B.C.

796473725

Some of the Principal Gods and Goddesses of Ancient Egypt

- **Amun:** The great god of Thebes.
- **Anubis:** Jackal-god patron of embalmers and guardian of cemeteries.
- **Aten:** The sun-disk.
- **Atum:** A creator-god.
- **Bastet:** The cat goddess.
- **Bes:** A curious dwarf-like fellow who was a domestic protector.
- **Geb:** The Earth god.
- **Hapy:** The Nile god.
- **Hathor:** A feminine cow-goddess with a horned headdress.
- **Horus:** A falcon god and the son of Osiris. Identified with the living king.
- **Isis:** Wife of Osiris and mother of Horus.
- **Khnum:** Ram-headed god who created people on a potter's wheel.
- **Khons:** The moon god.
- **Maat:** Goddess of truth, justice, and order.
- **Monthu:** Theban god of war.
- **Mut:** Wife of Amun.
- **Nekhbet:** Vulture goddess representing Upper Egypt.
- **Nephthys:** Wife of Seth and sister of Isis.
- **Nut:** The sky goddess.
- **Osiris:** Husband of Isis and father of Horus, god of the netherworld depicted as a mummified king.
- **Ptah:** Patron of crafts.
- **Ra:** The sun god.
- **Sakhmet:** The fierce lioness wife of Ptah.
- **Seth:** God of chaos, violence, and bad weather.
- **Shu:** The air god.
- **Taweret:** A goddess in the shape of a hippopotamus and a patron to women in childbirth.
- **Tefnut:** The goddess of moisture.
- **Thoth:** The divine scribe and the inventor of writing, associated with the ibis bird and sometimes an ape.
- **Wadjet:** A cobra goddess representing Lower Egypt.

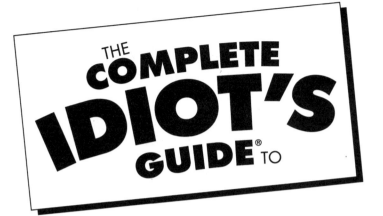

THE COMPLETE IDIOT'S GUIDE® TO

Ancient Egypt

by Donald P. Ryan

ALPHA

A Pearson Education Company

To Sherry and Samuel Ryan, who have tolerated my own version
of Egyptomania for many a year, and in appreciation of Maurice
and Lois Schwartz.

Copyright © 2002 by Donald P. Ryan

International Standard Book Number: 0-02-8642775
Library of Congress Catalog Card Number: 2001097245

04 03 02   8 7 6 5 4 3 2 1

Interpretation of the printing code: The rightmost number of the first series of numbers is the year of the book's printing; the rightmost number of the second series of numbers is the number of the book's printing. For example, a printing code of 02-1 shows that the first printing occurred in 2002.

Printed in the United States of America

Note: This publication contains the opinions and ideas of its author. It is intended to provide helpful and informative material on the subject matter covered. It is sold with the understanding that the author and publisher are not engaged in rendering professional services in the book. If the reader requires personal assistance or advice, a competent professional should be consulted.

The author and publisher specifically disclaim any responsibility for any liability, loss, or risk, personal or otherwise, which is incurred as a consequence, directly or indirectly, of the use and application of any of the contents of this book.

Publisher: *Marie Butler-Knight*
Product Manager: *Phil Kitchel*
Managing Editor: *Jennifer Chisholm*
Senior Acquisitions Editor: *Randy Ladenheim-Gil*
Development Editor: *Jennifer Moore*
Production Editor: *Katherin Bidwell*
Copy Editor: *Krista Hansing*
Illustrator: *Chris Eliopdous*
Cover and Book Designer: *Trina Wurst*
Indexer: *Brad Herriman*
Layout/Proofreading: *Brad Lenser, Mary Hunt*

Contents at a Glance

Contents

Foreword

Pyramids, tombs, mummies, giant statues, golden idols … nothing quite grabs the imagination like ancient Egypt. And it's not just because it's all so old. Even the ancients were astounded by Egypt. The ancient Greek traveler and historian Herodotus said that Egypt "has more wonders in it than in [any] country in the world, and more works that are beyond description than anywhere else." Ancient Babylonian kings were convinced that gold was as plentiful as dust in Egypt.

The modern fascination with Egypt dates to the eighteenth century when European intellectuals such as Wolfgang Amadeus Mozart looked to Egypt as a source of primordial wisdom, a wisdom that was beyond the philosophy of the Greeks or the ethics of the ancient Hebrews. Mozart even wrote an opera about ancient Egypt, "The Magic Flute" (premiered 1791, the year Mozart died)—an opera that has great music but zero information about the real Egypt. You can't blame poor Wolfgang—he died just a few years too early. In 1798, Napoleon Bonaparte brought a team of scholars with him during his abortive attempt to conquer Egypt. The French army was unable to hold on to Egypt and add it to Napoleon's empire, but the French *savants* began to systematically study ancient and modern Egypt in detail for the first time, bringing the wonders of Egypt to an awe-inspired public.

As archaeologists and linguists learned more and more about the real past of Egypt, Egypt's impact on the rest of the world only intensified. Eighty years after "The Magic Flute," a practicing Egyptologist, Auguste Mariette, wrote his own operatic plot, which became the basis for Verdi's *Aida* (premiered 1871), now adapted for Broadway with a score by Tim Rice and Elton John. The discovery of the tomb of Tutankhamun ("King Tut") in 1922 set off a new round of Egyptomania and was closely followed by a series of Hollywood films featuring reanimated mummies that continues to this day. And tales of ancient Egypt have been borrowed to throw light on modern politics: In his 1956 movie, *The Ten Commandments*, director Cecil B. de Mille made an appearance in the opening scene, explaining that his saga of an enslaved peoples' opposition to oppression was a story meant to inspire America and the Free World in the struggle against dictatorship in the twentieth century.

Egypt, more than any other ancient civilization, has been a mirror in which we liked to look at ourselves. But who were the ancient Egyptians really? How did they live, what did they believe, what did they hope for? What purpose did the pyramids actually serve? Why did the Egyptians mummify themselves—not to mention snakes, birds, crocodiles, mice, fish, and other animals by the millions? Why did they walk … well, walk like Egyptians? What really made the ancient Egyptians tick?

The Complete Idiot's Guide to Ancient Egypt, by Donald Ryan, is a book that will answer these questions. Ryan is an expert Egyptologist and an expert communicator, a guy you can trust to give it to you straight, give it to you right, and to not put you to sleep. In this book, Ryan draws upon his years of experience as an archaeologist and explorer of Egypt, as well as his talents as a storyteller and his knowledge of the off-beat and unexplored corners of Egyptology, to explain the mysteries of Egypt as few in the field can. This is a book that will introduce you to the history of Egypt, its strange gods, its customs, its art—everything you need to know to really understand the ancient Egyptians and their fascinating culture.

—Steve Vinson

Steve Vinson is an assistant professor of history at the State University of New York at New Paltz, where he teaches courses on the history of the ancient world. Vinson earned his Ph.D. in Egyptology at the Johns Hopkins University in 1995. He is the author of two books on ancient Egypt and a number of articles on ancient and Graeco-Roman Egypt, and on ancient ships, shipping, and nautical technology. He was a consultant to the Discovery Channel documentary "Cleopatra's Palace, In Search of a Legend."

Introduction

In the 1970s, millions of people waited in long lines to see a selection of objects from the tomb of Tutankhamun. The "King Tut" exhibition started a contemporary wave of enthusiasm for all things ancient Egyptian that hasn't wavered since. Museum exhibitions featuring Egyptian artifacts will always draw a crowd, and millions of tourists visit Egypt each year to see the remains of the ancient civilization for themselves.

Maybe you were one of those people who waited for hours to see the Tutankhamun exhibit, or maybe you've seen something intriguing about Egypt on television or read something in a book or newspaper. With me, it started when I was a small boy leafing through *National Geographic* and finding out about the great archaeological discoveries from Egypt's ancient sands.

In this book, we're going to survey the culture and history of ancient Egypt; in short, you'll be getting an introduction to Egyptology. In Part 1, "Egyptology: Laying the Foundation," we'll start by explaining what Egyptologists do and then provide some basic information about history and geography to set you on your way. In Part 2, "Life and Death in Ancient Egypt," we'll examine some of the life ways of the ancient Egyptians. In Parts 3, "The Pageant of History," and 4, "The Age of Empire," we'll take a romp through a history full of great people and events—pyramids, King Tut, Cleopatra, and even some of the stories in the Bible. In Part 5, "Changing Times, Ideas, and Influences," we're going to explore the latter days of ancient Egypt, examine a few controversial ideas, and look at the interesting effects Egypt has had on those who have come in contact with its intriguing remains. Last, but not least, Part 6, "Ancient Egypt in the Modern World," will offer some serious discussion about the future of Egypt's monuments and also provide you with some sound advice about how to visit the Land of the Pharaohs or become an Egyptologist yourself!

Obviously, there's a lot of ground to cover, and this book can provide you with only a mere sample of all that ancient Egypt has to offer. But after reading this book, you'll have a general feel for the subject and a sense of its many facets. If one aspect doesn't catch your interest, no doubt something else will—or, if you're like me, you'll find it all quite interesting.

Keep in mind that Egyptologists can be an argumentative bunch. Much of what is in this book can be argued in a variety of different ways, and that's part of the scholarly process. In this book, though, you're going to get my basic version of the subject; later, if you want to learn more, you can delve even further into whatever topic strikes your fancy. The last chapter of this book and the appendixes will aid you in pursuing your interest.

By the Way ...

Throughout the book, you'll find the following boxes or sidebars that offer all kinds of information you won't want to miss:

Pharaoh's Domain

In these boxes, you'll find information about some of the interesting people, places, and things of ancient Egypt.

Diggers

These sidebars will introduce you to a few of the archaeologists, Egyptologists, and other investigators of ancient Egypt.

Lost and Found

Archaeologists and Egyptologists are always making new discoveries and drawing new conclusions. Here you'll be privy to some of their findings.

Nile Notes

Fun facts about of the land of the Nile and its people will be floating by in these boxes.

Glyphs

Although they aren't as difficult to comprehend as ancient Egyptian hieroglyphs, there are a lot of terms that you'll want to know as you make your way through ancient Egyptian history and culture. Here you'll find their definitions.

Acknowledgments

Many thanks are extended to Sherry Ryan and my little assistant, Samuel; Mr. and Mrs. M.D. Schwartz; Randy Ladenheim-Gil, Jennifer Moore, Katherin Bidwell, Krista Hansing, and the other fine folks at Alpha Books involved in the editing and production of this book; my various scholarly cohorts, including Brian Holmes, Rick Reanier, Mark Papworth, David Hansen, Daris Swindler, Thor and Jacqueline Heyerdahl, Steve Vinson, Barbara Mertz, Mark Glickman, Joye Hardiman, Nick Reeves, and the gang from *KMT Magazine*; my many excellent colleagues in the Humanities Division at Pacific Lutheran University; and my loyal supporters, including Mr. Jeffrey Belvill, Johnny Rockne, Terry Griffin, Mary Russell, Hugh Crowder, Lynne and John Cole, Lisa and Richmond Prehn, Patricia Armstrong, Prof. Robert Ryan, and Jane Ho. Thanks to Egyptological colleagues who made suggestions, and special thanks to the technical editor of this book and an outstanding Egyptologist, Dr. David Lorton; another special thanks to R.J.W., who, 20 years ago, gave a young man a chance to visit Egypt for the first time.

Special Thanks to the Technical Reviewer

The Complete Idiot's Guide to Ancient Egypt was reviewed by an expert who double-checked the accuracy of what you'll learn here, to help us ensure that this book gives you everything you need to know about ancient Egypt. Special thanks are extended to Dr. David Lorton for his technical review.

David Lorton earned a doctorate in Egyptology at Johns Hopkins University. He works as a translator of books on Egyptology for Cornell University Press and has authored and co-authored books and articles on the subject of ancient Egypt.

Trademarks

All terms mentioned in this book that are known to be or are suspected of being trademarks or service marks have been appropriately capitalized. Alpha Books and Pearson Education, Inc., cannot attest to the accuracy of this information. Use of a term in this book should not be regarded as affecting the validity of any trademark or service mark.

Part 1

Egyptology: Laying the Foundation

Before launching into the history and culture of ancient Egypt, the novice Egyptologist should know some basic things: What happened to the ancient Egyptian civilization? How do Egyptologists learn about the past? How did Egyptology begin?

Once you have the answers to these questions under your belt, you'll also learn a little about Egypt's geography and history, to which we'll be adding more detail in future chapters. Finally, because much of our knowledge of the ancient Egyptians is based on what they themselves wrote, we'll take a look at their ancient language, including the fascinating hieroglyphic writing system.

Egypt: The Loss and Recovery of an Ancient Civilization

In This Chapter

- How we lost track of ancient Egypt
- Agents of transformation and destruction
- Old insights into Egypt
- Recovering the leftovers
- Different approaches of Egyptology

Ancient Egypt is old! How old? Well, many "ancient" Greeks and Romans visited Egypt in order to see the antiquities. In fact, when the Greek historian Herodotus claims to have visited Egypt in 450 B.C., the famous pyramids at Giza were already about 2,000 years old. This is a chronological distance about the same as between the time of Jesus and our present age! Before the building of those magnificent pyramids, what we call Egyptian civilization had already developed and flourished for about 500 years!

It Came and It Went

The ancient Egyptian civilization was certainly one of the most technologically and artistically sophisticated cultures that this world has ever seen. The

Egyptians sustained a sizable population and accomplished magnificent building projects, and their mighty army engaged in adventures abroad. They were governed by grandiose rulers and were supported by a vast civil and religious bureaucracy in a society maintained by farmers and craftspeople.

This unique civilization persisted for about 3,000 years, from about 3100 B.C. to 30 B.C. Given the complexity and longevity of this magnificent culture, perhaps it is surprising that it is essentially extinct. Yes, bits and pieces do survive, especially in certain agricultural and village practices, but the living grandeur of ancient Egypt is no more. Indeed, so much knowledge has been lost that a whole scholarly discipline appeared around 200 years ago with the aim of studying, reconstructing, and explaining ancient Egypt. It's called *Egyptology*, and its practitioners are *Egyptologists*. Even with the vast amount of information that has been recovered over the last couple of centuries, some might argue that we've still only scratched the surface, and a true vision of an amazing ancient reality has yet to be achieved.

Glyphs

Egyptology is the study of ancient Egypt.

Where Did It Go?

So what happened to ancient Egyptian culture and, thus, the need to rediscover it? You might say that it never really vanished, but was transformed. In future chapters, we will learn how the classical Egyptian culture flourished up until about 1000 B.C., after which it had a hard time maintaining its grip in the face of outside invaders who brought political domination and foreign cultural practices. After the time of what is called Egypt's New Kingdom (c. 1550–1069 B.C.), there were periods of civil disorganization during which rulers from such places as Nubia, Libya, and Persia held sway. (You'll read more about these invasions in Chapter 17, "Uninvited Visitors").

Lost and Found

The notion of the "rise and fall" of civilizations is disliked by some scholars. By what standards can you measure such things, especially on a large scale? On the other hand, a focus on transformation and change emphasizes that these are processes rather than merely events.

Alexander Came to Call

The Greeks, who became dominant in Egypt beginning in 332 B.C. with Alexander the Great's conquest of Egypt, had the biggest impact on Egyptian civilization. The Greeks were not content merely to rule; instead, they actively engaged in spreading their own culture. Many Greeks immigrated to Egypt and were widely established in Egyptian territory. The Greek language became the norm within the government and among literate people. In fact, the Egyptian city of Alexandria became the preeminent Greek cosmopolitan cultural center in the Mediterranean.

After about 300 years of Greek rule, the Romans incorporated Egypt into their own growing empire. Although they were not the cultural imperialists like the Greeks, they nonetheless had an impact on Egyptian culture.

Turning to God

Of vital importance, in terms of cultural transformation, was the introduction of major new religious philosophies that had a radical impact on the old Egyptian ways. Christianity appeared in neighboring Palestine during the first century A.D. and spread to Egypt relatively quickly, perhaps around A.D. 50. The religion shunned the ancient Egyptian gods, along with their priests, practices, and temples. A preference for the use of a modified Greek alphabet to write the ancient Egyptian language, especially for religious purposes, led to the eventual demise of the old cumbersome system of hieroglyphs. (See Chapter 4, "Glyphs," for more about this ancient form of writing.)

Perhaps the greatest transforming effect of all was the Arab invasion of A.D. 642. Arming themselves with their new Islamic religion, the Arabs established themselves in Egypt during a remarkable sweep across North Africa and many other lands. The impact was lasting. The Arabic language is spoken today in the Arab Republic of Egypt, and although there is still a Christian minority, Islam is the official state religion.

The subsequent history of Egypt is complicated. Turks ruled there for a time, and both the French and British were politically involved. It wasn't until 1952 that the Egyptians again were fully in control of their own country—it had been well over 2,000 years since they last controlled it. No wonder we are left to pick up the scattered pieces!

Hard Survivors

Unfortunately, the destructive processes of nature, time, and humans have not been particularly kind to the remains of ancient Egypt. Certain things have survived quite well, while others have left little or no trace. What have survived best are those special things that were built to last for all eternity: temples and tombs of stone. Many of these have survived fairly well, some incredibly so. But just because the temples and tombs have survived while there are few traces of other structures, such as houses, we need to be wary of gaining the impression that religion and death were the primary focus of ancient Egyptian existence.

Climate and location also play a huge role in preservation. Few of the villages where millions of

> **Nile Notes**
>
> Suppose that something terrible happened to wipe out our civilization, and archaeologists of the future excavated only our churches and other religious structures and our cemeteries. What a curious impression of our culture they might gain!

ordinary ancient Egyptians once lived have survived. Their homes were built of bricks of mud and organic materials, which have long since been broken down due to the annual flooding of the Nile, wind erosion, or other natural processes.

In the Nile Delta region in the north of Egypt, the climate is not well suited to preserving the past. The water table is high, the air can be humid, and even things made of stone can suffer considerable erosion. The drier climate in the south, though, has allowed for some remarkable preservation, especially for those things buried in the desert or hidden away in dry cliffs and valleys.

We can't lay the blame solely on nature, though. Humans, too, have had a significant hand in the loss of the ancient civilization. Apart from the cultural transformations noted, humans have destroyed many of the ancient artifacts. Some of the destruction has been in order to reuse some of the materials—ancient sites, for example, sometimes provided the raw material for new buildings. Pyramids were quarried for excellent stones, and the rotting debris of old town sites was sometimes mined for rich fertilizer.

The ancient site of Dimai, or Soknopaiou Nesos, to use its Greek name, stands silent and isolated in the desert on the north side of Egypt's Fayyum region, a mere shadow of its former splendor.

There have also been many examples of destruction of the ancient monuments by religious zealots and those seeking golden treasure. Old wooden funerary statues, coffin planks, and papyrus scrolls have served as fire wood for the living. Antiquities hunters and the sometimes crude methods of early archaeologists have all taken their toll.

Through Foreigners' Eyes

Until relatively recently, people in Europe, North America, and elsewhere were aware of the existence of ancient Egypt, but only indirectly. Egypt was known primarily from two sources: the Holy Bible (see Chapter 16, "Egypt and the Holy Book") and ancient Greek and Roman writers.

The Bible Tells You So

In the Bible, Egypt is mentioned numerous times. Notably, there is the highly cherished story of Joseph and his coat of many colors and Egyptian palace intrigue. The story of the Exodus, in which God delivers the Hebrew people from Egyptian enslavement, is a key story in the Jewish religion. Along with the accompanying spiritual and moral lessons, these biblical stories contained cultural and geographical data that shaped a vague notion of Egyptian society and places for readers of the Bible. Egypt in the Bible was portrayed as a powerful, industrious society that worshipped many gods and was ruled by a Pharaoh and his coterie of priests, governors, and functionaries. You'll have a chance to read more about Egypt's role in the Bible in Chapter 16.

It's Greek to Me!

Apart from the Bible, literate individuals could derive information about ancient Egypt by reading the surviving documents of old Greek and Roman writers who visited the land and wrote down their insights. As noted at the beginning of the chapter, one Greek author, Herodotus, is said to have visited Egypt around 450 B.C. He has left us with a lengthy and patchy—yet, at times, detailed—description of the land and culture.

Herodotus describes Egypt as a very odd place indeed, full of unusual customs and practices. The report contains quite a bit of anecdotal material that might not be wholly accurate. Herodotus's lengthy description of the Egyptians is sometimes so at odds with what we now know about that ancient civilization that some doubt that he ever actually went there! Perhaps he collected his information from the cosmopolitan visitors and sailors coming through the port of his Greek home town, Halicarnassus.

Pharaoh's Domain _____

Herodotus (c. 484–420 B.C.) was a Greek historian from the city of Halicarnassus, located on the Ionian coast of what is today Turkey. His principle surviving work is known as "The Histories." Along with a description of Egypt, it contains a vital record of the Persian Wars and other historical events around the time of what is called Greece's "Golden Age" in the fifth century B.C. Because of his early efforts at recording events, Herodotus is sometimes called "the father of history."

Despite the suspicion, it's likely that Herodotus did indeed visit Egypt, but he was doing so at a time when the glory days of classical Egyptian civilization were long over. The pyramids were already ancient, the mighty empire-building pharaohs had long been mummified, and Egypt was under the domination of the Persians. Herodotus was probably collecting information from a lot of people who themselves did not understand the monuments and much of the old culture. It was ancient to them, too, and was dying out.

Nile Notes

Many scholars think that late foreign visitors to Egypt, such as Herodotus, might have been gullible to fanciful stories told by creative guides or others who themselves were misinformed. Modern tourists can enjoy the same experience from informal guides at various archaeological sites who will be pleased to show you many secret "wonders." Don't forget to give them that big tip they're expecting!

Picking Up the Pieces

We'll look at the development of Egyptology as a scholarly pursuit in the next chapter, but, for now, let's take a look at the subject matter of that fascinating field of inquiry as it is practiced today. Egyptology is certainly one of the most interdisciplinary branches of learning to be found—that is, it incorporates insights, methods, and data from many different subject areas that are relevant to our search for the Egyptian past. It is a subject that you might classify within the humanities, yet it has aspects of both the social and natural sciences, and the fine arts as well. Let's take a look at some of the approaches.

Studying Texts

Fortunately, ancient Egypt was a literate society in the sense that there was a writing system, and there were people who could read and write. Many texts have survived, especially on formal monuments, and some Egyptologists are genuine experts in ferreting out the subtleties of these written materials (see Chapter 4 for more on this). A lot of Egyptology is text-oriented, and it is from inscriptions that we are best able to sort out many of the historical details that we now have.

Not surprisingly, many scholars continue to study and refine all that we can determine from what the Egyptians themselves wrote. Translating the words is one thing, but figuring out what they mean in the context of the ancient culture is vitally important. It's important, for example, to be able to tell the difference between a statement intended as religious propaganda and one meant as a public decree, or the difference between a historical account and a myth. These are things that must be carefully sorted out in our search for a reliable picture of the past.

> ### Lost and Found
>
> You might argue that in terms of surviving writing, Egyptology is somewhat spoiled by its riches. In places such as nearby Israel, where ancient inscriptions are few, archaeologists have become experts in identifying pottery styles through time, often to within a few years of their manufacture. In Egypt, the date and owner of an object, tomb, or monument can be identified merely by reading an accompanying inscription. As a result, there are few real pottery experts in the Egyptological world.

Ancient Art

Some Egyptologists specialize in art history. Much can be learned by the study of artistic and architectural styles and techniques, as well as their changes through the years.

Although much of the public might have the stereotypical notion that Egyptian art was essentially static through time, this is certainly not the case. Much of ancient Egyptian art is very symbolic, from the strong, idealized sculptures in stone representing the power of the ruler to the often subtle and esoteric meanings expressed on the walls of tombs and temples. The study of art provides insight in ways that other approaches cannot.

> ### Nile Notes
>
> Experts on Egyptian art can sometimes identify the handiwork of individual ancient artisans; tomb paintings, in particular, have been attributed to specific artists.

Too Many Cooks Do *Not* Spoil the Stew!

Most scholarly and scientific disciplines have something to contribute to Egyptology. Biologists can help reconstruct the environment and assist in studying mummies and the remains of other once-living things. Geologists can help us determine the sources of stone and precious metals, and chemists can add insights into various materials as well. Anthropologists can draw on their comparative knowledge of cultural practices to contribute insights. Engineers can help us understand the techniques of the past and help us protect the monuments for the future. And the list goes on. The end result is a growing and gradually more complete view of the ancient Egyptian past.

Dirt Diggers

Of all the approaches within Egyptology, *archaeology* receives the most attention. The public loves the glamour of discovery, and Egypt regularly delivers such glamorous discoveries. There's something about searching for and finding things of the past that has widespread appeal. The discovery of King Tut's tomb accelerated an interest that has barely slowed down since. Today, even relatively minor discoveries in Egypt have received significant public attention.

The Indiana Jones movies certainly have added to the mystique of archaeology, even though he's definitely a fictional character and his approach to antiquities is less than scientific. (And if someone tells you that someone is or was the living inspiration for that character, don't believe it: I.J.'s creators made him up!) But to the public, Indiana Jones has become a frame of reference for action and adventure in archaeology. Believe me, there can be lots of excitement in archaeology, but rarely the exaggerated swashbuckling that Indiana Jones serves up.

Archaeology usually involves some sort of careful digging. The level of difficulty of an archaeological project can vary, depending upon where you happen to be digging—consider the difference between excavating in a remote desert, where you have to bring all of your supplies, including water, with you, and digging in a highly populated region, where all the amenities are close at hand. No matter where the dig is, though, the work can be strenuous and expensive. And there is often a need for some of the specialists mentioned previously and a knowledge of history, hieroglyphs, and art.

Glyphs

Archaeology is the study of the human past. It tends to emphasize the physical remains of the past and has developed many of its own methodologies for excavation and artifact analysis.

Diggers

In North America, archaeology is generally considered to be a subdiscipline of anthropology. Part of this is the result of the historical development of those subjects: The cultural anthropologists learned about the living Native Americans, while the archaeologists examined the remains of their past.

Archaeologists from all over the world work in Egypt, including scholars from Britain, France, Germany, Australia, Poland, the Czech Republic, Japan, and the United States. Some even have permanent research centers based in Cairo or elsewhere in the country. And, of course, the Egyptians themselves are busy at work conducting their own explorations, along with taking responsibility for the antiquities in general and supervising the scientific activities of foreigners. You'll learn a lot more about archaeology in some of the chapters ahead.

Unsung Heroes

While archaeologists often get the majority of attention in the Egyptological world, some of the most important work is done by the *epigraphers*, specialists in recording the decoration and texts found on ancient monuments. In Egypt, where many human and natural forces continue to erode and destroy the ancient temples, tombs, and other antiquities, the epigraphers are racing against time to make permanent and accurate records of paintings and inscriptions that hopefully will survive if the original monuments do not.

Chicago House, based in Luxor, Egypt, is the most famous foreign mission involved in epigraphy. It is affiliated with the Oriental Institute of the University of Chicago and has been actively recording monuments in the Luxor area with photographs and line-drawings since it was founded in 1924. The work of the Chicago House epigraphers is extremely precise; they are not only actively involved in making records, but they also work on the conservation of the actual monuments.

Glyphs _____

Epigraphy is the art of recording inscriptions, and an **epigrapher** is the person who does the recording.

An Egyptologist examining an ancient tomb painting.

Lost and Found

Believe it or not, donkeys and horses have made a number of significant archaeological discoveries in Egypt. A stumbling horse, for example, found a strange underground passage in the Luxor area leading to a ceremonial statue. In the Bahariya Oasis, a donkey found what has become known as "The Valley of the Golden Mummies," a cemetery containing perhaps hundreds (or more) of gold-gilded burials.

The Real Things

So where are the remains of the ancient Egyp-tian culture to be found today? Large quantities of Egyptian antiquities have made their way to distant lands. We'll go into more detail about how that happened in the next chapter. Some of these exported antiquities are now in private hands, while others are housed in museums, where they can be enjoyed by the public. But much of what remains is still in Egypt … and perhaps the greatest treasures are yet to be discovered!

The Least You Need to Know

◆ The ancient Egyptian civilization thrived for about 3,000 years.

◆ Foreign invasions and new religions, languages, and cultures transformed the ancient culture, contributing to its loss.

◆ Until the field of Egyptology became established, the Bible and the works of old Greek and Roman authors served as limited sources of information about ancient Egypt.

◆ Egyptology employs a number of approaches to learn about the past, including the study of ancient texts, art, and the interdisciplinary practice of archaeology.

Rediscovering the Past

In This Chapter

- ◆ Napoleon invades Egypt
- ◆ Antiquities free-for-all
- ◆ Early Egyptologists
- ◆ Petrie sets some standards
- ◆ Modern Egyptology comes of age

As we saw in Chapter 1, "Egypt: The Loss and Recovery of an Ancient Civilization," a greater knowledge of ancient Egypt was lost long ago, and it would be many centuries before much of it was recovered. In this chapter, we're going to look briefly at this recovery process, including some of the key events and players. It's a story full of adventure, speculation, and genuine scholarship.

The Greeks, Again

As mentioned in the last chapter, the Greeks and Romans marveled at the remains of Egypt's past. Several travelers and writers have left us with some intriguing accounts. Apart from Herodotus, Greek writers Diodorus Siculus (c. 59 B.C.) and Plutarch (c. A.D. 50–120) provided some fascinating information, including insights into ancient mythology. Roman writer Strabo

(64 B.C.–A.D. 22) recorded a good deal of geographical information, as did Pliny the Elder (23–A.D. 79) The Romans, in particular, collected some antiquities and displayed them in Rome and Constantinople.

Travelers and Religious Pilgrims Drop In

Not too many works specifically address ancient Egyptian antiquities after the Arab invasion in A.D. 642, but a few travelers' comments survive, as do some observations made by Arab writers. Egypt was becoming a real center of Arab and Islamic culture, so it is no surprise that there doesn't appear to be an overwhelming interest in the debris of the distant past. During the European Middle Ages, though, travelers and religious pilgrims occasionally made their way into Egypt. Few ventured much farther south than the Cairo region, but a visit to the pyramids would not have been unusual.

Lost and Found

The Romans brought more than a dozen obelisks, stone shafts with pyramid-shaped tops, from Egypt to Rome. Others eventually ended up in such places as Constantinople (now Istanbul), Paris, London, and New York.

The interpretations of these early travelers were no doubt greatly colored by the Classical Greek and Roman writers and the Bible. The pyramids, for example, might have been viewed as the handiwork of Hebrew slaves (they weren't) or perhaps hollow granaries (wrong again), which relate to the biblical story of Joseph. Or, it might have been easy to envision that the Great Pyramid at Giza was built under the direction of the cruel pharaoh Cheops, as Herodotus reported (there is no evidence that Cheops was a particularly cruel pharaoh).

Diggers

Apart from lists of kings and such, few records demonstrate that the Egyptians themselves took much of an interest in exploring the remains of their own past. However, there are some rare examples: An Egyptian prince named Khaemwaset (c. 1250 B.C.) apparently took an interest in the monuments of some of his much earlier royal ancestors and engaged in some restoration work. Although this doesn't necessarily demonstrate a flair for archaeology, it does provide an ancient example of concern for the past.

Europeans Start Taking Egypt Seriously

Although these reports are interesting, what might be considered genuine exploration of Egyptian territory by Westerners didn't really begin until around the seventeenth and eighteenth centuries. During that period, some hardy European adventurers traveled south down the Nile, recording their observations and sometimes publishing them. The French Jesuit priest Claude Sicard (1677–1726), for example, set out on a mission to convert Egyptian Coptic Christians to Roman Catholicism. Whether successful in that regard or not, he managed to travel farther south—all the way to the Aswan region—than previous explorers and made plans, drawings, and written observations.

The Englishman Rev. Richard Pockoke (1704–1765) and Danish naval officer Frederik Norden (1708–1742) both explored Egypt around the same time, about 1737–1738. Trips up the Nile could be somewhat dangerous, with potential hostilities in those days, and it's surprising how persistent some of these early visitors were. Their reports were published and translated into other European languages, which served to pique further interest in the mysterious land of Egypt.

Meanwhile, back in Europe, objects from ancient Egypt were not unknown. Travelers and merchants brought back strange curiosities such as old amulets and other antiquities that no doubt invited plenty of speculation. Perhaps most strange was the trade in mummy products (see Chapter 8, "Mummies for Dummies"). A demand grew in Europe for ground-up Egyptian mummies because the resulting powder was believed to have medicinal benefits and also was a desired ingredient in some artists' paints.

Archaeological societies and museums formed in England and elsewhere during the 1700s, providing forums for learned men to discuss such things as Greek and Roman antiquities, the origin of such ancient sites as Stonehenge, the purposes of old stone tools found in the earth, and Egyptian antiquities as well. The British Museum in London, for example, was founded in 1753 and provided a home for a growing collection of antiquities from widely scattered locales.

Lost and Found

The British Museum was founded around a diverse collection of natural history specimens and artifacts, including some of Egyptian origin, that belonged to Sir Hans Sloane (1660–1753). The museum got its first mummy in 1756.

Napoleon the Egyptologist?

Between the odd objects and the scattered reports of travelers, the notion of Egypt as a strange and mysterious home to a lost civilization was reinforced. As unlikely as it might seem, it was a dramatic military adventure that finally created a scholarly discipline out of the study of Egypt's past.

In 1798, a huge French land and naval force under the command of Napoleon Bonaparte arrived in Egypt. The French, in intense competition with the British, were hoping to secure trade routes to the riches of India and the Far East. This well-planned expedition not only was composed of military personnel, but it also included a diverse group of nearly 175 scholars and special technicians whose job it was to observe and record the many facets of Egypt. There were natural scientists to study plants, animals, and other resources; surveyors; and mapmakers. Some noted the customs and practices of the native people, while others were artists and antiquarians with an interest in researching the remains of ancient Egypt.

These scholars accompanied the French army and conducted their work sometimes even in the heat of battle. Although it might all seem noble, there is little doubt that these scholars were sincere. It appears that their presence was not merely due to French cultural sophistication; the information that they gathered could be used by the likes of Napoleon to better control and exploit Egypt's people and resources. On the other hand, the French were quick to initiate a scholarly institution, the *Institut d'Égypte*, which they established in 1798.

> ### Nile Notes
>
> The artists accompanying Napoleon's expedition operated in the days before photography, yet many of their drawings exhibit almost photographic quality. One of their tools was a device called a camera lucida, which reflected an image to be drawn upon a piece of paper for tracing.

A drawing of the temple at Armant by Napoleon's artists.

(From Description de L'Égypte.*)*

The British quickly became aware of the French occupation of strategic Egyptian territory and brought their own fleet across the Mediterranean. A nasty battle at Aboukir, off the Egyptian coast, resulted in the destruction of the French naval force, effectively stranding Napoleon's army. His scholars continued their work, but the French eventually surrendered in 1801. The victorious English confiscated some of the choicer bits of antiquity collected by the French, including the famed Rosetta Stone that facilitated the eventual decipherment of the hieroglyphs.

Although the French were defeated, the scholars of Napoleon's expedition had a lasting impact—to such an extent that they are often credited with founding the field of Egyptology. Returning home with their notes and drawings, they edited a monumental report of their findings published under the title *Description de L'Égypte*. The sumptuous volumes comprising the report not only served as a magnificent research report, but they also stimulated an interest in Egypt within the literate communities in Europe. The *Description* is still considered a magnificent achievement today.

Welcome to the "Wild West"

After the French were defeated by the British, Egypt fell back under the control of the Ottoman Turkish rulers. It was up to them, for the time, at least, to decide to what extent foreigners would be allowed to conduct business or other activities in that land. One such ruler, Mohammed Ali, was somewhat open-minded about European contributions to a developing Egypt and invited foreigners to present their ideas for modernizing the country. This set the stage for one of the most intriguing characters in all the history of archaeology: Giovanni Battista Belzoni.

Circus-Giant Egyptologist

Belzoni was born in 1778 in Padua, Italy. He was a very large man and eventually ended up in London, where he played giants in the theater and performed a strongman act in street carnivals. Hearing of Mohammed Ali's desire for Western technology, Belzoni traveled to Egypt with the idea for a revolutionary waterwheel to be used in irrigation. The design failed to impress, leaving Belzoni, his wife, and a servant essentially stranded in Egypt without many funds.

Lost and Found

During the last several years, French archaeologists have located and studied the remains of Napoleon's destroyed fleet underwater at Aboukir. The findings have provided unique insights into the famous battle and serve as an example of how archaeology can be applied to relatively recent sites with interesting results.

Nile Notes

Despite his shortcomings (no pun intended), Napoleon Bonaparte, left a lasting positive mark by facilitating the group of scholars that accompanied his Egyptian expedition. In fact, in several cases, the *Description* is the only record of monuments, or portions thereof, that have since decayed or have been destroyed.

A portrait of Giovanni Belzoni.

At that time, a mad scramble for antiquities was about to begin, pitting rival nations against each other to compete for the best possible antiquities for their home countries and museums. Belzoni entered the fray when he accepted a commission from the British consul in Cairo to retrieve for the glory of Britain a large stone head from a temple about 400 miles upstream. This he was able to do, and thus began his career as an explorer, excavator, and collector. Among his many accomplishments, Belzoni …

◆ Was the first man known to excavate in the royal cemetery known as the Valley of the Kings.

◆ Was the first known Westerner to enter the sand-engulfed temple of Ramesses II at Abu Simbel.

◆ Studied the pyramids at Giza, which allowed him to discover the entrance to the pyramid of Khafra.

◆ Retrieved numerous objects of antiquity, both large and small, which made their way back to England and elsewhere.

The competition for antiquities was often ugly, and threats of violence eventually drove Belzoni back to England in 1819. He brought many antiquities with him, along with detailed records of some of his discoveries. He wrote a book that became quite popular, and he set up an Egyptian exhibition in London, contributing to his celebrity. Belzoni died in 1823 during a short-lived attempt to find the source of the Niger River.

Not Bad ... in His Day!

Belzoni became something of a folk hero in his day. To more recent scholars, however, he is often the character cited to represent the worst of the early nineteenth-century exploitation of Egypt's antiquities. His book unabashedly describes crawling through mummy-choked tunnels, using a battering-ram as a tomb-opening device, and accidentally dropping an obelisk into the Nile. These kinds of antics, unfortunately, were far from unusual in his day. But what sets Belzoni apart from many of his peers is that he actually recorded and mapped many of his discoveries and then published much of that information. That's a far cry from the random snatch-and-grab tactics of the average collector in those times!

> ### Nile Notes
>
> The complete title of Belzoni's popular book is *Narrative of the Operations and Recent Discoveries Within the Pyramids, Temples, Tombs, and Excavations, in Egypt and Nubia; and of a Journey to the Coast of the Red Sea, in Search of the Ancient Berenice; and Another to the Oasis of Jupiter Ammon.* The book was accompanied by 40 hand-colored plates, of which an additional 6 were later issued. Today it is a rare and very expensive collector's item.

Scholars and Artists, Take Note

The activities of Napoleon's scholars, and even the work of the likes of Belzoni, brought Egypt increasingly to the attention of more scholars. And with the puzzle of the hieroglyphs proclaimed solved in 1822 (see Chapter 4, "Glyphs,"), more scholars became interested in visiting Egypt to record and study its numerous monuments covered in hieroglyphs or other items of artistic merit.

Several expeditions set out with such purposes in mind. The decipherer of the hieroglyphs, the Frenchman Jean-François Champollion, along with the first Italian Egyptologist, Ippolito Rosellini (1800–1843), ventured out in 1828–1829 and returned to publish their findings. Even more ambitious was the Prussian expedition led by Karl Lepsius (1810–1884). Between 1842 and 1845 the well-organized and equipped expedition covered a tremendous amount of territory, all the while mapping, drawing, and collecting antiquities and making casts of others. They even ventured far south into the Sudan and east to Sinai and Palestine. The result of their achievement is a tremendous published report containing hundreds of accurate folio plates entitled *Denkmäler aus Aegypten und Aethiopien.* Like the French *Description*, this work is still regularly consulted today.

Cracking Down

With the increase in the number of scholars and laymen interested in Egypt, an unregulated antiquities market grew to meet the demand, and widespread informal digging and looting became increasingly common. Recognizing the potential catastrophic loss of knowledge as a result of such activities, Champollion and others formally expressed a desire for some sort of government control on the free-for-all antiquities grab in progress. In 1835, a government antiquities conservation ordinance was issued, although the effect was likely minimal.

Enter a Talented Frenchmen ...

Things finally began to change with the appearance in Egypt of a Frenchman by the name of Auguste Mariette (1821–1881). Mariette went to Egypt to collect early Christian (Coptic) manuscripts, but he ended up excavating pharaonic monuments instead and became one of the most significant individuals in the history of Egyptology.

> **Diggers**
>
> Careful archaeological methods were barely known in the early nineteenth century, and there are many examples of dubious excavation methods that make archaeologists cringe today. In 1837, for example, a British military officer named Richard Vyse and an engineer named John Perring used gunpowder to blast their way into the pyramid of Menkaura at Giza.

Mariette excavated numerous sites all over Egypt, amassing a collection that served as the basis for the first national museum in Egypt itself. He also became the first director of the Egyptian antiquities service in 1858, a government organization created to control activities involving the remains of Egypt's past, including issuing permits for excavation and attempting to reign in illicit digging and exportation of national treasures.

Mariette's successor, Gaston Maspero (1846–1916) was a true scholar and certainly one of the better directors of the antiquities service. He served during two periods: 1881–1886 and 1899–1914. Under Maspero's direction, the antiquities service matured into a professional organization. The supervision of archaeological activities increased, and the present Egyptian Museum in Cairo was opened.

Egyptian Archaeology Is Revolutionized

While the recording of texts and paintings in Egypt had been performed with relative competency for many years, excavation techniques remained somewhat crude during the late nineteenth century. And although a few people in Europe were precisely recording their excavations, what might be called modern archaeological technique was still in its very early stages. This changed, however, with big advances in Egyptian archaeology, and archaeology in general, made via the contributions of a brilliant Englishman by the name of William Matthew Flinders Petrie (1853–1942).

Trained in surveying, Petrie came to Egypt in 1880 to measure the pyramids in order to test a theory that their measurements embodied a mystical calendar. His findings showed otherwise, and thus began his long and stellar archaeological career, which lasted long enough to allow him to publish an autobiography entitled *Seventy Years in Archaeology*. Petrie's major contribution was to set high standards for archaeological excavation—a systematic approach that required the careful recording of objects as they were found, their conservation thereafter, and formal publication of the findings.

The Archaeological Record

Archaeology can often be a destructive process. When something is dug up, it is usually removed from its ancient context. Knowing exactly where something was found and with what other items is vital to understanding an object and its role in a culture. This contextual information is extremely desirable but is generally unavailable from random digging or for objects purchased from antiquities dealers, as was so often the case in early Egyptology. Petrie recognized the importance of recording the details as a dig was taking place because it was the only chance to get much of the information. His 1904 book, *Methods and Aims in Archaeology*, was a practical textbook of sound archaeological technique for others to follow.

Unlike many of his early peers, Petrie did not focus only on collecting the larger or prettier objects; instead, he was interested in retrieving the totality of information. He set an example by publishing many volumes dedicated to smaller objects or those related to everyday life. Petrie, who is often called "the father of Palestinian archaeology" for his pioneering work in the Holy Land, trained many of the better archaeologists of his day. Despite the notoriously spartan living conditions in his field camps, an apprenticeship with Petrie was probably one of the best archaeological educations available.

> **Nile Notes**
>
> Even with government controls, many travelers from Egypt in the late nineteenth century returned with all manner of interesting souvenirs. Antiquities dealers were more than happy to fulfill tourists' desires for artifacts, including mummies still in their coffins and even valuable papyrus documents from time to time.

> **Lost and Found**
>
> For an easy introduction to the subject of archaeology, check out *The Complete Idiot's Guide to Lost Civilizations*, by yours truly.

Nile Notes

The London-based Egypt Exploration Fund was founded in 1882 with the purpose of funding and facilitating the survey, exploration, excavation, and publication of Egyptian archaeological sites. Today it is known as the Egypt Exploration Society, and it remains very active in the sponsorship and publication of Egyptological activities.

Diggers

James Henry Breasted (1865–1935) became the first professor of Egyptology in the United States. He was particularly interested in historical inscriptions, and he traveled extensively in Egypt to record as many as possible. He was the founder and director of the prestigious Oriental Institute at the University of Chicago, and he initiated the famous Epigraphic Survey that is busy recording Egypt's monuments to this day.

Egyptology Blooms

The late nineteenth century was a very active time for archaeological work. More scholarly institutions and support societies were formed, and Egyptologists were becoming well-established members of museums and universities. Egyptology was truly beginning to mature. Many museums sponsored excavations in exchange for a share of the artifacts. The antiquities service in Egypt supervised this "division," keeping the objects that it felt were best suited for the national collection.

By the beginning of the twentieth century, Egyptology and archaeological excavation techniques had become quite sophisticated. Foreign scholarly institutions continued to establish permanent facilities in Egypt, which remain there to this day. And as is only right, more Egyptian scholars became involved in studying their past. Although initially directed by the French, the Egyptians took over responsibility for their own antiquities after their national revolution in 1952. Today the Egyptian Supreme Council of Antiquities manages and regulates all aspects of Egyptian antiquities. The council conducts many of its own excavations and conservation projects, maintains a number of museums within Egypt, and considers requests for foreign projects.

Over the centuries, the study of ancient Egypt moved from the merely speculative interest of the Greeks to the destructive looting and antiquities dealing of the early Western explorer-adventurers, to the rigorous and disciplined study of the past that it is today. And through it all, it's likely that Egyptologists have only scratched the surface of the past.

The Least You Need to Know

◆ Early European visitors occasionally took notice of Egyptian antiquities, although with only a limited knowledge of their meaning.

◆ The scholars accompanying Napoleon's invasion of Egypt are often considered the founders of Egyptology.

◆ During the nineteenth century, many antiquities collectors, scholars, artists, and excavators began working.

◆ William Matthew Flinders Petrie helped formulate modern archaeological methods for excavating in Egypt and elsewhere.

◆ Modern Egyptology is a sophisticated scholarly discipline involving Egyptians and other participants from around the world.

Ancient Egypt in Space and Time

In This Chapter

- ◆ The wonders of the Nile River
- ◆ Egyptian geography
- ◆ How Egyptian history is organized
- ◆ Time terms
- ◆ Dating the past

You probably already know that Egypt is in Africa, that a large part of it is desert, and that the Nile River runs through it. But there are some other aspects to Egypt's geography that will be important for you to know in order to make sense of the country's ancient past. In this chapter, we will consider the unique features of Egypt's geography that allowed the ancient civilization to flourish, and then we'll look at the system Egyptologists use to organize that culture's history.

On the Map

Egypt is situated in the northeast corner of the African continent. If you look at a modern map or globe, you'll see some straight lines on the south and west, and the Mediterranean and Red Seas on the north and east. These are modern political boundaries. Do not confuse them with the area of ancient Egypt—they aren't the same.

The civilization of ancient Egypt grew up around the Nile River. A lot of the area to the east and west on the modern map was desert then, just as it is today, and in ancient times as in modern ones, the vast majority of the population lived along the banks of the Nile or its triangular northern Delta. In concept, it's better to look at the land of Egypt in a way much different then the modern map. Think of it as looking like a beautiful lotus flower, with the Nile River forming its stem and the broad Delta as its bloom!

Map of Egypt.

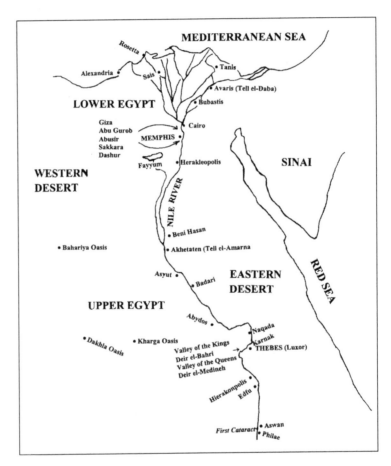

Gift of the Nile

The Nile is the longest river in the world, stretching about 4,200 miles. It has two major sources: the highlands of Ethiopia and the lakes in east Africa. These two Niles, known as the Blue and White, respectively, converge near the city of Khartoum, in what is today the country of Sudan. From there, the river flows through a series of six "cataracts," or rapids, until reaching the area of the modern city of Aswan. Flowing north for several hundred miles, the river splits into two major branches just past modern Cairo before emptying into the Mediterranean Sea.

The following statement by the Greek author Hecataeus (c. 300 B.C.) seems to be quoted in nearly every introductory book about ancient Egypt, so why not here as well? "Egypt is the gift of the Nile." Such a simple statement, but, oh, so true. It was the Nile River and its natural cycles that allowed Egyptian civilization to develop and thrive. Every year, the river would go through a flood stage, leaving in its wake a nutrient-rich deposit of silt that would renew the agricultural farmland. This process is known as the *inundation*. As you can imagine, the coming of the inundation was something of concern—too much water could cause some serious damage to human settlements, but, probably worse, too little could cause food shortages! A perfect inundation was obviously something desired by all, and, combined with intensive irrigation, such inundations turned Egypt into a fertile bread basket!

> **Nile Notes**
>
> During the time of the pharaohs, there were seven branches of the Nile flowing through the Delta region.

Glyphs

The **inundation** is the annual flooding of the Nile River, which produced a regular renewal of agricultural farmland. Due to the construction of dams in the vicinity of Aswan during modern times, this process, so important in ancient times, no longer occurs. The damming of the Nile has had radical implications for the future of the land of modern Egypt and its antiquities (see Chapter 20, "Facing the Future," for more details).

The Nile: The river that facilitated the development of the ancient Egyptian civilization.

(David Moyer collection.)

Black Land/Red Land

Because of the dark, fertile soil along the Nile, the Egyptians called Egypt "the Black Land," or *Kemet*, the Egyptian term. Kemet could also be contrasted with "the Red Land," or *Deshret*, referring to the adjacent desert regions.

Lost and Found

There survive in Egypt a number of ancient "Nilometers," instruments, so to speak, that allow for the noting of the varying height of the Nile. In its simplest form, a Nilometer might consist of a series of lines etched on rocks at the river's edge.

The Two Lands

The land of ancient Egypt can be divided into two geographically distinct areas: the generally narrow Nile Valley in the south and the broad Nile Delta in the north. The Egyptians themselves were very aware of this distinction, which they referred to as the Two Lands, and the unity of both territories of Kemet became a major concept in their notion of political unity and stability. One of the ancient capitals of Egypt, known by its Greek name, Memphis, was located near the junction of the Two Lands, as is the city of Cairo, the capital of modern Egypt.

Up Is Down

Because the Nile River flows from south to north, we refer to the Nile Valley as Upper Egypt (upstream), and the Delta as Lower Egypt (downstream). The unification of these areas was constantly reinforced in the titles and regalia of the ruler. For example:

- The king was often referred to as "Lord of the Two Lands."
- The king is frequently depicted wearing a double crown: a white crown representing Upper Egypt and a red crown representing Lower Egypt.
- One of the official names or titles of the king feature a sedge, a kind of aquatic plant (Upper Egypt) and a bee (Lower Egypt), and is translated as King of Upper and Lower Egypt.
- Another title of the king involves two goddesses: Nekhbet, in the form of a vulture (Upper Egypt), and Wedjat (Lower Egypt), in the form of a cobra.

Nile Notes

Don't forget: Upper Egypt refers to the Nile Valley in the south, and Lower Egypt refers to the Delta in the north.

And There's More!

As a geographical bonus, the ancient Egyptians were blessed not only with agricultural renewal, but also with a river that flowed north and prevailing winds that blew south.

This, of course, allowed for travel up and down the Nile because travelers could use the current to propel them north, to Lower Egypt, and the wind to propel them south, to Upper Egypt. This facilitated the transport of goods and political and military control.

The desert areas to the east and west of the Nile agricultural regions hemmed in the majority of the population, but several oases to the west were home to settlements from time to time. Southwest of modern Cairo is a region known as the "Fayyum" which was a Nile-fed lake. Today this lake, Birket Qarun, is brackish and greatly reduced in size, but the Fayyum still serves as a major agricultural region as it did in the past. The eastern desert features a chain of mountains from north to south and was regularly visited for quarrying and mining of precious materials such as gold. There were also routes to the east that provided access to the Red Sea.

Egypt's position at the northeast edges of the African continent was convenient for inter-action with the cultures of West Asia, including those in Palestine, Mesopotamia, and Persia. These interactions involved peaceful trade, domination, and invasion coming from both sides. The Mediterranean was an active place in ancient times and provided access to and from the land of Egypt, and it continues to do so today. The territory of Upper and Lower Egypt was also politically divided into traditional provinces that are referred to by their Greek name, *nomes.* Forty-two nomes could be found in Upper Egypt, and 40 were in Lower Egypt.

The geographical nature of the land also played a role in Egypt's belief system. To the west, where the sun set, lay the netherworld, or the land of the dead. Consequently, many cemeteries were established on that side of the Nile. The cycles of the Nile and agriculture also inspired religious notions of fertility and rebirth.

Pharaoh's Domain

The Nile inundation was represented by the Egyptian god Hapy, a somewhat strange-looking bearded fellow with a pot-belly and a headdress of aquatic plants.

Frameworks of Time

The ancient Egyptian civilization persisted for about 3,000 years, which is quite a sizeable time frame for any archaeologist or historian to work in. In an effort to organize where things fit chronologically, a system has been used to organize history into a series of time periods. Geologists have done a similar thing with their Mesozoic and Cenozoic eras, Jurassic and Pleistocene periods, and so on.

The traditional framework for organizing Egyptian history comes to us from an old source. An Egyptian historian and priest named Manetho (c. 305–285 B.C.) wrote down a list of kings organized into 30 dynasties. He probably had access to temple or other official records, and the list has proven to be relatively accurate. (An additional dynasty has been added to Manetho's list, bringing the number to 31.)

The dynasties themselves are further arranged into a series of kingdoms and periods. Now, technically, a dynasty should represent a related set of rulers. From what we now know, this doesn't always hold true in Manetho's system. In fact, there are even some cases of overlapping dynasties.

Our knowledge of the order of rulers is also advanced by the existence of several ancient Egyptian "king lists." One, for example, survives on a large stone fragment, three others were found in temples, and one was discovered on a sheet of papyrus. Unfortunately, most are incomplete, and occasionally they contradict each other. Some unpopular rulers were left off the lists or weren't included for other reasons. Nonetheless, they provide a lot of useful information.

Lost and Found

The original text of Manetho's work on Egyptian chronology is not known, but fragments of his work have come down to us by way of other writers of the first millennium, who copied from him extensively.

Although this dynastic system is not perfect and could use some revision, it is firmly entrenched in the world of Egyptology, it serves its purpose well, and it is a tool that is universally used. Here is how it's arranged, beginning with a period around the start of Egypt's time of civilization. (Note that many of the earlier dates are approximate and have been subject to debate.)

- Archaic, or Early Dynastic Period: Dynasties 1–2, c. 3000–2686 B.C.
- Old Kingdom: Dynasties 3–6, 2686–2181 B.C.
- First Intermediate Period: Dynasties 7–11, 2181–2055 B.C.
- Middle Kingdom: Dynasties 11–13, 2055–1650 B.C.
- Second Intermediate Period: Dynasties 14–17, 1650–1550 B.C.
- New Kingdom: Dynasties 18–20, 1550–1069 B.C.
- Third Intermediate Period: Dynasties 21–25, 1069–644 B.C.
- Late Period: Dynasties 26–31, 664–332 B.C.
- Although not within the traditional system, we can also add the Graeco-Roman Period when the Greeks and Romans ruled Egypt. Graeco-Roman Period, 332 B.C.–A.D. 395 (Ptolemaic [Greek] Period, 332–30 B.C.; Roman Period, 30 B.C.– A.D. 395)

Nile Notes

Many Egyptologist refer to a "Dynasty 0" to group a small number of rulers at the very beginning of the dynastic age.

The time leading up to the arrangement of the dynasties is usually referred to as the "Predynastic" period. This term is often vaguely used to describe the period of development leading to the classical period of Egyptian civilization, which the previous sequence describes. The term *prehistoric* also is sometimes used to describe anything preceding dynastic times, going as far back as the earliest humans to venture into the Nile Valley. But we'll be dealing with more of that in Chapter 9, "The Earliest Egyptians."

Not Exactly So

While Egyptologists might all use the system just described, they certainly don't all agree on exactly when everything happened. Dates for the lengths of reign for individual rulers are often disputed or revised as new information appears. There is also the problem of *coregencies*—a situation in which the reigns of two kings overlap in sort of a mentorship arrangement. This being so, you shouldn't be surprised upon opening two Egyptian history books to find different dates for the same time periods and events. Fortunately, the dates rarely vary by more than 50 years, although their certainty gets weaker the farther back you go in time. In this book, I prefer the chronological dates offered in *The Oxford History of Ancient Egypt*, edited by Ian Shaw.

Glyphs

A **coregency** is a situation in which rulership overlaps between two kings, typically father and son, usually to ensure a competent transition from one to the other.

Egyptian History in a Nutshell

Some easy ways are available to help you remember how Egyptian history is organized. Think of the Archaic Period as the old and formative time in the development of Egyptian civilization. The three kingdoms (Old, Middle, and New) were times when Egypt was generally unified, strong, and wealthy. Each kingdom period was followed by an intermediate period, or a time when Egypt was economically depressed, politically disunited, and vulnerable to foreign incursions. The Late Period is the prelude to the coming of the Greeks and Romans. With that in mind, we'll be filling in some of the exciting historical details in the chapters ahead!

A Note about b.c. and a.d.

You've probably noticed that most of the dates I've used so far in this book are followed by one of two abbreviations: B.C. or A.D. The calendar in common use today was created by Christians and begins its numbering system with the birth of Jesus:

◆ **B.C.** stands for "Before Christ" and refers to the number of years before the birth of Jesus. So, 300 B.C. is 300 years before Jesus was born. Note that the numbers get larger the farther in the past you go because we are counting backward from a particular date. As an example, 2000 B.C. is farther in the past than 300 B.C.

◆ Many people think that because B.C. means "Before Christ," then **A.D.** must mean "After Death." Not so. First of all, if that were the case, you'd have to add about 33 years (how old Jesus was when he died) to your actual date to account for the tenure of Jesus' life on Earth and then come up with a special term for dealing with those years. And, from a theological point of view, Jesus was only dead for a couple of days before being resurrected anyway!

Fortunately, we don't have to worry about all that: A.D. is actually an abbreviation for two Latin words, *anno Domini*, meaning "Year of Our Lord." From the perspective of a Christian calendar-constructor, every year since the birth of Jesus would be a Year of Our Lord. Unlike years dated B.C., years dated A.D. get larger the farther into the future you get. That's because we are counting forward from the date of Jesus' birth rather than backward from it.

Now there are some folks out there who don't care for the theological bias of these terms. Perhaps they don't share Christian beliefs, or maybe they simply feel that religion should not be imposed on such a universal apparatus as a calendar. To address those concerns, there is an alternative pair of terms that essentially mean the same things. The terms recognize that our current Christian calendar is entrenched in common use and is not going away, but the theological implications are neutralized:

◆ **B.C.E**, or "Before the Common Era," means the same as B.C.

◆ **C.E.**, or "Common Era," is the equivalent of A.D.

The term "Common" refers to the calendar dates that we all use in common, regardless of their origin and our personal beliefs. The B.C./B.C.E. and A.D./C.E. distinction is mostly known in academic circles, where it is unevenly applied. It's often a matter of personal choice, and occasionally it is an editorial policy, but B.C.E. and C.E. are being used more frequently, so it's best to recognize and understand them for what they are.

The important thing is to have a system that everyone can understand. In this book, we will use the traditional B.C./A.D. terms, which are familiar to more people.

Counting Backward

Another occasionally useful way of noting a point in time is with a B.P., or "Before Present," date. Essentially, B.P. means "years ago." So, if this is the year A.D. 2000 and I'm talking about 10 years B.P., I'm referring to the calendar year A.D. 1990. Or, to make matters slightly more complicated, if this is the year A.D. 2000 and I'm talking about 2500 B.P., I'm referring to the year 500 B.C.

Why would anyone want to do this? As you'll see when we briefly discuss dating techniques later, in some methods, such as radiocarbon dating, the age of an object is assessed from the time of the laboratory procedure. A date produced in the laboratory 10 years from now would be different (by 10 years) from a date provided today.

Round About Then

One last term that you'll come across in this book is *circa*, usually abbreviated with a simple "c." Circa means "about that time." It is useful for rounding off dates for a general discussion or for referring to dates that we can't pin down exactly.

Egyptian Time

The Egyptians had their own sense of time (calendars will be discussed in Chapter 6, "Science and Technology,") and often recorded their dates, but not in the same way we do. Dates were usually noted in terms of the occurrence of a given event during the reign of the ruling king. For example, such and such happened during year 4 of the reign of king so and so during the third month of an indicated season on day 3.

The Name Game

And since we're talking about reigns of kings, perhaps this is the time to mention a situation that might confuse beginners in Egyptology. Some of the rulers have been known by different names: a Greek version of a royal name derived from Manetho or other old sources, and an approximately reconstructed ancient Egyptian name. This is because the framework of Egyptian history from Greek sources was known well before the hieroglyphs were translated. So, the old Greek names have been around longer and are actually preferred by some, even in Egypt today. The following table shows some examples.

Glyphs _____

Many Egyptian cities and other sites have multiple names. In Upper Egypt, for example, Luxor (in Arabic) was known as Waset to the ancient Egyptians and later acquired a Greek name, Thebes.

Greek Names and Their Egyptian Equivalents

	Greek Name	Egyptian Name(s)
The builders of the three big Old Kingdom pyramids at Giza	Cheops Chephren Mycerinus	Khufu Khafra Menkaura
Name used by three Middle Kingdom pharaohs	Sesostris	Senusret Senusert Senwosret

continues

Greek Names and Their Egyptian Equivalents (continued)

	Greek Name	Egyptian Name(s)
Names used by New Kingdom pharaohs	Thotmose	Djehutymose or Tuthmosis
	Amenophis	Amenhotep
	Sethos	Seti

How Old Is It?

Determining age, or dating, is a crucial part of Egyptology, and there are a number of ways to go about it. We'll just take a quick look at three of the most important dating techniques that are used in Egyptology and archaeology in general.

Glyphs

In Egypt, a mound representing the accumulated debris of past human settlement is often referred to as a "tell" or "kom." Such mounds are often the obvious target of archaeological investigation.

Staring at Dirt

Analyzing layers of dirt or debris, or strata, in an archaeological site is known as stratigraphy. By looking at how layers of dirt and debris are positioned in an archaeological site, it's usually possible to tell which layer with its accompanying objects is older than another. The older ones tend to be below the younger ones, but it's sometimes not so simple because things can get mixed up through a variety of processes.

Stylin'

Another very important way to date old objects is by their style. You can tell that a Model T automobile is older than a Camaro by the way it looks. Likewise, this is true of many other kinds of objects because styles tend to change through time. This concept theoretically allows an expert to pick up a piece of pottery and tell whether it is a Predynastic pot or a much later Roman wine jar. There are also clever ways of ordering groups of objects based on their changing styles. This is called "sequence dating" or using the "seriation" method, as it is more commonly known among archaeologists.

Famous and Radioactive

Radiocarbon dating, or carbon-14 dating, has received a lot of attention. It's not used as much for material dating to the time of Egyptian civilization, but for objects that existed during the time before writing in that land, it is a very useful technique indeed. Without going into tremendous detail, this dating method is based on the notion that all living creatures absorb a kind of radiation from the atmosphere. When they die, this radioactive material begins to decay at a known rate. The amount of radioactive material remaining in an archaeological sample can be measured; thus, it can be determined how many years it has been since the sample was in a living state.

Although this technique works very well, it is not perfect. It works accurately only with uncontaminated organic materials, and the older the sample is, the wider the spread of possible dates. The technique also is good only for objects dating between about 400 and 50,000 years old, which isn't much of a problem for much of what is found of Egyptological interest. Very importantly, the dates are meaningful only in the sense that the sample is meaningful. For example, if I am trying to date an old building with a wooden beam, I might want to take into account the possibility that the wooden beam might be an old piece of wood reused from an earlier structure, so the radiocarbon date would be dating the wood, not necessarily the building in which it was found.

Radiocarbon dating can't pinpoint a specific day or year, but gives a range of years in which the date will fall, and this range gets wider the older the material!

Lost and Found

Some artifacts, including Greek coins and Egyptian beetle-shaped amulets called scarabs, are very portable. Finding one of these in your archaeological site doesn't guarantee that your site dates to the age of such objects by themselves. But it does mean that the layer in which they were found isn't older than such objects, unless it's been tampered with!

The Handwriting on the Wall

Fortunately, in Egypt, the plethora of inscriptions and our knowledge of art, history, and writing allows us to date things far more easily than in many other parts of the world. Also quite helpful are dates that can be verified from written sources outside of Egypt's borders, where precise dates can sometimes be more easily determined and then matched up with events taking place in Egypt. In short, the best approach to dating is based on the circumstance and, better yet, using a combination of methods.

Nile Notes

Known astronomical phenomena have also played an important role in fixing calendar dates to the framework of ancient Egyptian history. When the Egyptians noted certain periodic star positions, for example, we can use our modern knowledge of astronomy to pinpoint the year in which it happened.

The Least You Need to Know

- ◆ The Nile and its natural cycle allowed for an Egyptian civilization to flourish.
- ◆ The Egyptians divided their land into two primary divisions: Upper and Lower Egypt.
- ◆ Egyptian history is organized into a series of dynasties grouped into "kingdoms" and "periods."
- ◆ Archaeologists may use several different methods to determine the age of artifacts and monuments.

Chapter 4

Glyphs

In This Chapter

- ◆ Deciphering the hieroglyphs
- ◆ The language behind the script
- ◆ What they wrote on, what they wrote about
- ◆ Learning ancient Egyptian

Perhaps the greatest impediment to rediscovering the ancient Egyptian past was the mystery of the hieroglyphs, a puzzle that thwarted investigators for centuries. There seemed to be no end to these strange pictures that appeared in abundance on the walls of temples and tombs. What could these symbols possibly mean? Was it some form of mystical expression, "picture writing," or an actual writing system conveying the sounds of a language?

Animated Speculation

The answer? *Hieroglyphs* are an actual form of writing, or language expressed in symbols. But the road to the discovery was long, and there was a lot of wild speculation before the issue was resolved. Let's look at some of the earlier ideas.

Take the hieroglyph that represents the *m* sound in the ancient Egyptian language. It is depicted with the picture of an owl. Now after the loss of knowledge of the hieroglyphs after the first few centuries A.D., this owl became a mystery. Could it, for example, be some sort of philosophical statement in and of itself? Wisdom, perhaps? After all, the Bible refers to "the wisdom of Egypt," and we all know how wise owls are!

Glyphs

The proper term for the Egyptian writing system is **hiero-glyphs,** not "hieroglyphics," as is so commonly but incorrectly used. The word **hieroglyphic** is an adjective that refers to a kind of pictorial script.

And if we maintain the opinion that the Egyptians were mystical, as evidenced by the numerous temples along with such ideas of ancient secret knowledge passed down to medieval masons, then voilà—we are left with an inscrutable mystery subject to our own speculative interpretations. In fact, it was not uncommon for would-be translators to propose lengthy, complex, and abstract interpretations of a mere handful of hiero-glyphic characters!

Just As It Appears?

Another idea was that the hieroglyphs represented a form of picture writing—that is, the characters themselves represented what they depicted. Our owl hieroglyph, then, would represent that very thing, an owl. Now we look at what appears in front and what appears behind, and we have a story, so it seems. Let's say that we have three hieroglyphs: an owl, a man with a stick, and some legs facing the opposite direction. The imaginative transla-tor might propose that what we have is the story of an owl who was whacked with a stick by a man who turned and left in the aftermath. This method, though, was obviously quite subjective and involved a great deal of imagination—and if we follow through with the owl example, we might be tempted to propose some sort of story to explain why the bird deserved such treatment.

Lost and Found

The irregularly shaped Rosetta Stone is 3 feet, 9 inches tall; 2 feet, 4 inches wide; and 11 inches thick. It weighs just less than 1,500 pounds. In its complete form as a standing stone stele, or tablet, it probably stood between 5 and 6 feet tall.

Meet the Rosetta Stone!

The age of speculation eventually came to an end with the chance discovery of a chunk of stone by one of Napoleon's soldiers in 1799. While maintaining fortifi-cations in the Delta town of Rosetta, a large fragment of black granite was found. One face of the stone was completely covered with three kinds of ancient writing displayed in three groups. The top portion contained an inscription in the mysterious hieroglyphs, the middle contained a cursive script known as Demotic, and at the bottom was Greek. The French recognized the poten-tial importance of the stone and had it sent off to Cairo.

The Greek inscription on the stone could be read because the knowledge of that ancient language had never been lost; there were plenty of European scholars capable of reading it. The Greek inscription indicated that the stone was a decree dating to 196 B.C. during the reign of Ptolemy V. The actual historical context of the inscription is not itself of profound importance. The key lay in the possibility that the Rosetta Stone might contain an identical inscription written in multiple languages and scripts, including the hieroglyphs! Copies of the stone were made and sent to scholars in Europe, who got busy comparing the Greek text to the undeciphered scripts above it. Meanwhile, the Rosetta Stone was confiscated from the French by the British, who still retain it. It can be found today in the British Museum in London, where it is a major attraction.

The Rosetta Stone.

(Courtesy of the British Museum.)

The decipherment didn't take place overnight. A number of small steps made by different scholars contributed to a final conclusion. It had been proposed, for example, that a series of hieroglyphs specially enclosed in an oval symbol, or *cartouche*, were the names of the royalty mentioned in the Greek text. This proved to be correct. Others made a surprising bit of progress with the cursive inscription.

Glyphs

A **cartouche** is an oval-shaped symbol that contains the hieroglyphs for the names of Egyptian royalty. Cartouches often make it reasonably easy to date monuments and objects to the reign of a particular ruler or individual.

After several years of study, a young French prodigy named Jean-François Champollion proclaimed in 1822 that he had solved the puzzle: The hieroglyphs were basically phonetic in nature. By comparing the alphabetic Greek royal names with the individual hieroglyphs found in the cartouches, he was actually able to identify several phonetic signs. From there, rapid progress was made in further decipherment, and Champollion himself went on to write, among other things, a grammar and dictionary of ancient Egyptian.

Diggers

Jean-François Champollion (1790–1832) was a French scholar credited with the decipherment of Egyptian hieroglyphs in 1822. He was a master of many languages—even as a child, he had studied Hebrew, Arabic, Coptic, and Chinese. In 1826, he was made conservator general of the Egyptian antiquities in the Musée du Louvre in Paris, and he led a scholarly expedition to Egypt in 1827. Champollion accomplished much in his relatively short life and is generally considered one of the founding figures in Egyptology.

An Egyptian hieroglyphic text telling how King Tuthmosis III ordered the dredging of a clogged canal. His name is found in the oval, or cartouche.

All in the Family

The decipherment of the hieroglyphs revealed the ancient language behind the script. Linguists classify ancient Egyptian today as a member of the Afro-Asiatic language family (formerly called "Hamito-Semitic"), a family that incorporates the Semitic languages such as Hebrew, Arabic, and Akkadian, and a number of African languages as well.

> **Nile Notes**
>
> The alphabet that we use contains seemingly arbitrarily shaped characters used to express sounds in our language. But if we go back far enough, we can learn that the letter *A* once was represented by an ox head (take a look at it upside down), and the sound *B* was represented by a symbol of a house, or "bet," as it was called in Phoenician.

Different Times

Languages, of course, change through time. Word usage changes, new words are invented, pronunciations might differ with dialects, and even spelling might evolve.

Compare the works of Chaucer, Shakespeare, the King James Bible, and so forth with contemporary English, and it's easy to see. In the case of Chaucer, it's often barely comprehensible to a modern audience in its original form. And as for Shakespeare, nobody today really communicates in such a florid manner regularly, unless someone is a member of some sort of medieval times re-enactment group. The dynamic of change applies to ancient Egyptian, and Egyptologists have identified five stages of the language through its 3,000 plus years of written history. Here are the five stages of Egyptian language:

- **Old Egyptian**—The language of the oldest known texts, best represented from the monuments of the Old Kingdom, including the famous Pyramid Texts.
- **Middle Egyptian**—The classic form of the language, which was probably spoken from around the time of the Middle Kingdom but persisted in written form into much later periods.
- **Late Egyptian**—The spoken and literary language common during the New Kingdom.
- **Demotic**—The stage of the language common during the Late Period.
- **Coptic**—The latest known stage. It still survives in the liturgy of the Coptic Christian church.

Different Scripts

Along with the different stages of the language, there were four primary scripts for writing Egyptian:

◆ **Hieroglyphs**—A script that incorporated pictorial symbols and was used primarily in formal inscriptions.

◆ **Hieratic**—A cursive form of hieroglyphs that was especially useful for writing on papyrus (paper) and other informal writing surfaces.

◆ **Demotic**—An even more cursive form of writing that was used during the Demotic stage of the language.

◆ **Coptic**—An especially interesting script because it is the latest stage of the Egyptian language. It is written with a modified Greek alphabet, including the vowels (which, as I'll mention later, were not actually incorporated in the other scripts.)

A sample of the cursive hieratic script.

(From Life in Ancient Egypt, *by A. Erman.)*

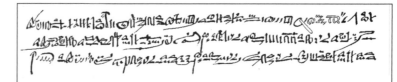

How It Works

Let's return to the hieroglyphs. This is basically how the script works: First of all, vowels were not commonly represented in the phonetic script. Basically, the symbols represent words composed with their consonants. How odd this seems to those familiar with European languages! Obviously you can't pronounce words without vowels. (If you don't believe me, try a few combinations with consonants. *M* + *n* and *b* + *v*, for example, will produce some interesting effects!) Ancient Egyptian is by no means alone in this writing phenomenon. Arabic and Hebrew are both commonly written without vowels, and anybody who knows these languages will tell you that they're not really necessary if you understand the grammar. But without going into the big discussion about how that all works, trust me—it's possible.

This and That

You should also know that the ancient Egyptian language contained some sounds that don't appear in English. A couple seem to be sounds made in the throat, while another seems to be a "kh" sound familiar in German and Hebrew.

Did I mention that hieroglyphs can be written from left to right, and also right to left, and also top to bottom? If you know the script, it doesn't really matter, so the hieroglyphs could be arranged artistically as space or need required on various objects or monuments.

Lots of Glyphs to Go Around

Hundreds of individual hieroglyphic signs exist, but only a couple dozen of the signs are alphabetical—that is, one sign signifies a single sound. Numerous other signs stand for combinations of two consonants, and yet others stand for three.

Now perhaps you are wondering, how is it possible to tell the difference between words with the same combination of consonants but no vowels? Take the two letters representing the sounds "b" and "t." To use English, we could arrive at numerous words including *bait, bet, bit, boat, boot, bite, but, beat, bat* (and which one? the stick or the flying beast?), *beet*, and so on. Well the Egyptians had a nice way of dealing with this. They had hundreds of nonphonetic signs known as determinatives, which were usually found at the end of the word and indicated which of the possible choices was the intended one. After a man's name, for instance, often comes a hieroglyph depicting a seated man, and a seated woman follows the name of a female. Verbs dealing with human motion might show some walking feet, and a word indicating a kind of cow might show just that: a cow. A cumbersome system, you say? Absolutely, but it worked, and the world would have to wait some time before a simple alphabet would be invented and applied to various languages.

Diggers

The Englishman Thomas Young (1733–1829) came to nearly the same conclusion as Champollion—that the hieroglyphs were basically phonetic. And although Champollion has long received the credit, even his work was built on the ideas of others who perhaps deserve a share of the recognition.

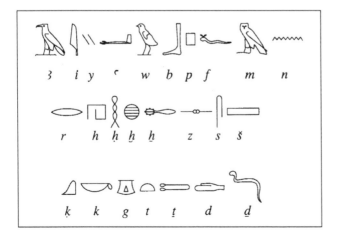

The Egyptian hieroglyphic alphabetical characters.

Writing Surfaces

Most people are familiar with the idea of grandiose temples and other monuments covered with hieroglyphs carved in stone. Fortunately, stone wasn't the only material available for writing. Much more portable and convenient was a kind of paper known as *papyrus* manufactured from an aquatic plant, *Cyperus papyrus*, which grew along the Nile. Although the exact method of manufacture cannot be confirmed, the paper seems to have been made with overlapping strips of the inner pith of the plant. Under pressure, natural adhesives aid in binding the materials together. Individual sheets or lengthy scrolls could be produced in such a manner. Scribes wrote on papyrus with a reed pen typically dipped in black or red ink.

> **Glyphs**
>
> **Papyrus** is a kind of paper manufactured from the inner pith of the papyrus plant, *Cyperus papyrus*. An individual document written on such paper is known as a **papyrus,** (plural: **papyri**). An **ostracon** (plural: **ostraca**) is a piece of broken pottery or a flake of stone that serves as a writing surface.

> **Lost and Found**
>
> Hundreds of examples of ancient Egyptian graffiti have been found. Many of these are simply names of individuals scratched on rock, but others provide some real historical insights into history and even the environment!

A number of letters on papyrus survive, as do many complete scrolls bearing funerary texts such as the so-called Book of the Dead, as recovered from tombs. Keep in mind that papyrus is a very fragile commodity, and only a minute fraction of the documents that once existed have likely survived.

Other writing surfaces included flat flakes of stone, typically limestone, and broken pottery shards, which Egyptologists refer to as "ostraca" (singular, "ostracon"). These were readily available for quick notes and short documents. Because of their durability, many of these documents have survived, some with quite interesting contents!

What Were They Writing About?

The Egyptian uses of writing were much the same as they are today, including letters of communication between individuals, business transactions, construction plans, complaints, requests, receipts, and so forth. Some fine examples of literature are known, sometimes in multiple copies, as recorded by students in scribal schools. Among the more interesting are "instructions," bits of sage advice to guide the student to a better life made with better choices.

There are also plenty of writings relating to religious themes of the living and the deceased. Temples and tombs, especially in the dryer parts of the land, offer us a plethora of such inscriptions.

Talk Like an Egyptian

What did ancient Egyptian sound like? No one knows, for sure. The situation with the lack of vowels certainly complicates things, but that hasn't discouraged some scholars from giving it a try. At least two approaches have been taken to reconstruct the spoken language. One is to look at ancient documents using Egyptian words, but written in another script that indicates the vowels. Correspondence between foreign and Egyptian royalty, for example, has been found with Egyptian names spelled out. This can really shed some light, but the words used tend to be limited. There is also the problem that the Egyptian names were written with a foreign script that might itself offer only an approximation.

> **Diggers**
>
> With Hollywood's desire for a certain sense of authenticity, American Egyptologist Stuart Smith was hired to write Egyptian dialogue for several blockbuster films, including *Stargate*, *The Mummy*, and *The Mummy Returns*. Although we aren't sure exactly how ancient Egyptian was pronounced, Smith produced some reasonable approximations that might be the closest thing that the public will likely hear of the old language. And it's a great way to employ an Egyptologist!

Another technique is to study texts written in the Coptic script, which does indicate the vowels, and then try to work backward. Given the lengthy life span of the Egyptian language and its changes through time, this method cannot guarantee complete results, but it does provide some insights.

How, you may ask, are Egyptologists able to discuss these words among themselves if they can't even pronounce them? The answer is relatively simple. We usually insert a short vowel, typically *e*, between consonants. For example if we have glyphs representing the consonants *w*, *b*, and *n*, we would say "weben." A couple of other informal rules are used as well. Yes, it is a contrived system that all students learn, but the ultimate purpose is that we are able to communicate with each other.

> **Lost and Found**
>
> Some ancient scripts still lack credible decipherment. These include Linear A, found in the Mediterranean; the Indus Valley script, found in Pakistan; and the curious symbols known as Rongo-rongo, found on remote Easter Island in the middle of the Pacific.

Glyphs Are Your Friend

At first glance, hieroglyphs look intimidating in the extreme. It must take years and years for an

Egyptologist to be able to deal with those things! Not necessarily so. With some good books or an introductory course, you will be amazed at how quickly you can actually read many inscriptions. It helps, too, that many surviving inscriptions are written in formulas that repeat themselves often. Many tourists have benefited from a study of cartouches, especially the more common ones, which allow them to delightfully identify royalty on monuments of different periods, with the side benefit of impressing their friends. One book, *How to Read Egyptian Hieroglyphs,* by Mark Collier and Bill Manley, has been somewhat of a bestseller in Britain and provides a relatively gentle approach to this whole business.

I found learning to draw the hieroglyphs especially fun, but, of course, the quality of output varies from person to person. An excellent book by Henry Fischer, *Ancient Egyptian Calligraphy,* provides a good start in drawing glyphs that are uniformly recognizable.

Egyptian Grammar School

Those bold enough to want to really learn the grammar behind the script can anticipate some exciting challenges. The grammar of ancient Egyptian can be very unlike English. And when it comes to verbs, you're in for a real treat. The whole matter, again, is complicated by the lack of vowel structure, which might more readily lead you to distinguish one verbal form from another. On the other hand, a sound knowledge of ancient Egyptian grammar will unlock the door to numerous intriguing texts and inscriptions.

Close Encounters with Sir Al

The classic text on the subject is *Egyptian Grammar,* by Sir Alan Gardiner. This mighty work has served as both curse and savior to several generations of students. It is a big, heavy book that serves as an instructional grammar and reference book. Those who have progressed through the book will know that Sir Al takes no prisoners. The book includes exercises requiring translation from Egyptian to English, and vice versa, and grammatical concepts and terminology that might make your head spin. The satisfaction that comes as a result of learning Egyptian grammar, though, is well worth the effort.

Diggers

Sir Alan Henderson Gardiner (1879–1963) was one of the world's greatest Egyptologists and was the author of more than two dozen books and 200 scholarly articles. In particular, his book on ancient Egyptian language and writing, *Egyptian Grammar,* has influenced several generations of students.

Much progress in the study of Egyptian linguistics has been made since Sir Alan's *Grammar* was last updated in 1957. However, the volume is still quite relevant and available, and many professors continue to use it in their teaching. Especially useful is the hieroglyphic sign list found in an appendix at the back of the book. It contains a list of the most common hieroglyphs, organized by category and accompanied by insightful explanations of their meanings.

A more updated approach to Egyptian grammar can be found in the new and highly regarded book by James Allen, *Middle Egyptian: An Introduction to the Language and Culture of Hieroglyphs.* The book is loaded with interesting examples and exercises, and it takes care to explain the grammatical terminology in ways that are likely comprehensible to the average reader.

> **Nile Notes**
>
> Apart from its last vestiges found in the Coptic language, the ancient Egyptian language is dead. The modern language of Egypt is Arabic and was introduced by the Arabs beginning around A.D. 642.

Show Me the Words!

Where we have words, it's not surprising that we also have a dictionary—several, in fact. In the early twentieth century, a big effort was made to collect all known Egyptian words and organize them. The result was the impressive multivolume *Wörterbuch der Aegyptischen Sprache*—that's German for Dictionary of the Egyptian Language. It's huge and it's expensive, and if you do find your Egyptian word of interest, you'd better be able to deal with German if you want to know the translation!

Of more practical use to many beginners (and professionals, too) is Raymond Faulkner's *Concise Dictionary of Middle Egyptian.* It's a single, relatively inexpensive volume, and it contains the majority of words that a student might encounter while studying Egyptian. Plus, the translations are in English. As scholars continue their work, new words continue to be collected and old meanings are refined. It's a continuous process that leads to further understanding.

The Least You Need to Know

- The Rosetta Stone provided the key to the decipherment of the hieroglyphs.
- The ancient Egyptian language developed through recognizable stages and was written in different scripts.
- The hieroglyphic and cursive scripts included hundreds of different signs.
- Egyptologists aren't exactly sure how the ancient language was pronounced.
- Learning Egyptian need not be intimidating, and it can be a lot of fun!

Part 2

Life and Death in Ancient Egypt

The remarkable artifacts left over from the civilization of the ancient Egyptians sometimes overshadow the fact that these were people very much like us, albeit from a far different culture. It's now time to look at the lives of the people who created this amazing civilization.

In this section, we're going to look at some of the basics of ancient Egyptian society. What did the Egyptians eat? What kind of jobs did they have? How was their society organized, and how did they view the world? Of course, there will be a whole chapter on mummies and such, but just keep in mind that ancient Egyptian civilization was all about living, whether here or in the afterlife, and it is the job of Egyptologists and archaeologists to rediscover the once vibrant existence of this great civilization.

Chapter 5

Daily Life

In This Chapter

- ◆ Egyptian family life
- ◆ Jobs for all
- ◆ Royal responsibilities
- ◆ Pharaonic clothing and cuisine
- ◆ Good times!

Although it's easy to stand in awe of the ancient Egyptians and their many accomplishments, it's important to remember that they were people just like you and me, and they had the same needs as everyone else. In this chapter, we're going to look at ancient Egyptian daily life, including what they ate, what kind of jobs they had, and how their society was organized.

Domestic Life

The typical family in ancient Egypt included a husband and wife and their children. Marriage was an arrangement between the couple or their families, and the woman brought a dowry into the relationship. There is no evidence of any special marriage rituals, although they might have thrown a party to celebrate the occasion. Typically, relationships were monogamous, with the exception of the ruler, who sometimes had quite a few wives. It wasn't particularly difficult for couples to get divorced, and what divorces there were probably resulted mostly from incompatibility. When there was a divorce, the wife got all of her stuff back!

Lost and Found

Much of what survives from ancient Egypt comes from specialized sources—temples and tombs—that often were designed to last through time. Most of the ordinary, everyday stuff was perishable and simply didn't survive. But fortunately for us, the Egyptians loved life so much that they wanted it to continue in a similar way in the afterlife. Consequently, Egyptians included all kinds of objects from daily life in the tombs of their dead, and in some of the more expensive tombs they even painted scenes of daily life on the walls! Egyptologists have gleaned much of their information about Egyptian daily life from what they've found buried with the dead.

Lacking sophisticated medical knowledge, giving birth could sometimes be a dangerous thing, as could infancy and childhood. It was common for women to have several children in order to ensure the perpetuation of the family. Evidence suggests that the ancient Egyptians truly cherished their children, both boys and girls. The kids often assisted their parents in household or professional tasks and were expected to look after Mom and Dad in their old age.

Nile Notes

Egyptian girls were often married between the ages of 12 and 14. Marriages between half-siblings and cousins were possible.

Pharaoh's Domain

In Egyptian texts, the wife is often referred to as "the mistress of the house." During the New Kingdom, the term "beloved sister" was sometimes used, referring to a special sort of closeness rather than a formal kinship relationship … unless you were the king.

Gender Roles

Men and women had certain gender roles in Egyptian society. The women were usually household managers whose job it was to bear and raise children and maintain the home. They also ground grain and baked, and some engaged in textile production. The men were employed in any number of professions, from agriculture and crafts to government bureaucracy. Typically all government officials were males, although some women were priestesses or filled other religious roles. Even though they were rarely involved in government, in many legal situations, women had equal status to men and could own and manage land and engage in business dealings.

The Royal Family

The family situation of the rulers was often altogether different. Polygamy was not unusual, and the king might have a chief wife plus a few minor ones, and perhaps maintain a concubine. It was not uncommon for the pharaoh to marry his sister or daughter. This served the purpose of keeping the ruling line close-knit, but it was generally not practiced outside of the royal family. Examples of royal intermarriage can also be found in Egyptian mythology, in which both the gods Osiris and Seth married their sisters. It was possible for a pharaoh to take on foreign brides for diplomatic purposes as well.

Going to Work!

As is typical of complex societies, the Egyptians lived in an occupationally diverse and socially stratified society. At the bottom were what are commonly called peasants. Egypt was a large agricultural society, and the majority of people were farmers or did farm-related work. Maintaining the crops and irrigation was difficult work!

There were also all manner of different craft specialists, such as pot-makers, butchers, and carpenters. Many of these skills were probably handed down from generation to generation, and it wouldn't have been unusual for a son to follow exactly in his father's professional footsteps. There were also slaves in Egypt, who were typically prisoners of war, but not enough of them that the Egyptian economy was dependent upon them.

Lost and Found

In Egyptian art, men are typically depicted with reddish skin and women with yellowish skin. It has been suggested that this might be representative of their traditional roles: The men worked outdoors in the sun, and the women worked mostly inside the home.

Sowing, hoeing, and plowing. Some of the hard work required of an Egyptian farmer.

(From Life in Ancient Egypt, *by A. Erman.)*

Upper-Class Employment

The elite jobs, those of government officials and bureaucrats, were reserved for literate males. The literacy requirement kept most of the powerful jobs out of the hands of the commoners. Schooling in reading and writing wasn't available to everyone, but people who mastered those skills could be employed in thousands of elite positions. The overall literacy rate in Egypt seems to have been no more than 5 percent of the population, at its greatest.

A fascinating and humorous text from the Middle Kingdom, called *Satire of the Trades*, offers insights into the nature of the hard-working working class. In the text, a student is lectured on how most everybody's job is no good except that of the scribe. Here's a sample of some of the negative opinions offered:

◆ Carpentry will make your arms tired.

◆ Potters live a dirty and grubby existence.

◆ Clothes washers and fishermen face the danger of being eaten by crocodiles.

◆ Masons are dirty and wear loincloths made of twisted rope.

◆ Arrow makers get harassed all day long by mosquitoes and gnats in the marshy water.

◆ Farmers work harder than most and suffer horribly.

As a copying and writing exercise in a scribal school, advice such as this probably got the attention of the students! "Listen and learn," was the usual attitude at school, and mistakes could be rewarded with a good beating from the instructor.

Nile Notes

The Egyptian word for the king was *nesu*. I personally prefer the term *ruler* over *king* because the *king* has too many connotations based on European notions. As a living god on earth, the Egyptian ruler was not equivalent to a Renaissance monarch. The word *king*, however, is widely accepted, and we'll use it once in a while here. The term *pharaoh*, as a designation for the Egyptian king, actually wasn't used as much until the New Kingdom. It is derived from the Egyptian words, *per-aa*, meaning, "The Great House" and referring to the palace, or the center of kingship (similar to the modern use of the term "The White House" to represent the American presidency).

It's Good to Be the King

At the other end of the social spectrum from the lowly farmer was the ruler. The king of Egypt was considered to be the living embodiment of the god Horus, the son of the god Osiris. As such, the pharaoh was thought to represent the people on earth to those in the divine realm. He was the divine absolute ruler of Egypt for a life term.

Glyphs

Maat is the Egyptian concept of truth, justice, and cosmic order. It was represented by a goddess portrayed with a feather upon her head.

The ruler had many responsibilities, including making decisions, appointing officials, and handling the usual day-to-day activities of someone of such a high office. He also had divine responsibilities, including the maintenance of *maat*, which is the concept of truth, justice, and cosmic order. *Maat* is the opposite of the undesirable state of chaos and could be upheld by striving to do that which is right and just. Keeping the forces of chaos at bay included fending off Egypt's enemies. As you'll find out in later chapters, this was a *big* responsibility!

What's in A Name?

A look at the typical names and titles of the king of Egypt is instructive. Usually there were five associated with the ruler:

- A Horus name, identifying the king as the living Horus.
- The "nebty" or "Two Ladies" name, associating the king with Nekhbet, the vulture goddess of Upper Egypt, and Wadjyt, the cobra goddess of Lower Egypt.
- The Horus of Gold name, reinforcing the notion that the ruler is the living incarnation of the god Horus.
- The "prenomen," a coronation name in a cartouche preceded by his title as King of Upper and Lower Egypt.
- The "nomen," a second "family" name in a cartouche preceded by the title, Son of the Sun.

A full listing of these names and titles makes for a cumbersome bit of writing. The nomen is the name by which we usually refer to the rulers, e.g. Amenhotep, Ramesses, and so on. In the case of multiple kings with the same name, for example, eleven fellows named Ramesses, the prenomen allows us to tell them apart.

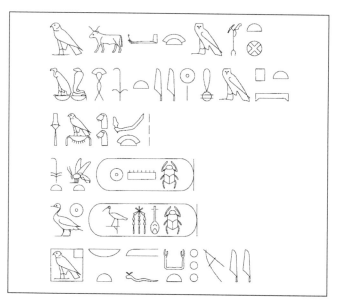

An example of royal names and titles, in this case, that of Tuthmosis III: Horus, "strong bull arising in Thebes"; Two Ladies, "enduring of kingship like Ra in heaven"; Horus of gold, "powerful of strength, holy diadems"; King of Upper and Lower Egypt, "Menkheperra"; Son of the Sun, "Thutmosis, beautiful of forms."

The power of kingship was also symbolically manifested in the form of special crowns, scepters, and other royal regalia. There was a red crown to symbolize Lower Egypt and a white crown representing Upper Egypt. Worn together, it was clear who was the ruler of the Two Lands. There was also a blue war crown symbolizing the pharaoh as a mighty warrior. Two scepters, the crook and flail, seem to symbolize the pharaoh as the good shepherd of his people, guiding them like a concerned father.

A sketch of the New Kingdom pharaoh Merneptah as depicted on the walls of his royal tomb. Merneptah is wearing a royal headdress known as the "nemes." Note the cartouches with his prenomen and nomen.

(From Atlas de l'Histoire de l'Art Égyptien, *by Prisse d'Avennes.)*

All the King's Men

Fortunately, the ruler didn't have to keep chaos at bay by himself—he was served by a pyramid of bureaucrats, whose jurisdictions covered Egypt and any outside lands under its control. The highest official below the ruler was known as the *vizier,* who served as a prime minister of sorts. He was handpicked, of course, and was often a member of the royal family or the son of a previous vizier.

Other very high and important offices included Treasurers, High Priests, and the Overseer of Works, who supervised the royal building projects. The next tier of workers included other overseers of all kinds. (See Chapter 10, "Age of Pyramids," for some Old Kingdom examples.) There were also military and priestly hierarchies. Special offices emerged from time to time, such as a Viceroy of Kush, who directed Egypt's domination over Nubia in the New Kingdom. And there were, in some periods, the governors of the various "nomes" or provinces, who maintained their own bureaucracies.

Glyphs

A **vizier** is the highest office in the Egyptian governmental hierarchy below the king. The word was derived from Turkish imperial terminology.

You've Been Drafted!

The Egyptian government extracted taxes from its people in the form of goods such as wheat, cattle, or other products. The supreme ruler also was able to draft people, so to speak, for national service. This might have involved serving in the army for a while or perhaps working on a pyramid or some other laborious project that required lots of manpower.

In short, Egypt was a highly stratified society, and although it was possible to move up through the ranks, most people probably stayed in the social and professional class they were born into. The educated elite ensured that their children would remain elite, too, by educating them.

Everyday Things

Now that you know a little bit about how ancient Egyptian society was organized, let's look at some of the details of daily life and how the Egyptians met their needs for food, clothing, and shelter.

House and Home

In the earliest times, the ancient Egyptians probably lived in a hut made of sticks plastered with mud and roofed with thatch. As villages became permanent features on the landscape, the average house was built of mud bricks with a flat roof. Most of them probably consisted of a living room and storage and sleeping rooms, with a little back courtyard for cooking and other activities. A lot of domestic activities were carried on outside of the house proper, so a great deal of interior space wasn't necessary.

Houses could come in all sizes, of course, depending upon one's wealth, from the simplest varieties described previously to two-story villas with numerous rooms. Royal palaces, too, could be made of mud brick, with wooden ceilings supported by pillars. Few remains of royal palaces have survived, but from those that do, archaeologists can tell that some were quite elaborate and included painted walls and clever architecture.

> **Pharaoh's Domain**
>
> Everybody loves cats, and so did the Egyptians. They made nice domestic household pets, as did dogs and even monkeys on occasion.

> **Nile Notes**
>
> Even with all of the cultural changes that have occurred in Egypt since the time of the pharaohs, much of the ancient lifestyle of ordinary people remains the same. It is most readily seen in the numerous agricultural villages along the Nile, where many of the activities of daily life are virtually unchanged from ancient times.

Because they were built of mud brick and other perishable materials, not many Egyptian homes or settlements have survived. Archaeologists, however, have been able to excavate a few unusually well-preserved domestic sites including: the New Kingdom workmen's village of Deir el-Medineh, the Middle Kingdom pyramid town of Kahun, and the short-lived Amarna Period city of Akhetaten. Each has given us special insights into daily life, but because each was a rare, somewhat specialized, settlement, we should be careful about generalizing from them. Still, people in pyramid towns needed homes and food like everyone else, and we are lucky that some of these sites have survived.

There probably weren't many of what we would call "cities" in ancient Egypt. Perhaps Memphis and Thebes might fit the bill because they probably had relatively high populations. Smaller "towns" serving as administrative centers were likely the norm, with the majority of people living in what we might characterize as "villages."

What's for Dinner?

Now that we know where the ancient Egyptians lived, let's take a look at what they ate! The two big staples of the ancient Egyptian diet were bread and beer. The bread was made from flour ground from barley or emmer wheat, and the beer was brewed from barley. Bread was produced in flat, oval, triangular, and cone-shape loaves.

Surprisingly, archaeologists have found loaves of bread in tombs, where they were left as offerings or food provisions for the deceased. Now that's some stale bread!

A variety of vegetables was available, including chickpeas, fava beans, lentils, lettuce, onions, and cucumbers. Meat was quite expensive, especially the larger animals such as cows. Wealthy folk went hunting for wild game such as antelope and gazelles. Domesticated goats and sheep weren't quite as costly and were a source of milk products such as cheese. There were also pigs. Lacking refrigeration, meat had to be consumed right away. The average Egyptian, however, probably enjoyed fish and some tasty ducks for a little protein in the diet. Ducks and geese were kept in pens, and the Egyptians ate their eggs. For a little variety, mice and hedgehogs were sometimes eaten as well.

Food could be spiced up with a little salt, parsley, coriander, cumin, and other enhancements. Available fruits included figs, dates, and grapes. The ancient Egyptians produced a lot of wine, including the traditional variety made from grapes, but also others types manufactured from pomegranates and dates. For sweetening up one's life, honey was a real favorite.

The Egyptian kitchen was generally an open-air affair. A large domed oven was typical, and ceramic pots were used for certain types of cooking. Kitchen utensils included long sticks for poking at things in the oven, copper knives, and wooden spoons and spatulas. Food could be grilled, boiled, fried, roasted, or baked.

Pharaoh's Domain

A typical Egyptian workman's lunch might consist of bread and onions slugged down with a jar of beer. Delicious!

Lost and Found

The Greek historian Herodotus mentioned that the pig was a taboo creature in ancient Egyptian society, but no Egyptian evidence confirms this. In fact, archaeologists have found lots of pig bones while excavating settlement sites.

What Am I Going to Wear?

Clothing in ancient Egypt ranged from the minimal—or nothing—to the expensively elaborate. Like many things in Egyptian society, clothing and status were often linked. For the male laborer, a simple loincloth might suffice, and children often ran around naked. For more general wear, a wrapped skirt or kilt reaching to at least the knees was common for both men and women. More elite women often wore a sheath dress, which was basically a cloth tube with shoulder straps. For party wear, the dresses were often much more elaborate, with shawls and cloaks serving as accessories for chilly evenings.

Generally, the cloth used in Egypt was linen manufactured from flax, and there were different grades of quality. White seems to have been the usual color, but some of the dresses had patterns, fringes, or beading. During some time periods, pleats, longer sleeves, and tunics were all the rage. And what about underwear? Both men and women could wear a triangular loincloth beneath their other clothes.

It's likely that many Egyptians went barefoot, but sandals were also worn. Men's hair was generally short, and women wore theirs long and straight. Wealthier individuals of either sex might have worn wigs, some of which were made of human hair, while some priests shaved their heads, if not their whole bodies. Egyptian children, both boys and girls, typically had their head shaved except for a long lock of hair on one side, the "side lock" of youth.

It was quite common for Egyptians to use eye paint to accentuate their eyes. They were noted for their personal cleanliness and bathed regularly. The Nile was always there for a bit of washing up, and some of the nicer homes had a place to shower with water poured from a clay jar.

Pharaoh's Domain

The Egyptian game of *senet* was played on a game board marked out with squares. Players threw dice or sticks to move around the board in what was an ancestor to many similar games enjoyed today. Senet boards have been found in tombs, and replica versions can now be purchased and played in the twenty-first century.

Let Me Entertain You

Like people everywhere, the ancient Egyptians liked to have a good time. They participated in sports such as running, jumping, wrestling, and stick fighting, as well as board games involving strategy and chance. Fishing and fowling were enjoyed along the banks of the Nile, with participants throwing sticks to knock out the desired birds. Some things never change—kids back then enjoyed playing with toy animals and dolls as well.

The Egyptians also loved a good party. The fancier ones included dancers, musicians, and singers. Musical instruments included the harp, lute, lyre, flutes, drums, rattles, and other noisemakers while lots of good food and wine were consumed.

A lovely Egyptian musician plays the lute.

(From Atlas de l'Histoire de l'Art Égyptien, *by Prisse d'Avennes.)*

Paying the Bills

Barter was the name of the game when it came to paying bills. There was no coinage, but there was a general sense of how much things were worth. Quantities of desirable and useful products, such as wheat, were a regular unit of exchange.

Raising a family, earning a living, preparing food, paying bills … sounds familiar, doesn't it? Even though our modern cultures are quite different in the details from those in the distant past, we have a lot in common—and it's this common sense of humanity that connects us with all people, past, present, and future!

The Least You Need to Know

- The traditional family unit was the core of Egyptian society.
- Men and women each had their different, but vital, societal roles, and Egyptian women had more legal rights than in any other ancient Near Eastern society.
- Egyptian society was highly stratified, as reflected in such things as housing, clothing, and professions.
- The role of the pharaoh was that of divine supreme ruler for life.
- The ancient Egyptians were similar to us today in many ways, although the details of their society vary considerably.

Chapter 6

Science and Technology

In This Chapter

- ◆ Math and measurements
- ◆ Calendars
- ◆ Bricks and pots
- ◆ Stones, gold, gems, and wood
- ◆ Donkeys, boats, and baskets

The ancient Egyptians were very skilled and creative people. They quarried and moved large blocks of stone for hundreds of miles, built massive monuments such as the pyramids, and created complex, intricate jewelry. Although this ancient culture did not have the advanced knowledge of science and technology that we have today, the scientific and technical competence of the Egyptians was impressive. In this chapter, we'll take a look at just a few of the notable scientific and technological developments of this ancient culture.

The Numbers Game

As we marvel at the ancient Egyptian's incredible architectural achievements— the pyramids, the Sphinx, obelisks, and temples—it's easy to jump to the conclusion that they were masters of arithmetic, geometry, trigonometry, and physics. That's not necessarily so. Although we don't have a lot of written

Lost and Found

The most complete of the few surviving ancient Egyptian mathematical texts is known as the Rhind Papyrus. It was found in the mid-nineteenth century, and most of it resides in the British Museum. The papyrus is a mathematical textbook with a wide number of problems and solutions.

information specifically addressing such matters, it seems that the Egyptian understanding of mathematics was somewhat rudimentary, which makes their architectural achievements even more impressive!

In terms of arithmetic, the Egyptians worked in base 10, which is the same system we're generally accustomed to today. They had symbols representing 1s, 10s, 100s, 1000s, and so on, and numbers could be indicated by repetitions of these symbols. With these numbers they could easily add, subtract, multiply, and divide with whole numbers. They also were somewhat adept at fractions, although their methodology for computation would probably seem cumbersome to us. They did not use zero.

Despite their apparent limited knowledge of advanced mathematics, the Egyptians could readily calculate length, volume, area, and slope. This can be confirmed by looking at the proportions of finished monuments, which would have required at least some ability in these matters to be constructed.

Egyptian numerals.

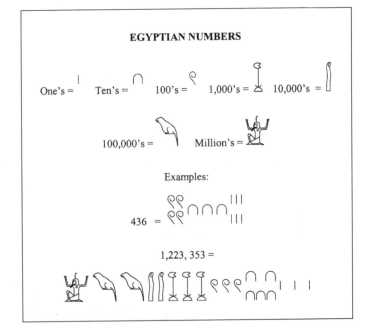

EGYPTIAN NUMBERS

One's =   Ten's =   100's =   1,000's =   10,000's =

100,000's =   Million's =

Examples:

436 =

1,223, 353 =

Sizing Things Up

Standards of measurements were of great importance in all ancient civilizations, especially in those such as Egypt where they didn't use what we'd call "money." Some sense of uniformity in size, weight, and volume was essential for such things as managing land, fair commerce, accounting, and construction. The standard Egyptian unit of measurement for length was the royal cubit, which was based on the length of the pharaoh's forearm. A cubit was about 20.5 inches in length and was divided into seven palm-breadths composed of four finger widths. Larger measurements such as the "rod," equaling 100 cubits, could be used for great lengths.

For volume, the "hekat" or standard "wheat-measure" was used not unlike the "bushel" is used today. It was probably equivalent to about a gallon. Additionally, there were smaller measures such as the "hin" or "jar," ten of which made a "hekat." For weight, including precious materials such as gold and silver, a unit known as a "deben" was used, weighing about 91 grams and composed of 10 "kites."

> **Nile Notes**
>
> Although a measurement based on a pharaoh's forearm might seem fairly arbitrary, depending upon the size of the current king, standardized cubit sticks have been found that provide a degree of uniformity.

Calendar

Like many ancient civilizations, the Egyptians produced a civil calendar to keep track of time and events. While some of the other nearby cultures based their calendars on the cycles of the moon, the Egyptian calendar was arranged around the sun. The Egyptian year consisted of 12 months of 30 days each. Five extra days were added to the end, for a grand total of 365 days a year. The year was also divided into three seasons: inundation, winter, and summer. Each day was divided into 24 hours, 12 of day and 12 of night. This calendric arrangement was adopted by the Romans and eventually became the basis for the system we still use today.

You might be aware that an actual year on Earth lasts 365.25 days. Given this phenomenon, we need to correct our modern calendar periodically so that it keeps up with that of nature. That's why we have a "leap year" every four years, adding an extra day for adjustment. The Egyptians, unfortunately, didn't use such a correction, so, consequently, the civil calendar was essentially six

> **Pharaoh's Domain**
>
> The three Egyptian natural seasons would correspond approximately to our calendar months as follows: inundation, mid-July until mid-November; winter, mid-November until mid-March; summer, mid-March to mid-July.

months off to the astronomical year after 730 years! Fortunately, nature is a reliable calendar, and such observable phenomenon as the rise of certain stars in certain places probably announced to the Egyptians the coming of seasons even if their civil calendar was incorrect.

Medicine

Egyptologists have been able to learn about ancient Egyptian health problems and their medical treatments by examining mummies and skeletal remains. Furthermore, several medical papyri have been discovered, and they address a variety of ancient concerns, including study of the eye, gynecology, and internal problems. Given the nature of warfare in ancient times, it is not surprising that traumatic injuries and their treatments were described in the medical papyri as well.

Nile Notes

The average life expectancy of ancient Egyptians was between 30 and 36 years.

Pharaoh's Domain

We have evidence that some of the ancient Egyptians were afflicted with bilharziasis (schistosomaisis), a tiny parasite hosted by snails in slow-moving water such as irrigation canals. This disease remains a problem even today in Egypt's extensive agricultural areas.

Lost and Found

Veterinary texts have also been found describing the treatment of various animal ailments.

There were several kinds of physicians and medical specialists in ancient Egypt. A surgeon of sorts and experts in snake and scorpion bites might accompany desert workers or soldiers.

The ancient Egyptian understanding of the human body and how it works was quite different from ours. It was thought, for example, that the heart rather than the brain was the center of thought and emotion, and the Egyptian perception of the nature of circulation and bodily fluids was far from modern. Yet, perhaps the Egyptians were successful from time to time in treating a variety of ailments.

Egyptian medicine seems to have been a combination of practical or rational approaches mixed with the magical. A physical remedy such as a poultice or pharmaceutical recipe might be combined with an incantation, a magic spell, or the wearing of a magic amulet. There were also patron deities for such things as healing (Thoth), disease (Sekhmet), and scorpions and snakes (Selqet). Some of the remedies called for exotic products that likewise blurred the line between the physical and supernatural realms.

Dentistry was also practiced, but it's unclear to what extent. Because of their coarse diet, especially bread, which can contain a lot of grit from the threshing process, it is common to see a great deal of dental attrition in the remains of ancient Egyptians. They wore their teeth down, and gum disease and oral abscesses were not rare. There must have been at least a few dental specialists because a dental bridge has been found in the Old Kingdom, secured in place with gold wire.

Technology Time

Having addressed a few of the interesting notions about "science" and ancient Egypt, let's take just a brief look at a few of the many interesting aspects of ancient technology. Many topics could be covered, so I'll have to be selective and offer up a few facts about some of the more common subjects. For starters, let's look at one of the most basic of all substances, mud and clay.

Baking the Clay

The remains of ancient pots are one of the most common and useful artifacts examined by archaeologists. Because these pots are made of baked clay, they tend to survive for long periods of time. And because they often break, they were continuously produced. The sizes and shapes of the pots give us an idea about their function, but, perhaps more importantly, their different styles through time serve as a very useful dating tool.

Pots could be made by hand or in a mold, but techniques involving spinning, such as using potter's wheels, were far more efficient. Decorative and functional features including handles could be shaped into the clay before firing. Pigments could also be added to provide a little color. Egyptian and foreign styles of pottery can give us great insights into trade and international commerce in ancient times.

A very special type of ceramic material often associated with ancient Egypt is called *faience*. It was typically shaped in molds for amulets, inlays, and small figurines, but it could also be used in plates

Diggers

Alfred Lucas (1867–1945) was a British chemist who applied his scientific skills to the study of ancient Egypt. He is especially famous for his role in conserving the many objects from the tomb of Tutankhamun. His book, *Ancient Egyptian Materials and Industries*, is still a basic resource on Egyptian technology.

Nile Notes

Most sources of clay contain slight chemical differences from each other. Some archaeological methods allow us to actually identify the very source location of the clay from which an individual pot was made. This is very useful, of course, in tracing trading practices, including imports and exports.

Glyphs

Faience is a type of ceramic material made from quartz. It was typically glazed in blue or green and was formed into amulets, funerary figures, and occasionally plates and other vessels.

and other vessels. Its usually glassy green- or blue-glazed surface gives it its distinct and desirable character.

Muddy River

One benefit of living along a river such as the Nile was an endless supply of building material in the form of mud. Temporary "wattle and daub" shelters—that is, woven sticks covered with mud—seem to have been common in prehistoric days. Starting at least around the beginning of dynastic times, the use of brick in major construction became very common. The bricks consisted of mud and sometimes clay mixed with straw as a binder; they were pressed into rectangular wooden frames and then typically dried in the sun. Bricks of this sort are still manufactured and used in the villages of Egypt today.

Structures of all sizes could be built of mud brick. Huge brick walls from ancient times can be found in Egypt—some are the remains of buildings, and others are enclosure walls. Mud bricks could be incorporated in vaulted and domed ceilings and as floor pavements. And, surprisingly, the constructions weren't necessarily ugly! Mud brick architecture could be spruced up by white-washing, plastering, and painting.

Cutting and Chiseling

Stone, of course, was an essential building material in ancient Egypt, and the three most common types in use were granite, sandstone, and limestone. Sources of stone can be found far and wide, and the Egyptians were not averse to establishing quarries in distant places to obtain the best quality material for special projects. Some of the most desirable granite, for example, was found far south in Aswan, yet it was shipped hundreds of miles to the north for use in pyramid building and other projects.

Lost and Found

The remains of a huge obelisk sit in a granite quarry in Aswan. At 128 feet long, it would have been one of the largest pieces of stone quarried in Egypt, had it not cracked in the quarrying process. Because the work was abandoned before completion, it has provided Egyptologists with wonderful insights into the quarrying process.

The difficulty of quarrying and shaping stone varied, depending on the nature of the stone. Sandstone and limestone are relatively soft, and copper and stone chisels and hollow copper drills and saws were used to cut them. Granite, a much harder stone, was more difficult to cut. Egyptians used hard stone pounding balls to free blocks of stone from quarries, a task accomplished by hand that must have been utterly exhausting and mind-numbing.

Gold and Other Malleable Metals

Something about gold makes it universally appealing. It seems that most cultures throughout the world, ancient and modern, valued this gleaming metal, which can be easily manipulated and transformed into treasures of all sizes. Egypt was no different. The ancient Egyptians considered gold to be the flesh of gods, most notably the sun god, Re.

With the discovery of King Tut's tomb in 1922 and its enormous number of golden or gilded objects, the world evermore associated gold with the wealth of ancient Egypt. The main sources of gold in Egypt were from Nubia and the Eastern Desert. Although silver was available, it didn't seem to have the same sort of appeal as gold during much of pharaonic times.

Copper was especially desirable for tools and other utilitarian items. Extensive remains of copper mining have been found in the Sinai, and copper was in such heavy demand that it was also imported. Copper smelting, which involves melting copper ore to refine it, began in Egypt during Predynastic times. Bronze (copper plus an alloy, such as tin) also was in use early on, but not extensively until much later.

> ### Nile Notes
>
> The oldest known geological map comes from ancient Egypt and shows gold mines in the Wadi Hammammat in the Eastern Desert. The map dates to the reign of Ramesses IV (c. 1150 B.C.) and resides in the Egyptian Museum in Turin, Italy.

Gemstones were prized, and materials such as turquoise, carnelian, garnet, and jasper were mined or otherwise collected or imported and frequently were used in jewelry. One of the most exotic gems was lapis lazuli, a deep blue stone from Afghanistan. An extensive bit of trading and transport was required before this stone could make its way to Egypt.

Wood!

I've mentioned stones and such, so perhaps it would be appropriate to mention another essential material that can be carved and shaped for any number of functions: wood. Egypt, with its desert climate, didn't have many stands of tall trees, but smaller trees such as acacia, tamarisk, and sidder were sufficiently abundant and were used to make smaller items. For larger objects, including furniture, statues, and even coffins, several small pieces of wood were often skillfully joined together. If large planks were needed for boats or special projects, they could be imported from Lebanon or Syria. Special wood, such as the exotic black ebony, could be obtained from Nubia through trade. The Egyptians utilized a variety of wood-working tools, including chisels and mallets, adzes, drills, and saws. They also occasionally manufactured things from ivory, which was obtained from hippo teeth or imported elephant tusks.

Getting Around

Moving from one place to another doesn't seem to have been that difficult in ancient Egypt. Trails and roads connected villages and districts, and travel on foot would not have been unusual. Donkeys, though, were a common mode of transportation. As able beasts of burden, they could assist in many of the smaller domestic and economic chores and also could work in caravans.

Caravan routes traversed the Eastern Desert to quarry and mining sites and the Red Sea. Other trails led out to oases or other remote regions. A major thoroughfare known as "The Ways of Horus" led across the northern Delta into the Sinai and parts to the east.

> **Nile Notes**
>
> Although the camel is often iden-tified with Egypt today, it didn't feature regularly as a beast of burden until relatively late, per-haps during the ninth century B.C.

> **Glyphs**
>
> **Papyriform** boats are those whose shape imitates that of old papyrus vessels, most notably by their upturned bow and stern.

> **Pharaoh's Domain**
>
> The Twenty-sixth Dynasty pharaoh Necho II (c. 600 B.C.) is said to have commis-sioned an expedition of Phoeni-cian sailors to circumnavigate Africa. Leaving from the Red Sea and returning through Gibralter, the trip took three years.

The River Road

The Nile provided a veritable highway for the transport of people and goods. As noted in Chapter 3, "Ancient Egypt in Space and Time," the current of the river flows north, while the winds tend to blow south, allow-ing for travel in either direction. The Egyptians had many boats to take advantage of this gift of nature. Dating back to Predynastic times, there are many depictions of boats on pottery vessels and in rock art. Although the details are often hard to sort out, some of these early boats seem to be made of bundles of papyrus with upturned bows and sterns, a feature later imitated on wooden boats.

Boats came in all sizes, from little papyrus fishing skiffs to huge wooden barges capable of carrying many tons of material. Many boats featured an upturned bow and stern. These *papyriform* vessels seem to imitate the shape of old papyrus boats. Surviving examples of Egyptian boats indicate that rope was widely used to tie planks of various sizes together.

Despite their ability to construct sophisticated river craft, the Egyptians were not known for great seafaring prowess. Other peoples in the region of the Near East, such as the Phoenicians, were quite adept at sea travel, and many of them no doubt carried out extensive trade visits throughout Egyptian history. There is little evi-dence that the Egyptians ventured regularly across the

Mediterranean or had an interest in extended exploration by sea. There is at least one notable exception, though: an expedition down the Red Sea coast to the exotic Land of Punt during the New Kingdom reign of Hatshepsut. Even then, they probably hugged the coast.

Tying Up Loose Ends

When you're dealing with huge and magnificent temples, tombs, and pyramids, it's easy to forget the small stuff. Some of the so-called "mundane" technologies such as rope and basketry played a vital role in both the everyday and the extraordinary doings of the Egyptians. How are you going to drag those big blocks of stones or lower them onto a barge without rope? How will you tie up your donkey or hold your fishing raft together? Baskets can be put to use for any number of purposes, including transporting and storing food and objects and moving dirt in construction projects.

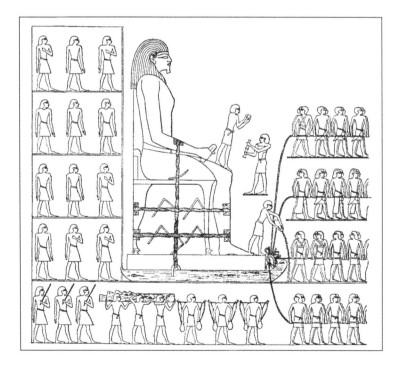

A colossal statue being moved on a sledge pulled by large number of workmen.

(*A. Erman,* Life in Ancient Egypt*)*

Yes, ropes and baskets served a myriad of important functions. They were made from natural fibers including those derived from some grass and palm species and papyrus. Ropes were made of all sizes—from string to cable—to serve different functions. Baskets were woven in several different styles and sometimes were attractively decorated.

Lost and Found _____

Some large-diameter ropes made from papyrus were found in one of the quarries from which the stone for the Giza pyramids was hewn. A radiocarbon date demonstrated that they were much younger than the pyramids (from around the first century B.C.), but they still provide us with well-preserved examples of ancient rope and evidence of the long-term use of the quarry.

We'll be exploring some more developments in Egyptian science and technology in future chapters—they're hard to avoid when considering such things as building pyramids and making mummies!

The Least You Need to Know

- ◆ Ancient Egyptian mathematics weren't terribly sophisticated by modern standards.
- ◆ Ancient Egyptian medicine was a combination of practical and magical treatments.
- ◆ The Egyptian solar calendar is the foundation for the one we use today.
- ◆ The Egyptians mined and imported copper and were very adept at working with gold and gemstones.
- ◆ The Egyptians were masters of working with stone and wood.
- ◆ Less "glamorous" industries, such as the making of pots, ropes, baskets, and bricks, played vital roles in ancient Egyptian culture.

7

Religion: Organizing the World

In This Chapter

- ◆ The way the world works
- ◆ Creation stories
- ◆ Loads of gods
- ◆ Egyptian temples
- ◆ Priests in action

One of the most profound differences between ancient Egypt and our modern technological world is the way we perceive our universe and how its many parts work and interact. The development of science over the last few hundred years has provided us with models for explaining many things around us. Religion continues to play an important societal role, but it occasionally conflicts with science. In the United States, the separation of church and state is seen as a major societal principle. In ancient Egypt, religion seems to have permeated most everything. In this chapter, we'll take a look at the Egyptian world view and the role that religion played in that view.

Lost and Found

Egyptologists are not sure how or when some of the earliest Egyptian religious concepts came into being. The earliest written religious texts from ancient Egypt come from the time of the Old Kingdom. They were written on the walls of several pyramids and are known as the "Pyramid Texts." These difficult-to-comprehend writings provide some insights into the abstract thinking of the ancient Egyptians and continue to be studied.

Gods for Everything

Most people are aware that the Egyptians recognized many gods—hundreds of them, in fact. There seems to have been a god linked to or representative of nearly everything in the world, from the physical facets of nature to abstract notions of the human condition. Great natural features, such as the sun, the moon, and the Nile, were thought to be gods, but there were also certain gods that an Egyptian could appeal to if pregnant or bitten by a snake. There were plenty of gods to go around to suit any given occasion, and two or more gods could even be combined.

The Egyptians believed that the gods were the forces behind the phenomena that they observed or otherwise experienced. Today, for example, we explain weather by the complex interaction of various—and, ideally, predictable—physical factors. To the Egyptians, no such complexity was necessary. A god was behind the action, and that explained it!

Many Egyptian gods were associated with and depicted as animals, which is probably due to certain characteristics that the gods were thought to have. For example, Sakhmet, a fierce goddess, was depicted as a lioness, and the god Anubis, the protector of the cemeteries, was a jackal, a kind of wild dog that roams the hills by night. Many gods were portrayed as *anthropomorphic*—that is, in human form; at other times, these same entities might be portrayed with human bodies and the heads of the animals they were associated with. (Some Egyptologists believe that this stems from the practice of priests sometimes wearing animal masks.) The Egyptians seemed satisfied with either depiction; whatever way the gods were depicted, they were considered to be the personification of reality and concepts. Very few people probably claimed to actually see these gods in the form that they were depicted in art, yet the people felt the gods' presence and believed that they could be appeased and appealed to.

Nile Notes

In his *Histories,* the Greek historian Herodotus noted that the Egyptians were "religious to excess, far beyond any other race of men."

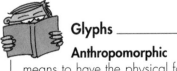

Glyphs

Anthropomorphic
means to have the physical form of a human.

A View of the World

To understand the Egyptian world view, it's useful to see how the people viewed the structure of the universe. Looking around them, the ancient Egyptians saw the same things that we do: the sky above, with the sun, moon, and stars, and the Earth below. Whereas we believe that there is a vast expanse of space filled with stars, planets, and constellations, the Egyptians had other ideas.

The Egyptians believed that their world was basically surrounded by water. The sky was thought to be the edge of the eternal waters, as represented by the goddess Nut. The Earth, represented by the god Geb, was separated by the air god Shu. On the opposite of the Earth was a parallel land of sorts, a netherworld known as the Duat, which was home not only to the blessed dead, but was full of devious creatures, demons, and damned souls as well.

How might they have formed such beliefs? The Egyptians did not know that the Earth travels around the sun in a regular orbit. Instead, they believed that the cycles of night and day were created by the sun god making a westward journey across the sky. After traveling beneath the Earth into the land of darkness, the sun god was triumphantly reborn each day in the east.

Nile Notes

Whereas the Egyptian deities rarely, if ever, showed their actual faces to the average Egyptian, the gods were believed to be able to communicate their will through dreams. The tricky part was in the interpretation! And occasionally, the gods served as oracles when their cult statues were paraded through town during festivals. A voice from the vicinity of the statue borne by priests or a slight tip of its carrying bier might provide an answer to a commoner's question.

With this sort of thinking, the daily travels of the sun became a repetitive cosmic drama. The movement of the sun could be seen as a great divine boat traversing the waters of the sky, or perhaps it was propelled by great celestial wings, like a slowly flying falcon. Or, the round ball of the sun might have been pushed across the sky by a great cosmic dung beetle, an insect that lays its eggs in dung and then pushes it across the ground, forming a round ball. In some examples of religious art, the goddess Nut is seen spread out across the universe, swallowing the sun, which travels through her body during the 12 hours of night to be reborn in the usual way the next day. Ancient Egyptians could believe all of these things to be true at the same time without contradiction—each way of representing something was simply a different facet of the same phenomenon.

In the Beginning

Most humans are curious about their ultimate origins. So, too, were the Egyptians. There were several versions of the creation story, of which the following scenario is representative: Before creation, eight gods existed in the eternal waters of Nun in a time of infinite darkness and nothingness.

The eight precreation gods represented various abstract concepts of this boundless watery void. Out of this void appeared a primeval mound, from which emerged a creator god by the name of Atum. Atum then proceeded to create a male and female pair of gods who started the process of the formation of the known universe. The first couple, Shu, representing air, and Tefnut, representing moisture, became the parents of Geb, the Earth, and Nut, the sky. Artistic depictions survive showing Shu (the air) separating Geb (the Earth) from Nut (the sky). Geb and Nut, in turn, produced two more pairs of important gods, Osiris and Isis, along with Seth and Nephthys. This first and vital group of nine early gods is known as the *Ennead*.

Another later version of the creation scenario involves Ptah, a god associated with crafts, as an intermediary in the creation process. As the ideas of things were conceived by the creator, the god Ptah spoke their name, and they were converted into reality. And where did people come from? The ram-headed god Khnum created them on a potter's wheel.

Glyphs

The first group of nine gods from Egyptian creation are known as the **Ennead** and consist of Atum, Shu and Tefnut, Geb and Nut, Osiris and Isis, and Seth and Nephthys.

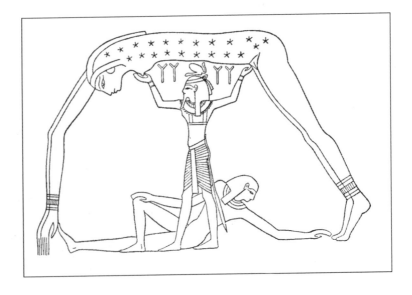

The god Shu (air) separating the Earth (Geb) from the sky (Nut).

(After The Mummy, *by E.A.W. Budge.)*

Pick a God, Any God ...

Different gods could be associated with different cities, towns, or places. Ptah, for example, was the favored god of Memphis, while Amun became closely associated with Thebes. Gods often appeared in triads of a paired male and female deities plus their offspring. At Memphis, Ptah and Sakhmet were at home with their son, Nefertum, and at Thebes, Amun and his wife, Mut, could be found with their son, Khonsu. During most of Egyptian history, there seems to have been no real national requirement to worship any one god, and the Egyptians were apparently able to pick and choose whichever ones appealed to them or might be helpful to them in any given situation.

The gods were also sometimes mixed and matched. Ptah, for example, was occasionally combined with another favorite god of Memphis, Sokar, who was associated with the dead (as was Osiris); thus, Ptah-Sokar-Osiris was worshiped as a composite entity. The sun god, Ra, was joined with other gods, including Amun, Horus, Atum and Monthu, to be envisioned as Amun-Ra, Ra-Horakhty, Ra-Atum, and Monthu-Ra. The modern Western mind rebels at such concepts, but the Egyptians didn't see these seemingly contradictory propositions as an intellectual fallacy. To them, these various divine incarnations and permutations not only explained the workings of the world, but also provided viewpoints that acknowledged different perspectives of what we might consider to be one phenomenon.

Egyptian Gods: The Short List

Here's a very short list of some of the principal gods:

- ◆ **Amun:** The great god of Thebes.
- ◆ **Anubis:** The jackal-god patron of embalmers and guardian of cemeteries.
- ◆ **Aten:** The sun disk.
- ◆ **Atum:** The creator god.
- ◆ **Bastet:** The cat goddess.
- ◆ **Bes:** A curious dwarf-like fellow who was a domestic protector.
- ◆ **Geb:** The Earth god.
- ◆ **Hap:** The Nile god.
- ◆ **Hathor:** A feminine cow-goddess with a horned headdress.
- ◆ **Horus:** A falcon god and the son of Osiris. Identified with the living king.
- ◆ **Isis:** Wife of Osiris and mother of Horus.
- ◆ **Khnum:** Ram-headed god who created people on a potter's wheel.
- ◆ **Khons:** The moon god.
- ◆ **Maat:** Goddess of truth, justice, and order.

- ◆ **Monthu:** Theban god of war.
- ◆ **Mut:** The wife of Amun.
- ◆ **Nekhbet:** Vulture goddess representing Upper Egypt.
- ◆ **Nephthys:** Wife of Seth and sister of Isis.
- ◆ **Nut:** The sky goddess.
- ◆ **Osiris:** Husband of Isis and father of Horus, god of the netherworld depicted as a mummified king.
- ◆ **Ptah:** Patron of crafts.
- ◆ **Ra:** The sun god.
- ◆ **Sakhmet:** The fierce lioness wife of Ptah.
- ◆ **Seth:** The god of chaos, violence, and storms.
- ◆ **Shu:** The air god.
- ◆ **Taweret:** A goddess in the shape of a hippopotamus and a patron to women in childbirth.
- ◆ **Tefnut:** The goddess of moisture.
- ◆ **Thoth:** The divine scribe and the inventor of writing, associated with the ibis bird and sometimes an ape.
- ◆ **Wadjet:** A cobra goddess representing Lower Egypt.

Some depictions of some of the principal Egyptian gods. From left to right: Isis, Osiris, Horus, Seth, Bes, and Bastet.

(After The Mummy, *by E.A.W. Budge.)*

Polytheism and Monotheism

There is no doubt that the Egyptians were *polytheists*—that is, they worshipped many gods. Some scholars, though, suggest that there are inklings of the belief in a supreme god to be found among the numerous theological concepts.

One of the more interesting religious phenomena in Egypt was the emergence of the god Amun, whose cult was centered at Thebes, especially during the New Kingdom, when huge temples were built for him. Amun was considered a great, infinite, and unknowable divine presence, and he came to be perceived as almost a universal god incorporating all of the other gods. This might be as close to monotheism as the Egyptians ever got, although during the famous Amarna period (see Chapter 14, "An Empire Is Built"), the worship of the sun-disk Aten was promoted as superior to all other gods.

Glyphs

Polytheism is the worship of many gods. **Monotheism** is the worship of one god.

High Drama

Many stories about the different gods tied a lot of diverse ideas together. Some of these myths played a significant role in understanding life and death, and one of the most powerful was that of Osiris and Seth. Osiris was killed by his brother, Seth, the god who personified evil and chaos. After Osiris's body was wrapped as a mummy, he was "resurrected" and served as the king of the afterlife. Osiris plays an important role in the Egyptians' notions of a life after death, which was very real to them. Osiris was believed to have been buried at Abydos, which was a cult center for his worship.

After killing Osiris, Seth continued his mischief and battled it out with Horus, the son of Osiris. At one point, Seth wounded one of Horus's eyes, but it was restored by the god Thoth. The phases of the moon were thought to replay this drama regularly, with the waning of the moon representing Horus's damaged eye and the waxing moon representing its restoration.

Horus eventually triumphed over Seth, which was a worthy role for the ruling pharaoh, who was thought to be the living incarnation of Horus. After all, it was the ruling pharaoh's job to triumph over chaos, violence, and confusion. The pharaoh's father, the previous ruler, was thought to be Osiris.

Mansions for the Gods

Ancient Egyptians built temples to the various gods all over Egypt, including at the gods' cult centers. A temple was a specific area or building established as a holy space separated from the profane world. There was no single plan for all temples, but many featured courtyards and a series of rooms, with entrance to the smallest

Pharaoh's Domain

When depicted in animal form, the god Seth is a very odd creature, with a long snout, short ears, and a pointy, upright tail. There have been many attempts to try to identify this creature with a known animal. The possibility remains that it is purely a mythological creature. To Egyptologists, it is known as "the Seth-animal."

rooms restricted to a small number of qualified priests. Inside the restricted area was a shrine, which contained a stone, bronze, gold, or gilded wood image of the god to whom the temple was dedicated. The statue was considered to be a resting place for the god, who could visit or inhabit the image if it so chose and consume the offerings presented to it.

Priestly Duties

The pharaoh served as the supreme high priest and intermediary between humans and gods. Making sure that all was in order with the universe was one of the king's primary concerns, and service to the gods was a big part of this responsibility. It was thought that attending to the gods was required to ensure that the sun was reborn again each morning and to keep chaos at bay. The pharaoh himself, in theory, at least, was supposed to conduct the daily temple rituals. Of course, this was a physical impossibility because there were temples throughout Egypt, so it was necessary to have priests associated with every temple to do the necessary deeds. However, the pharaoh was often symbolically present by means of his statues or by his images on temple walls and probably physically participated in the most important events or festivals.

Some depictions of some of the principal Egyptian gods. From left to right: Anubis, Maat, Ptah, Ra, Thoth, and Tawaret.

(After The Mummy, *by E.A.W. Budge.)*

There was a hierarchy of priests, and, until the New Kingdom, most seemed to have been part-timers recruited from the upper classes. With the building of huge temple complexes in the New Kingdom, a large number of priests became necessary to attend to everything from cleaning the sacred buildings to making accounts of the temple estates, income, and expenditures. The priests at the top of the hierarchy performed the necessary rituals three times a day. In the morning, a qualified priest approached the inner sanctum of a given temple and opened the shrine. The priest bathed, clothed, and otherwise prepared and renewed the image of the god and performed rituals to ensure a hospitable home for the god. Finally, the priest left the god a tasty meal.

A Couple of Big Ones!

Two of the biggest and best-preserved temples in ancient Egypt are in modern Luxor, the site of ancient Thebes. Beginning in the twelfth dynasty of the Middle Kingdom, religious structures were established at a site known as Karnak. With subsequent rulers adding onto the site, especially from the New Kingdom onward, this is now a sprawling complex of structures covering over 247 acres and is principally dedicated to the god Amun. The site is an extremely complex mix of pylons, columns, walls with carved reliefs, obelisks, statuary, and even a sacred lake.

The Karnak Temple was connected to what is referred to as the Luxor Temple, on the southern end of Thebes, by an avenue of ram-headed sphinxes. The spectacular Luxor Temple was built primarily by the New Kingdom ruler Amenhotep III and, like Karnak, was augmented by later additions.

> ## Nile Notes
>
> Egyptian priests cannot be equated with Christian pastors or Jewish rabbis. They didn't conduct rituals before a body of parishioners, nor did they offer personal counseling. Some types of priests were apparently knowledgeable in healing and magic, however, and were thus able to occasionally assist the needs and desires of individuals.

> ## Nile Notes
>
> Many of the temples in Egypt were probably painted in gleaming white and bright colors. Most of the coloring has long ago worn away, and the monuments tend to appear a uniform light brown. Traces of paint can still be found on less exposed surfaces, giving us an idea of their once splendorous condition. Some of the temple doors were once sheathed with sheets of copper or gold, and some of the painted decorations were also encrusted with semiprecious stones. Needless to say, those particular features are long gone!

Honoring the Dead

Apart from the temples dedicated to the gods, mortuary temples were dedicated to the memory of the formerly living gods on Earth, the pharaohs. The pharaohs built these monuments in honor of themselves during their lifetimes, and some of these buildings are the most impressive surviving stone structures in Egypt. While relatively small mortuary temples or chapels were built alongside pyramids during the Old and Middle Kingdom, huge and grandiose independent buildings were constructed during the New Kingdom to serve the dead kings who were buried a distance away in a mountain valley. These temples, too, required priests and rituals to maintain the cult of the dead pharaoh.

Pharaoh's Domain

Several special individuals were deified after their deaths and were worshipped accordingly. Two of the most famous were architects. Imhotep was involved with the works of the Third-Dynasty ruler Djoser. Amenhotep, Son of Hapu, was associated with the Eighteenth-Dynasty King Amenhotep III.

There are also instances of temples and religious cults dedicated to the divine ruler even before he died! Ramesses II was especially notable in this regard and had numerous giant statues and other monuments to himself created throughout the land. Although such state temples were restricted to the priests, religious rituals could be carried out by ordinary people at the funerary chapels of private individuals.

It's Festival Time!

If average Egyptians ever got to visit a temple, they probably didn't get to see much. The only time that someone might see the image of the god (that was usually hidden away in the restricted part of the temple) was during special festivals but even then, the image was probably concealed in a shrine. There was an annual festival calendar for various gods in various places. Two of the biggest events took place at Thebes. During the Opet festival, the image of the god Amun was carried by priests during a procession between the Karnak and Luxor temples. During the annual Valley Festival, the images of Amun; his wife, Mut; and their son, Khonsu, were carried to the western side of the Nile river to visit special cult sites, such as the royal mortuary temples.

The grandeur of the Karnak Temple complex is evident even in its ruined state, as depicted by the artists of Napoleon's expedition.

(From Description de L'Égypte.*)*

One of the most unusual festivals was known as the *Heb-sed*. This festival was a ritual meant to demonstrate the vitality of the living god-king. Special festival facilities were set up, and, among other activities, the king had to ritually renew his power and fitness by sprinting around a track. Traditionally, it is said that the Heb-sed occurred during the thirtieth year of a ruler's reign and then perhaps every few years thereafter. A few rulers seemed to have bucked the trend, though, and celebrated theirs on earlier occasions.

Glyphs

The **Heb-sed** festival was a ritual to renew the vitality of the ruler. It is thought to have been celebrated on the occasion of the king's thirtieth year of reign.

Special Animals

The Egyptians believed that some animals were representative, if not actual incarnations, of certain gods. At Memphis, the sacred Apis bull was considered to be a living incarnation of the god Ptah in animal form. The beast bore special markings and was treated quite well. When it died, it was buried in royal splendor, and a search was begun for its divine successor.

Some species of animals were held as sacred, not as gods themselves, but as living representatives of a particular god. Ibises could represent the god Thoth, falcons could symbolize Horus, and so forth, with crocodiles, cats, rams, and other animals filling the bill for other gods. At some cult centers for various gods, a person could essentially sponsor the burial of a representative animal as a kind of votive offering, in hopes of receiving divine goodwill.

Small-Time Worship

The average Egyptian didn't participate in the big temple rites, but worship could be conducted at small shrines. Little shrines were sometimes included in homes for private worship.

The Egyptians believed in the power of magic, and there were a number of ways in which it could be invoked, including incantations and spells in an attempt to channel divine forces for healing or other purposes. Amulets were popular as ways to ward off the bad and hopefully attract the good. An amulet in the form of the restored eye of Horus, the Udjat, could be worn for good health. A cat representing the goddess Bastet might offer protection, and a scarab beetle might assist in the maintenance of one's very existence!

Lost and Found

Scarab amulets are one of the most commonly found Egyptian artifacts. The Egyptian name for the beetle and the word for "existence" are very similar, so the two concepts became linked. The scarab beetle lays its egg in dung, which it rolls in a ball from which little beetles eventually emerge into existence.

The Least You Need to Know

- ◆ Ancient Egyptians believed that the Earth existed in a great bubble, with the sky above and a netherworld below.
- ◆ The Egyptians had numerous ways to explain the origins of the world and its natural phenomena.
- ◆ Egyptian gods were often depicted in animal, human, or composite forms.
- ◆ The ruler of Egypt was the supreme high priest but was assisted in the worship of the gods by a large hierarchy of other priests.
- ◆ Temples dedicated to the gods were established throughout Egypt.

Chapter 8

Mummies for Dummies

In This Chapter

- ◆ Concepts of the spirit
- ◆ Journeying through the netherworld
- ◆ Making mummies
- ◆ Coffins and grave goods
- ◆ Tomb robberies

When people think about ancient Egypt, mummies and tombs are probably what first come to mind. This isn't surprising, given the technical achievements of burial monuments such as the pyramids or the discovery of remarkable tombs full of exotic objects. And as the remains of ancient people, mummies have a certain kind of creepy appeal.

But before we unravel the mysteries of the mummy, it's necessary to point out that Egyptians were not obsessed with death. They were obsessed with life and wanted it to continue after the physical death of their mortal body. Furthermore, just because the vast majority of artifacts that we have from this ancient civilization are related to death and religion—temples, mummies, tombs, and so on—this doesn't mean that death and religion were the primary obsessions of the ancient Egyptians. These simply were the things that were built to last, often in stone, or that were situated in dry locations.

Multifaceted You!

The Egyptians believed that the human body was made up of both physical and spiritual components, as follows:

- The physical body itself, with the heart as the center of intellect and emotion
- The *ka*, or life force
- The *ba*, roughly translated as one's soul
- The shadow
- The name

Glyphs

The Egyptian concept of the **ka** refers to one's life force. The **ba** can be roughly translated as one's soul. The ba was often depicted as a bird with a human head.

Lost and Found

Many copies of the so-called Book of the Dead have survived. Ancient Egyptians could buy or commission these expensive scrolls and even have them personalized with the name or picture of the deceased. Although they address the afterlife, these books were not referred to as Books of the Dead by the ancient Egyptians, but were known as the Book of Coming Forth by Day.

The body was considered to be the earthly home of all these entities. Upon death, preserving the body was a means of providing a home for the spiritual elements, such as the *ka* and the *ba*, which Egyptians believed continued to exist after the body ceased to function. It was important to perpetuate a person's name, too, because it was thought to be the embodiment of the complete person.

Taking the Trip

Let's pretend that you are an ancient Egyptian who just died. It's time for your spirit to take a trip through the netherworld. It's a crazy voyage full of spooky creatures bent on tricking you into making fatal mistakes. Fortunately, there's a handy guidebook available to help you navigate such perils. In the Old Kingdom, magical funerary texts were available in some of the pyramids for the king to use. In the Middle Kingdom, these kinds of texts became more accessible to the population at large and were sometimes written on wooden coffins. From the New Kingdom onward, scrolls popularly referred to today as the Book of the Dead served as a guide to navigating the netherworld.

It's Judgment Time!

Your soul, having successfully traversed the terrifying obstacles of the netherworld, reaches the judgment hall, where your ultimate fate will be determined. The trial to determine your fate takes place in front of the god Osiris, who is seated on a throne.

Forty-two judges, or assessors, are in attendance to quiz you on the goodness of your life. You are asked several questions, and you give the so-called Negative Confession, in which you deny having committed any and all wrongs, including having murdered, stolen, cheated, caused pain and suffering, and other offenses.

After your proclamation of innocence, you come to the moment of truth. The god Anubis places your heart on one pan of a giant scale, and on the other pan Anubis places *maat*, the concept of justice and right behavior, which is represented by a feather. The ibis-headed god Thoth stands by and takes notes.

Your heart and the feather of truth had better balance, or you are doomed! An odd and frightening creature with the head of a crocodile, the forefront of a lion, and the hindquarters of a hippo waits to devour you if your heart is heavier than the feather, at which point you would become a nonentity for eternity. If your innocence is confirmed, then you become an *akh*, an "effective spirit," and you will live for eternity.

A judgment scene from the Book of the Dead in which the deceased's heart is being weighed by Anubis against the feather of truth, representing maat. Thoth takes note, and the Devourer waits hopefully.

(Courtesy of The British Museum.)

Making Mummies

For the ka and ba to continue after an individual's death, ancient Egyptians needed to preserve the body and sustain its surviving spiritual elements—the ka and the ba. (The ba could leave the body, visit places, and return; the ka rarely left the tomb.) There was good reason, then, to keep the body intact.

How did the Egyptians figure out that mummification would preserve their dead? Egyptologists aren't certain, but perhaps it began with the realization that bodies interred in simple graves in the dry, hot desert had a tendency to remain more or less intact, albeit dried out. Attempts to keep the bodies intact by wrapping them and burying them in simple coffins are known from Predynastic times. From the later Old Kingdom onward, ancient Egyptians manipulated the body in order to preserve a living semblance so that its spirits might recognize it and find it hospitable.

By the way, the word *mummy* is derived from the Persian word *mummia*, which refers to bitumen or tar. The use of resins during mummification could give a tar-like appearance to some of the ancient preserved bodies.

> ### Nile Notes
>
> The ancient Egyptians weren't the only ones who practiced intentional mummification. It was also performed by other ancient cultures on every continent except Antarctica. The practice continues today, in a way, in the American funeral industry.

The Dirty Details

According to the Greek historian Herodotus, the process of mummification took 70 days. Professional embalmers made a small slit in the abdomen of the deceased, through which they removed all of the internal organs except for the heart. The liver, stomach, intestines, and lungs were retained and were mummified separately. Embalmers also removed the brain, using the classic method of inserting a hook through the nose, using the hook to mash up the brain, and pulling out or draining the residue—not a job for the squeamish.

A natural chemical drying agent, known as *natron*, was used to dry out the body. The natron was placed in small bags within the body cavity, and then the entire body was covered with natron or perhaps even soaked in a solution of the substance. Afterward, the body was washed out, perhaps with palm wine; then aromatic, and perhaps preservative, oils and resins were applied. The abdominal cavity was packed with different substances, including straw, sawdust, or wads of linen.

> ### Glyphs
>
> **Natron** is a naturally occurring white chemical substance that was used in the mummification process as a dehydrating agent. Its main components include salt and sodium bicarbonate. An area known as the Wadi Natroun in Egypt's Western Desert is a plentiful source for this substance.

The body was then typically wrapped in bandages or swaths of linen. Protective and magical amulets were sometimes mixed in the wrappings. A special scarab-shaped amulet bearing excerpts from the Book of the Dead was occasionally placed over the area of the heart. These heart-scarabs could serve as a substitute in case anything happened to the original. Flimsy jewelry suitable for burial purposes has been found on many mummies, although precious jewelry was often buried on the bodies of elite persons. The faces or whole heads of some bodies were covered with a funerary mask that would show the deceased looking good even if his mummified face wasn't.

The internal organs that were kept after evisceration were also mummified and routinely placed in four vessels known as *canopic jars*. The lids of the jars usually depicted the heads of the four protective sons of Horus in either their animal or their human forms. The canopic jars and their contents—along with the mummy in its coffin—were an important component of the physical burial of the deceased.

Enclosed for Longevity

The actual procedures of mummification varied through time. There were also different qualities of mummification available, depending upon how much one might care to spend. The same was true of coffins, which show a great variety of style and quality. Relatively simple decorated rectangular coffins were common in the Middle Kingdom, and the classic "mummy case" appeared not long afterward, with its shape in the form of a human body complete with painted face and hands. Elite individuals sometimes had multiple coffins, perhaps even gilded or made almost entirely of gold, as was the case of some royal burials. Large stone sarcophagi with heavy lids could secure the coffins of the most elaborate of burials.

Lost and Found

The intact mummy of the New Kingdom ruler Tutankhamun contained more than 140 amulets in its wrappings, as well as real daggers and incredible pieces of ornate jewelry.

Glyphs

Canopic jars are four jars, usually made of stone, which held the mummified liver, stomach, intestines, and lungs of the deceased. Their lids were in the shape of the four protective sons of Horus.

Not for the Queasy

One of the most singular and intriguing recent examples of what might be called experimental archaeology was conducted by a team led by American professor Bob Brier and anatomist Ronald Wade. Using ancient tools and procedures, they conducted experiments in ancient Egyptian mummification on the cadaver of a modern 76-year-old human male. Most of the entrails were taken out through a small incision in the abdomen, and the brain was removed through the nose. The body was then covered with natron imported from Egypt. The experiment was a great learning exercise, and Brier and Wade were successful in producing a modern Egyptian-like mummy.

A classic example of a high-status Egyptian coffin from the Eighteenth Dynasty.

(David Moyer collection.)

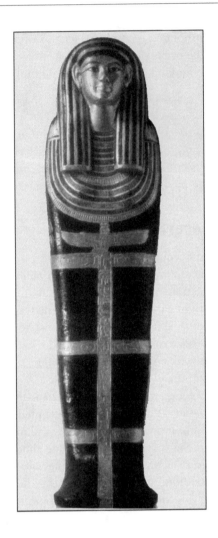

Tombs

The quality of burials also varied considerably through time. The poorest of laborers might be placed in a hole with a few items such as a pot, a knife and other tools, and maybe a comb or other personal items. At the other extreme, the pyramids and other royal tombs took years to build and involved a tremendous number of resources. In between the two extremes are simple one-room tombs carved into rock, just big enough to hold a coffin or two and a few items. High-ranking officials had more elaborate settings of chapels bearing decorated walls.

Most tombs consisted of two parts: the actual subterranean burial site and a place above the burial site where offerings could be placed to sustain the ka of the deceased. In its simple versions, a stone tablet, or *stele*, might note the location of the burial, where plates of food could be left during festivals or whenever desired. More deluxe were superstructures with small chapels and, if affordable, a professional priest who could regularly make the offerings. On the largest of all scales were the New Kingdom royal mortuary temples, built apart from the actual secluded burials and which probably required a permanent staff dedicated to the cult of the deceased ruler.

Lost and Found

Some of the most extraordinary mummies from ancient Egypt are some of the most recent. During the period when the Romans ruled Egypt, painted portraits of the deceased were sometimes affixed to the outside wrappings at the head of the mummy. Generally referred to as "Fayyum Mummy Portraits" after the region where many have been found, these eerily realistic paintings allow one to look virtually into the face of individuals who lived and died 2,000 years ago.

Feeding the Ka

The burials included items, many of them symbolic, that were intended to help the ka pursue a happy afterlife. Funerary texts on stone tablets or decorated on the walls of expensive tombs represented offerings to the deceased. A typical text described presenting the deceased with large quantities of bread and beer, meat, fowl, linen, alabaster, and other items. Painted scenes of daily life and work, nice meals, and good times were not unusual.

As a life force, it was thought that the ka required at least some sort of food, so, apart from offerings in writing or decoration, actual quantities of food were often placed in the tombs. A number of examples have survived, including prime cuts of preserved beef and birds such as ducks, which were themselves mummified and wrapped. Wine, oils, linen, clothing, and sometimes furniture have been found in some of the more expensive burials. When it came to royal burials, it wasn't unusual to include everything but the kitchen sink!

To assist the deceased in the afterlife, many burials included artificial servants. Wooden figures or even model scenes could do the job, but the most popular version of this idea was the *shabti* (also

Glyphs

A **stele** (plural **stelae**) is a stone or wooden tablet usually bearing inscriptions and scenes at the top. Archaeologists have found numerous stelae bearing funerary inscriptions, and there are also larger stelae bearing royal inscriptions, such as the Rosetta Stone. **Shabtis** are servant figurines placed in tombs to do the bidding of the deceased in the afterlife.

referred to as "ushabti" or "shawabti.") Shabtis were little figures made of wood, stone, or faience that were placed in the tomb to do the bidding of the deceased. Some tombs included a shabti for every day of the year or more! Some of them were little specialists who were experts in different tasks.

These Late Period shabti figurines are ready and willing to do the bidding of the deceased.

(David Moyer collection.)

Last Trip Down the Road

Egyptian funerals were loaded with rituals. A procession including a priest, family members, and other mourners carried the coffined mummy to the tomb, where the coffin was stood on end. Some very esoteric ceremonies then took place, including the "Opening of the Mouth" ritual, which was intended to animate the mummy of the deceased. Offerings were given, and a banquet was held. The mummy was then placed into its appropriately provisioned tomb and the door closed (hopefully, but rarely, for good).

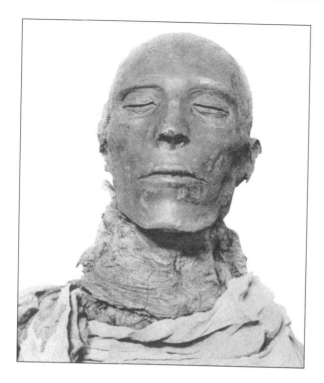

A splendid example of high-quality mummification: the mummy of the pharaoh Seti I.

(*From* The Royal Mummies, *by* G.E. Smith.)

Purloining the Perished

The practice of burying the dead with the things of this life proved to be quite a temptation for those who had little respect for the deceased. Of the innumerable ancient tombs in Egypt, relatively few have survived intact. In the case of the richly furnished royal tombs in the Valley of the Kings, none completely escaped the attention of tomb robbers.

The tomb robbers were particularly interested in finding materials that could either be sold or used without their original source being known, or materials that could be recycled and thus made anonymous. In the first case, materials such as linen, oils, and perfume were sought by thieves. For recycling, gold or other precious metals could be melted down, and expensive woods and ivory could be recarved. To the tomb robber, few things were sacred. In most cases, they seemed to have no qualms about tearing through a wrapped royal mummy to remove jewelry or other valuable items.

Lost and Found

In places where small tombs were located quite close to each other, the robbers' work could sometimes be made easier by busting through the wall of one tomb into the one next door. Some archaeologists have been surprised to find that what appeared to be intact doorways leading to unviolated tombs had been robbed through adjacent chambers.

Tomb robbery was definitely a problem in ancient Egypt, and, amazingly, we have old records to prove it. Several papyrus documents from the late New Kingdom have been found that include transcripts of interrogations, and even confessions of ancient tomb robbers. Some of the accused were beaten, and those found guilty no doubt suffered an unpleasant death. Ancient graffiti even has been found near the tombs, written by officials inspecting their security.

Animal Mummies

As noted in the last chapter, animals, too, could be mummified. Some, such as the sacred Apis bulls kept at Memphis, were mummified because ancient Egyptians believed that they were living incarnations of a particular god. The Apis bulls were not only mummified, but they also were placed in mammoth stone sarcophagi and were interred at Sakkara in extensive underground galleries.

Pharaoh's Domain

Animals of all sizes that were related to certain gods were often mummified in large quantities. The largest mummified animals include bulls and crocodiles. On the other end of the scale, scarab beetles and even shrews have received the mummy treatment.

Archaeologists have even found an underground complex of tunnels filled with more than a million small ceramic jars, each containing a mummified ibis. Mammoth quantities of cat mummies and others representing sacred animals have been found elsewhere. In the Valley of the Kings, a mummified dog and a few monkeys have been found in a small tomb, suggesting that they might have been royal pets.

Where'd They All Go?

Considering that intentional mummification was practiced in Egypt for more than 2,000 years, it's possible that over that time, hundreds of thousands, if not millions, of human mummies were buried. They are still plentiful in Egypt today, but their numbers have decreased considerably.

In approximately the twelfth century A.D., ground ancient mummies became a hot commodity in Europe, where the substance was used as medicine to treat a variety of conditions. Many pharmacies carried "mummy" as a regular product, and the demand was filled in Egypt by pulling ancient bodies out of their graves. Apparently the demand was so great that some unscrupulous individuals engaged in making their own mummies from recently dead individuals and pawning them off as the ancient real thing.

Many mummies were collected as souvenirs, especially in the nineteenth century, and they ended up in Europe and North America. Some of the stinkier ones were thrown away, but lots survive in museums around the world. As entertainment for the curious—but often called educational exercises—mummies were sometimes unwrapped in public. Although some of this was cheap showmanship, much was learned, and several scholars looked upon the study of mummies as serious research.

Modern research has shown that we can learn about the ancient Egyptians from their mummies. More sophisticated techniques, such as x-rays and CAT scans, are far less intrusive then the old methods of dissection. The ancient Egyptians would no doubt be appalled if they knew that they were being pulled out of their tombs and poked, prodded, and put on display. But if modern science, through its research, has taught us the importance of preserving the receptacles of those ancient spirits and, especially, perpetuating their names, then the Egyptian deceased should be confident of their ultimate survival.

> **Nile Notes**
>
> Mummies have been exported for other purposes, too. A nine-teenth-century American paper manufacturer attempted to make paper out of old linen mummy wrappings, and a huge quantity of cat mummies was shipped to Britain for use as fertilizer.

The Least You Need to Know

◆ The ancient Egyptians loved life and wanted it to continue—in a good way—in the afterlife.

◆ Before enjoying the afterlife, the deceased had to pass through the netherworld and survive judgment.

◆ Mummification was an attempt to preserve the body as a home for its spirits.

◆ Styles of tombs, coffins, and grave goods varied through time and according to the status of the deceased.

◆ Tomb robbery has taken place in both ancient and modern times.

The Pageant of History

When people think of ancient Egypt, they often imagine pyramids, temples, and mummies. Nothing wrong with that, but keep in mind that ancient Egyptian civilization wasn't always there and didn't appear out of thin air. People roamed the land of the Nile for tens of thousands of years before any pyramids were built or hieroglyphs were written.

In the next few chapters, we're going to briefly survey the development process of ancient Egyptian civilization. In many ways, the details are still sketchy, if not somewhat mysterious. Nonetheless, we'll see how, in just a few hundred years, the ancient Egyptians went from living in relatively simple agricultural communities to building massive pyramids requiring great organization, command of resources, and good technical skills. It's an amazing story full of drama and historical uncertainty.

The Earliest Egyptians

In This Chapter

- ◆ Historians of prehistory
- ◆ Stone Age folk
- ◆ Agriculture comes to Egypt
- ◆ Predynastic cultures
- ◆ The development of civilization
- ◆ Unifying the Two Lands

For eons, humans lived a relatively simple lifestyle, gathering the available resources of the land and hunting and fishing. And then, around 10,000 years ago, something extraordinary happened. In several places around the world, some of these groups of people began to settle down, live in villages, and tend crops and animals. This idea caught on and spread far and wide. Then, in a just a few places, beginning around 5,000 years ago or so, some societies that were significantly more culturally complex began to emerge from this agricultural foundation. Egypt was one of them, and the explanations for these changes continue to challenge archaeologists. In this chapter, we're going to take a look at the earliest days of that land and how the Egyptian civilization might have emerged.

Prehistoric History

Archaeologists and Egyptologists have specific uses for the words *prehistory* and *history*. *Prehistory* generally refers to the time before written records, and *historical* times are those when such records are available. In Egypt, for example, writing appeared around 3100 B.C., and the time before that is considered prehistory in Egypt. Archaeologists who deal in such preliterate time periods are often called *prehistorians*.

Without the luxury of texts, prehistorians scrutinize a wide spectrum of physical evidence. Their techniques are often meticulous in their attempt to squeeze the most data out of whatever they might uncover. Prehistorians tend to be multidisciplinary and are interested not only in stone tools and other artifacts, but also in reconstructing the total physical and cultural environment to the extent that it is possible. Ask them to read some hieroglyphs, and many wouldn't know where to start. But give them a trowel and turn them loose, and they'll come up with information that won't appear in any ancient text. Although perhaps their areas of interest don't have the glamorous appeal of pyramids and golden mummies, their work is essential for understanding the thousands of years that led to the development of the classic Egyptian civilization.

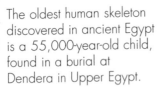

Glyphs

Prehistory is the course of human events before the time of writing. It is often studied by archaeologists, who can be referred to as **prehistorians.**

Lost and Found

The oldest human skeleton discovered in ancient Egypt is a 55,000-year-old child, found in a burial at Dendera in Upper Egypt.

Glyphs

The **Paleolithic,** or Old Stone Age, is characterized by the use of stone tools and hunting and gathering. It extends from about 2 million years ago to 10,000 years ago, roughly corresponding to the geological Pleistocene epoch.

Out of Africa

The current scientific consensus is that humans originated in Africa and spread out from there. The remains of an early type of human known as *Homo erectus* have been found in East Africa and Israel, suggesting that these early humans migrated from Africa, through Egypt, and into Europe and Asia perhaps 1.8 million years ago. Although skeletal remains of this human ancestor haven't been found in Egypt, numerous examples of very ancient stone tools have been found there, suggesting that parts of Egypt were inhabited by people perhaps 300,000–400,000 years ago and probably much earlier.

Archaeologists refer to these early days of humanity as the *Paleolithic,* or "the Old Stone Age," a time period characterized by the use of stone tool technology and a lifestyle based on hunting, gathering, fishing, and foraging. Don't let the name of the time period confuse you, though—people during that time probably had a variety of different products made from different materials, not just stone. The stone items, though, are what typically survive from such a distant past and thus must serve as the basis for a good deal of archaeological research.

How Did They Live?

One way to examine the social structures of the past is to compare them to those of similar peoples today. The few surviving hunter-gatherer groups around these days tend to be organized into small groups, and they more or less live within the natural carrying capacity of the land. They seem to be generally egalitarian, sharing their resources among their group.

Hunter-gatherers tend to move around a lot, taking advantage of food and other resources during different seasons of the year. As a result, they tend not to have a lot of permanent buildings or large possessions that they would have to cart around with them. But, fortunately for us, they have left a lot of stone spear points and other stone tools lying around for archaeologists to find.

Do keep this in mind: The environment in Egypt has experienced substantial climatic changes. In much of prehistoric times, wide portions of the Western Desert, for example, were very habitable. There were savanna-like grasslands and lakes of various sizes. Animals more reminiscent of modern southeast Africa roamed the region where today there is little more than sand.

> ## Nile Notes
>
> A popular image of Paleolithic times is that of a harsh existence with people regularly on the edge of starvation and a high mortality rate. Studies of modern hunters and gatherers, however, suggest that these people have a relatively content existence, with lots of leisure time. On the other hand, studies of the remains of early people suggest that they didn't live very long.

A Radical Change

As I noted, humans hunted and gathered on Earth from their earliest days, until something dramatic and still somewhat unexplained occurred about 10,000 years ago. At that time, a major shift in lifestyle occurred. In just a few places at first, people started settling down, raising crops, keeping animals, and constructing permanent buildings and villages.

One thing led to another. People needed to harvest and store grain, so they produced a lot of pottery and different kinds of tools. The food surplus created by domestication and agriculture meant that more people could live together in much larger groups. This revolutionary new way of living is often referred to as the *Neolithic*, or New Stone Age, and is sometimes called the "Neolithic Revolution." This change in lifestyle had profound effects.

Glyphs

The **Neolithic** is a period in a given culture when the hunting and gathering lifestyle gives way to permanent settlements, the tending of plants and animals. Stone tools are still widely used, and pottery and other new kinds of tools reflect the new way of life.

Pharaoh's Domain

Maybe at our core we are still hunters and gatherers, and these primal instincts manifest themselves in modern society by a fascination with the unknown and the seeking of lost information—archaeologists and Egyptologists, for instance.

The earliest known evidence for this Neolithic phenomenon comes from the Near East, in the area around modern Iraq. From there the notion of agriculture apparently gradually spread to neighboring areas. In Egypt, it appeared around 7,000 years ago, and emmer wheat and barley were the crops of choice.

The First House Plants?

Plants are considered to be domesticated when they are altered in some way that makes them more useful to humans. It can involve something as simple as pulling weeds from a favorite stand of wild wheat or as complicated as organized agriculture involving the selective breeding of crops. Many domesticated plants are distinguished from their wild brethren by attributes that, while making them useful to a hungry human, make it difficult for them to survive on their own in the wild. For example, humans want the seeds of wheat to stay on the plant, where they can be removed at will, rather than having them disperse as nature would require in the wild. Some plants became completely dependent upon humans for their existence—and vice versa!

Taming the Beast

A number of animals were domesticated during the Neolithic period as well. Did you know that the wild equivalent of that peaceful, slow-moving, domesticated cow in the field can be a ferocious untamed animal? To make cattle more useful to humans, a process took place that probably involved the capture and breeding of the slow, fat ones to the point where a cow gives milk, provides meat, and is well behaved, if not trustworthy. This process took place in the Near East with goats, sheep, dogs, pigs, and several other popular beasts.

Life in the New Stone Age

Although you might think that the farming life sounds pretty good compared to a hunting and gathering lifestyle, some consider the Neolithic to be the downfall of the human species. Archaeologists have found ample evidence that with growing populations living in permanent settlements and accumulating private possessions and differing levels of wealth, disputes and fighting become commonplace. The assumed egalitarian existence of hunters and gatherers is transformed as chiefs or leaders with more power than others emerge. Furthermore, we find that humans begin to alter and transform the natural environment in radical ways.

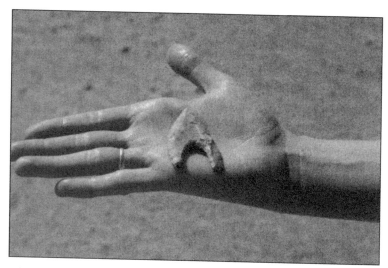

A prehistoric stone projectile point from Neolithic times found in the Fayyum region. Just because they were growing plants doesn't mean that hunting was abandoned!

Revolutionary Forces

A number of theories exist about why the Neolithic revolution occurred, but there are not yet any firm conclusions. Some prehistorians have suggested that perhaps it was an accident: A few wild wheat stalks dropped their seeds near camp, and a surprised hunter/gatherer returned later to see plants growing near the site of his lunch. Or maybe it was an intentional invention encouraged by the changing environments after the Ice Age about 10,000 years ago.

Other historians suggest that it could be the result of pressures from expanding populations. A rather fun (but seriously presented) idea is that the desire to produce beer was the incentive! For whatever reason, the revolution happened, and from that Neolithic foundation, great ancient civilizations arose in several places in the world, beginning around 5,000 years ago.

After the end of the Ice Age, deserts began replacing grassland in Egypt, perhaps leading to

Nile Notes

Although we tend to look at animals or plants as being domesticated or undomesticated, it's not that black or white. Domestication is not a single event, but a process that takes place over time.

the concentration of people in the Nile Valley and Delta regions. And then, perhaps around 5500 B.C., domesticated wheat and barley, along with goats and sheep, were likely introduced into Egypt from the area of Syria-Palestine to the northeast, where they had already been in use about 2,000 years. Cattle, however, seem to have been a mainstay of a prehistoric culture in the Western Desert and were likely domesticated in Egypt or elsewhere in Africa earlier on to become a particularly valuable resource. Some of the earliest evidence of Egyptian agriculture has been found in the Fayyum region, which had a far more lush environment in the past than it does today. There, stone sickle blades and grinding stones along with silos and other agricultural artifacts suggest that people in that area led a farming lifestyle but also hunted and fished.

Lost and Found

In some parts of Egypt, it is possible to find the scattered remains of stone tools and the bones of ancient creatures, including fish, lying out in the middle of the desert! Environmental changes have left them "stranded" in now inhospitable surroundings.

Predynastic Times

In Egypt, the Neolithic time period leading up to the civilization of cultural complexity is generally referred to as the Predynastic period, beginning about 7,000 years ago. As I've already mentioned, the lack of written documents tends to make the study of this period quite different from what you find later during literate dynastic times. Prehistorians have been busy at work on the subject for perhaps a hundred years now. Many sites have been examined, and a cultural chronology of sorts has been devised based on artifacts found in graves and ancient settlements. Actually, it's more like two parallel chronologies, one for Upper Egypt and one for Lower Egypt. Because we don't have texts and don't know what the earlier people in Egypt called themselves, prehistorians have named the various cultures that they encounter after the sites where they are first or best represented.

Diggers

Gertrude Caton-Thompson (1888–1985) was a British archaeologist and explorer who spent many years working in Egypt. Her special area of interest was prehistoric times, conducting notable work in such places as the Fayyum and the Kharga oasis.

In Upper Egypt, these Predynastic cultural phases are organized as follows: Badarian (c. 4400–4000 B.C.), Naqada I (c. 4000–3500 B.C.), Naqada II (c. 3500–3200 B.C.), and Naqada III, which is also known as the Protohistoric Period (c. 3200–3000 B.C.). Most of the Predynastic period in the Delta is perhaps best represented by what's called the Maadi Cultural Complex (c. 4000–3200 B.C.)

Given the difference in archaeological preservation and degree of exploration, the sequences from Upper Egypt have been based more on cemetery sites than settlement sites in the Delta. But even in the cemeteries of Lower Egypt, a difference between the Two Lands can readily be seen.

In both Upper and Lower Egypt, we find that technology became more sophisticated over time. Trade may have played a role in the development of the Two Lands, and the Delta region was well situated for the import of foreign goods and culture. The Upper Egyptian Naqada II culture is especially noteworthy, with major sites at Naqada, Hierakonpolis, and Abydos. Their pots were often painted with geometrical and representational designs. The latter often depict boats, leading prehistorians to conclude that travel and commerce were important. The components of Naqada II culture began making their way into the Delta, and, by the time of Naqada III, the Upper Egyptian culture had spread over all of Egypt.

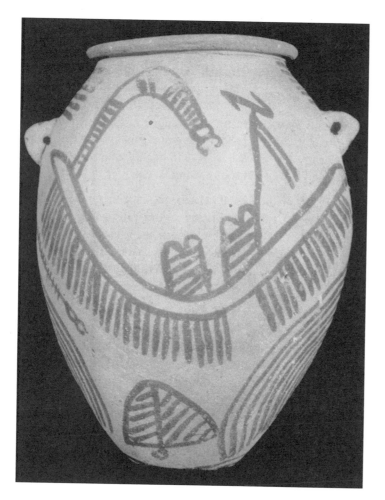

A Predynastic Naqada II pot decorated with a boat.

(David Moyer collection.)

The Road to "Civilization"

Before turning to the specifics of Egypt, it's time once again to address another vital notion: What is a civilization? The word has its origins in the Latin word *civitas*, which means "city." The term implies a densely populated and organized living center. That term seems inadequate, though, because what we mean by a civilization requires much more than an extra-large village or a city. Many scholars today prefer the term *complex society* to *civilization*—even then, it is much easier to describe than it is to define.

A complex society tends to have a ranked social, political, and religious system—that is, kings, bureaucrats, priests, merchants, slaves, peasants, generals, soldiers, and so forth. Plus, it has a lot of artisans and occupational specialists. Contrast that to the hunters and gatherers and perhaps even many of the early agricultural societies, where people could probably do each other's jobs without much training.

Complex societies tend to build large religious or political structures, such as temples and palaces, and most have some sort of writing system. All these signs of a complex society are evidenced in the things that archaeologists dig up. In an ancient city, you can expect to find the sophisticated homes of the wealthy and the decrepit little shacks of the poor. Burials, likewise, tend to show a difference in wealth, and you might find many kinds of workshops belonging to a variety of crafts specialists. The grave goods of various Naqada II burials, for example, vary in terms of quantity, variety, and quality, thus demonstrating an increase in craft diversity and the power and status of individuals.

> **Nile Notes**
>
> Besides Egypt, other early complex societies emerged in Mesopotamia, China, Mesoamerica, and Peru.

> **Lost and Found**
>
> A **complex society** is characterized by such features as class, wealth, and status differences; political, economic, and religious elites; craft specialists; relatively large populations; monumental architecture; and writing.

The temples and palaces speak for themselves, especially if there is writing on the walls, and this is exactly what is found in Egypt. Just as the change to agriculture is of great interest to archaeologists, the origins of civilization, or complex societies, pose another huge problem for scholars to solve.

Complex societies didn't develop everywhere, and the timing of those that did is interesting. A number of theories try to explain it. One of the most prominent ideas is that the practice of organized irrigation might stimulate the creation of cultural complexity by the need for decision makers and a variety of different jobs. Writing might develop for record-keeping and communication, and differences in wealth might arise as some irrigated lands flourished more than others.

Others have suggested that population growth inspired cultural complexity because of the need to deal with the requirement of more people. But couldn't the converse be argued as well, that complex cultures might provide conditions conducive to population growth? Another interesting theory involves warfare and population. As populations increase and resources become limited, a group might choose to conquer its neighbor. In doing so, status and wealth differences are created between the two, and the characteristics of complex societies develop as a result. Still other ideas suggest climate change as playing a significant role.

In short, we don't really know how the ancient civilizations came about. In some cases, they seem to appear almost instantaneously, a phenomenon that has given rise to all manner of exotic explanations. One scholar, G. Elliot Smith, was impressed by similarities in ancient civilizations in diverse corners of the world and advocated a single origin for all civilizations: Egypt. And from there it all spread, far and wide. Others have even called upon visitors from outer space. (We'll deal with some of that silliness in Chapter 19, "Alternative Theories.")

It is possible, too, that certain characteristics of Egyptian civilization might have been introduced from elsewhere. Mesopotamian architectural features, characteristic cylinder seals and even a few artistic motifs, were present in Egypt during the crucial time period. If that's not direct evidence of cultural influence, it's probably at least evidence of trade!

> ### Nile Notes
>
> Although in some instances it looks as if civilizations instantly appear, we shouldn't forget that one inch of dirt separating a buried Neolithic village from a city built on top might represent a couple hundred years of change and development. We should likewise remember that certain important things, such as the unwritten exchange of ideas, do not leave direct traces for the archaeologist to examine.

Unifying the Two Lands

Both the ancient Egyptian lists of kings and Manetho, the Egyptian historian discussed in Chapter 3, "Egypt in Space and Time," attribute the origins of ancient Egyptian civilization to the unification of Upper and Lower Egypt. The first king of the first dynasty, and presumably the unifier, is noted as Meni or Menes. What sort of evidence is there of this being truly the case? We've already seen that this notion of the Two Lands played a very symbolic role in kingship and culture, and, given the eventual dominance of the Predynastic Naqada II culture, the suggestions seem to be that the south overwhelmed the north culturally, if not militarily. This is a tempting conclusion, but the fact remains that it is very difficult to come to definitive conclusions during this crucial time period, the very beginning of Egyptian "history."

The Least You Need to Know

◆ Early humans probably lived in, or at least passed through, Egypt on their journeys out of Africa.

◆ The earliest Egyptians were likely hunters and gatherers who also fished.

◆ Agriculture and permanent villages appeared in Egypt at least 7,000 years ago, setting the stage for an increasingly more complex society or "civilization."

◆ How ancient agriculture developed and how complex societies evolved are two puzzling questions for prehistorians.

◆ Traditional ancient Egyptian historians consider the civilization of ancient Egypt to begin with the unification of the Two Lands, Upper and Lower Egypt.

Chapter 10

Age of Pyramids

In This Chapter

- ◆ The early days of civilization
- ◆ A well-organized society
- ◆ Fancy graves and pyramids
- ◆ A mystery tomb
- ◆ Ambitious rulers

Whatever the ephemeral details of the actual unification of Upper and Lower Egypt might be, the results of the process would have amazing cultural consequences over the next 3,000 years. The combination of a ruler with command over Egypt's many resources, along with an industrious and talented people, produced a civilization like no other. Within a few hundred years of unification, the Egyptians would go from building structures of mud brick to constructing massive stone pyramids that continue to astound and impress.

Dynasty Zero

It is quite likely that this fellow named Menes, who is said to have unified the Two Lands, was not the first to rule Egypt. There is evidence of kings who might predate the unification, including one known as Scorpion. Egyptologists have placed these kings in a "protodynastic" period that is often referred to as "Dynasty 0."

At the Upper Egyptian site of Hierakonpolis, a cache of objects bearing their names was excavated in the late nineteenth century. One of these objects is a ceremonial stone mace head depicting an individual wearing the crown of Upper Egypt, holding a large hoe, and perhaps carrying out some sort of agricultural ceremony. A glyph of a scorpion near his head seems to indicate his name, Scorpion. Behind him are poles with dead lapwing birds hanging from them, which can be interpreted as representing conquered peoples. Some scholars think that this might depict a conquering Upper Egyptian ruler just before the unification of the Two Lands.

One of the most intriguing artifacts from ancient Egypt is another object from Hierakonpolis that likewise relates to this controversial time period. It is a decorated commemorative stone made of green slate and called the Narmer palette. On one side, an individual named Narmer is depicted wearing the white crown of Upper Egypt and smiting an enemy. On the other side, he is shown wearing the red crown of Lower Egypt. There is a lot of violent imagery suggesting that Narmer is victorious and rules both lands. Many Egyptologists have argued that the Narmer palette commemorates the actual event of the unification. Narmer, then, might be the legendary Menes. Lacking an ancient written explanation, however, the palette is subject to other interpretations.

> ### Nile Notes
>
> The interpretation of art can be a tricky thing. It's important to try to understand the intent of a given object as manufactured by its maker and also attempt to suspend personal biases. In many cases, the best that can be done is a well-argued guess.

The Narmer palette.

(After The Mummy, *by E.A.W. Budge.)*

It's important to note that in Dynasty 0, the names of rulers begin to appear drawn or carved in what is called a *serekh*, which resembles a rectangular palace facade. This sort of protocartouche (you'll recall from Chapter 4, "Glyphs," that a cartouche is an oval-shape symbol containing the hieroglyphs for the names of Egyptian royalty) was typically surmounted by a falcon, probably representing the god Horus with whom Egyptian rulers would be divinely identified. This trend continued well into Dynasty 3.

Glyphs

A **serekh** is a rectangular motif on which was typically written the names of many of the earlier kings of Egypt. It was usually surmounted by a falcon representing the god Horus or, on a couple of rare occasions, the enigmatic "Seth-animal."

The Fighting Hawk

Whatever role Scorpion and Narmer might have played, the unification of Upper and Lower Egypt seems to be confirmed under an early king of Dynasty 1, a fellow with the royal name of Hor-Aha. Hor-Aha means "Fighting Hawk," and, interestingly, his second royal name was "Men," thus dragging him into the Menes debate. Regardless, Hor-Aha is responsible for establishing the capital of Egypt at the site of Memphis, which is just south of modern Cairo. Memphis was strategically situated at the juncture of the Two Lands, thus greatly contributing to the command and control of both the Nile Valley and the Delta.

Except for funerary monuments, there aren't a great deal of sites that have been explored for Dynasties 0 through 2. Some of the earliest remains of these crucial time periods are buried deep below the debris of later settlements, have long been destroyed by the deteriorating effects of Nile flooding, or are otherwise inaccessible or poorly preserved. However, the royal grave sites and a few impressive burials of important officials can provide us with some insights.

By the way, the typically rectangular brick tombs of the early dynasties are usually referred to as *mastabas*, the Arabic word for "bench," referring to their shape. Later in the Old Kingdom, such mastabas were built of stone and served primarily as burials for royal family members and important officials. Large numbers of these sorts of tombs can be found in the vicinity of such royal cemeteries as those at Sakkara and Giza.

The royal burial ground for the earliest dynasties was at the sacred site of Abydos in Upper Egypt. The royal burials there usually consisted of brick-lined chambers for both storage and burials. Some

Glyphs

The early rectangular-shape tombs are referred to as **mastabas,** an Arabic word meaning "bench."

Lost and Found

Archaeologists working at Abydos have excavated an interesting tomb to which they have given the name "U-j." It dates to around the time of Dynasty 0, and although it was well robbed in antiquity, surviving labels from some of the burial goods give us some of the earliest examples of what might be considered writing from ancient Egypt. The grave also contained a large number of ceramic jars imported from Palestine.

seemed to have been quite well equipped with food and other supplies for the afterlife. When excavating these graves, archaeologists were surprised to find dozens, and occasionally hundreds, of related subsidiary burials. Most of the remains therein were found to be that of young men. It is possible that these were human sacrifices, probably servants or retainers who were killed to accompany the ruler in the afterlife. Fortunately, this practice seems to have been exclusive to the First Dynasty.

Number Two

Throughout the Early Dynastic Period, the development of a distinct, centralized Egyptian society and state continued. If the data about the First Dynasty is fairly elusive, that about the Second Dynasty is even more so. We know the names of several kings, each following the practice of presenting their names in a serekh. But near the end of the dynasty, we have a bizarre permutation of that tradition: A ruler by the name of Peribsen displayed his name not with Horus, but with the Seth-animal. Seth, you might recall, was the devious twin brother of Horus. Egyptologists have speculated that there was likely some sort of political upset at this time. Whatever it might have been, it seems to have been resolved by his successor, Khasekhemwy, whose serekh is surmounted by both Seth and Horus. These kinds of situations beg for interpretation, but the evidence is limited. And we don't see Seth alone on a serekh again.

Serekhs bearing the names (from left to right) of Early Dynastic rulers Hor-Aha, Peribsen, and Khasekhemwy. Note the roles of Horus and Seth.

Like his predecessors, Khasekhemwy was buried at Abydos. His tomb featured a huge number of storerooms full of grave goods. More importantly, it is perhaps the earliest large-scale construction utilizing stone, a trend that was taken to extreme proportions in the years that followed. It should also be noted that some of the most important royal officials and family members (most of whom were no doubt one and the same) had truly impressive tombs at Sakkara, the necropolis adjacent to the capital at Memphis. This gives some serious hints of a growing bureaucracy and the nature of the distribution of power.

Pharaoh's Domain

A huge walled enclosure made of mud brick can be found at the site of Hierakonpolis. Nicknamed "the Fort" by archaeologists, it seems to date to the time of Khasekhemwy. It's possible that it is somehow related to his burial, but its function remains unknown.

Royal Concerns

As an archaeologist and Egyptologist, I've always felt uncomfortable with the fact that so much of Egyptian history is based on the acts of rulers and their monuments, especially the funerary monuments. In many cases, this is hard to avoid because these artifacts have best survived. And on the positive side, royal remains such as elaborate burials and pyramids are the byproducts of power, economics, and other essential variables. The fact that a ruler is capable of sacrificing retainers or building an impressive burial structure can tell us a lot about the state of society. The nature of the grave goods, too, can give us a lot of information about such things as available resources, trade relations, and status. Fortunately, as we shuffle into the Old Kingdom, there are increasingly more documents to help us more fully fill in the picture. By the way, although I'll be mentioning pyramids here and there in this chapter, they'll get special attention in Chapter 11, "Pharaohs' Mountains."

The Old Kingdom

With the Third Dynasty, we have the onset of what is called the "Old Kingdom." As mentioned back in Chapter 3, "Ancient Egypt in Space and Time," this somewhat artificial chronological structure portrays periods classified as "kingdoms" to be times of political unity, economic wealth, and cultural sophistication. This seems to be a very appropriate description for most of the Old Kingdom (c. 2686–2125 B.C.) comprising Dynasties 3 through 6. In this arrangement of time, we can't necessarily argue for a clear break between the earliest dynasties and those of the Old Kingdom, with the latter being a development of the former. Some real architectural changes can be seen in the Third Dynasty, though.

Djoser Rules!

Not much is known about the first ruler of the Third Dynasty, Sanakhte, but his successor is one of the most famous and impressive individuals in Egyptian history. His name is Netjerikhet, better known as Djoser. It is during the reign of Djoser that we see some major indications of the growing power and sophistication of Egyptian society. Djoser built for himself an incredible funerary complex at Sakkara on an architectural and artistic scale hitherto unknown. Rather than constructing a mud-brick mastaba as had been previously common, Djoser built his tomb out of stone—stone bricks and blocks.

The design of this tomb was changed in the process of its construction. The end result was essentially six mastabas stacked one atop the other, forming a step-pyramid over subterranean burial passages. The surrounding funerary complex is perhaps even more impressive. It uses stone to imitate palatial architectural elements of wood and other perishable materials, thus preserving them in perpetuity. The complex also contains an artificial Heb-Sed court along with shrines and other dummy features in stone.

Lost and Found

A mummified foot was found in one of the underground passages beneath Djoser's step-pyramid. It's possible that this is all that is left of the great ruler and builder.

Credit for these provocative innovations is given to Djoser's architect, Imhotep, who was also a high-ranking official and a priest of Heliopolis, a religious center for the worship of the sun not far north of Memphis. Such was his reputation that he was deified in later ages and was revered as a great sage and physician. He likely has a tomb at Sakkara. Despite attempts to locate it, it has yet to be discovered. Very little was known of Djoser's successor, Sekhemkhet, until the discovery of his unfinished pyramid (you can see more specifics of this intriguing find in the next chapter).

A Remarkable Time of Building

During the Egyptian Fourth Dynasty, there was an intense spurt of monumental building in Egypt, unsurpassed anywhere else in the world at that time. The new dynasty was led by a ruler named Snefru. Building on the experience of his predecessor, Snefru created the first true pyramid, setting a vigorous trend for others to follow. He built two large pyramids in an area south of Memphis called Dashur. A text dating to his reign brags about an expedition to Nubia which returned with 7,000 captives and 200,000 head of cattle. Other expeditions during his rule, though, engaged in peaceful trade to retrieve wood and other goods from Syria-Palestine.

The immense power, organization, and control of the Old Kingdom state is represented in Snefru's son and successor, Khufu (Cheops), who built what is known to the world as the Great Pyramid at the site of Giza, just north of Memphis. Up until the nineteenth century, it remained the world's largest construction. We'll talk more about this amazing structure and others in the next chapter. Herodotus describes Cheops as a mean and ruthless ruler, although Egyptologists have found little evidence substantiating such a claim. Perhaps he was under the impression that the only way such a massive structure as the Great Pyramid could have been built would have been under intense duress!

Khufu's son, Djedefra, had a short reign of about eight years. He started to build a pyramid at a site named Abu Rawash, but the monument was never finished. Interestingly, Djedefra was the first Egyptian ruler to incorporate the name of the sun god, "Ra," into his name. He was also the first to use the title "Son of the Sun," which became a regular component of Egyptian royal titles.

Pharaoh's Domain

Snefru had a reputation as a good ruler. Perhaps this is reflected in his name, which means, "to make good or beautiful."

Another son of Khufu, Khafra (Chephren), exercised his might by building a pyramid at Giza nearly as large as that of his father! Along with this was an impressive funerary complex that included the famous mammoth sculpture known as the Great Sphinx. After Khafra, the pyramids began to decline in size. His successor, Menkaura (Mycerinus), built a much smaller pyramid on the Giza plateau. The ruler that followed, Shepsekaf, chose to be buried in a mastaba.

Lost and Found

Despite the lasting fame of Khufu, the builder of the Great Pyramid, the only known sculpture of this great ruler is a small ivory carving less than three inches tall that bears his name.

A Mysterious Discovery

In 1925, a photographer with an American archaeological expedition was setting up his tripod near the Great Pyramid when one of its legs slipped, revealing a plastered surface. Upon inspection, it covered a shaft that eventually was excavated to a depth of about 100 feet. The shaft led to a room sealed with limestone blocks, apparently undisturbed since antiquity. The chamber contained the remains of all sorts of funerary equipment. Much of it had been gilded, but the wood had rotted from underneath. This excavation, as you can imagine, required an incredible amount of patience and documentary excellence on the part of the archaeologists involved! When reconstructed, the tomb's contents included some chests, a carrying chair, a bed and a canopy, and two armchairs. A set of four intact canopic jars was found in a sealed niche. It appeared to be the tomb of Hetepheres, the wife of Snefru and the mother of Khufu.

Diggers

George Andrew Reisner (1867–1942) was one of America's greatest Egyptologist. He spent much of his career excavating pyramids and their surrounding temples and adjacent cemeteries.

Pharaoh's Domain

The Giza plateau is a limestone plateau located just south of modern Cairo on the western side of the Nile. The plateau is the site of the massive pyramids and funerary complexes of the Fourth Dynasty pharaohs Khufu, Khafra, and Menkaura. Many hundreds of subsidiary burials are likewise found in the vicinity.

A sealed sarcophagus stood in the chamber, and, in 1927 it was finally opened with much anticipation. It was empty, leaving the Egyptologists with a genuine puzzle. There have been at least a couple of suggested scenarios to explain the empty sarcophagus. One idea suggests that Hetepheres was originally buried south at Dashur and that her tomb was robbed and her mummy was destroyed. What was left of her burial was then transferred to Giza (Khufu perhaps not being informed that his mom's mummy was missing, thus the empty sarcophagus). Another idea is that this was the original tomb for the queen and that her body was transferred to a small subsidiary pyramid near her son's giant monument. We might never know for sure.

Old Kingdom Times

The Old Kingdom was indeed a time of great wealth and creativity. There were few threats from abroad, and the Egyptians engaged in vigorous trade and occasionally raids to secure whatever resources they might desire. Sculptures in both wood and stone demonstrate extraordinary artistry, whether carved in relief or three dimensions.

Very telling are the huge number and variety of titles of officials involved in the Egyptian royal government during this time. Here is just a sample:

◆ Royal scribes, secretaries, and seal-bearers

◆ Overseers for dozens of things, including ships, household goods, linen, all the trees of Memphis, beef fat, boat nets, the duck pond, granaries, and ladies of the harem

◆ Directors of wheat measurers, brewers, hairdressers, interpreters, scribes, singers, and gold smelters

◆ Inspectors of dancers, manicurists, prophets, priests, and sculptors

◆ Eye physician of the palace

◆ Bookkeeper of the royal documents

◆ Carpenter of the Great Dockyard

- ◆ Royal Sandal-Bearer
- ◆ Sole companion (of the ruler); a funny title to us because it could be held by several individuals at the same time

During this period, the system of hieroglyphs became ever more developed, to the point that it was fully expressive in communicating the Egyptian language. Although there are few known texts from the Old Kingdom as compared to later historical periods, much of what has survived is very insightful. The oldest ancient Egyptian religious documents are the Pyramid Texts, carved on the inner walls of Old Kingdom pyramids, beginning with the last king of the Fifth Dynasty. Autobiographical statements found in the tombs of bureaucrats who proudly served their rulers also provide us with valuable insights.

Sunny Days

During the Fifth Dynasty, there was a spurt of activity in further developing the sun cult. Its first ruler, Userkaf, built a temple to Ra at Abusir, a practice that was followed by some of his dynastic successors. Userkaf's sun temple included a large, stubby obelisk atop an elevated platform surrounded by a walled ceremonial complex.

There is an increasing trend of smaller, cheaper, and more simply constructed pyramids. The pyramid of Unas contains the first example of Pyramid Texts, a trend that continued into the Sixth Dynasty. In the Pyramid Texts, it's possible to see that the sun cult that was dominant in these days was being joined in popularity with that of Osiris, the god of the dead.

Going Downhill?

The smaller pyramids and other declining building projects during the Sixth Dynasty suggest that the glory days of the Old Kingdom were near their end. Beginning at least during the reign of the last three rulers, Pepi I, Merenra, and Pepi II, there is evidence that regional governors were gaining more wealth and power. The central

> **Nile Notes**
>
> One of the most famous autobiographical inscriptions from the Old Kingdom comes from the tombs of Weni at Abydos. Weni served under three rulers of the Sixth Dynasty: Teti, Pepi I, and Merenra. During his long career, his jobs included confidante to the king, military leader, judge, and governor.

> **Lost and Found**
>
> An ancient document known as the Papyrus Westcar tells stories set in the time of the Old Kingdom, although the papyrus itself dates to hundreds of years later. These interesting tales include an attempt to cheer up Snefru with a boatload of scantily clad rowing girls (and a subsequent miracle), a magic show for King Khufu, and a story of the divine births of three Fifth Dynasty kings.

authority of the ruler of Upper and Lower Egypt was weakening. Egypt was about to become immersed in civil conflict.

The Least You Need To Know

- ◆ The earliest historical periods in Egypt, Dynasties 0–2, are often referred to as the Early Dynastic or Archaic Period.
- ◆ Egyptian civilization truly flourished during the Old Kingdom, Dynasties 3–6.
- ◆ The many grandiose monuments of the Old Kingdom are a reflection of Egypt's power and wealth.
- ◆ The Fourth Dynasty is particularly known for its gigantic pyramids, with the Great Pyramid at Giza being the largest.
- ◆ The preeminence of the sun cult during the Old Kingdom is evident by pyramids, royal titles, and sun temples.

Chapter 11

Pharaohs' Mountains

In This Chapter

- From brick mastabas to stone step-pyramids
- The massive pyramids of Giza
- A lost pyramid and buried boats
- The Great Sphinx
- More pyramids, large and small
- Construction mysteries

The pyramids of Egypt are perhaps the most readily identifiable symbols of that ancient civilization. They have been looked upon with awe for thousands of years, and they continue to command a good deal of attention even now. Overall, there are more than 90 known pyramid structures—of various sizes and designs—from ancient Egypt.

In this chapter, we'll take a closer look at the pyramid phenomenon during the Old Kingdom, including the building of the Great Pyramid, the Sphinx, and some other less famous but equally-as-interesting monuments to the dead. We'll also begin to consider just how the ancient Egyptians actually managed to build these massive structures. (In this chapter, I'll be considering only the explanations accepted by Egyptologists; alternative viewpoints regarding the pyramids will be noted in Chapter 19, "Alternative Theories.")

Stairway to Heaven

As you already know, the pyramids of Egypt were built to hold the remains of the rulers of Egypt, who were considered to be living gods on earth. The pyramidal shape itself is quite important: Some scholars argue that it represents, in stone, a version of the primeval mound or hill found in the old Egyptian creation stories. Perhaps it was inspired by the natural cycle of the Nile. As the Nile receded every year after the Inundation, mounds of fertile earth would appear. As such, it represents regeneration and resurrection. The pyramids also rise to a point aiming at the heavens, where the ruler's soul will take its place among the immortal stars.

Nile Notes

Some skeptics like to point out that an intact pyramid burial has never been uncovered. Empty pyramids and sarcophagi, they insist, suggest that maybe the pyramids had some function other than that of burial. Keep in mind that few intact royal burials have been found at any time in Egyptian history, but there's plenty of evidence of robbery. The practice of burying royalty with grandiose grave goods was an alluring attraction to thieves at all times of Egyptian history.

One Giant Leap

As mentioned in the previous chapter, many of the early dynastic graves were rectangular mastabas made primarily of brick. During the Third Dynasty, the innovations of Djoser and his architect Imhotep resulted in the amazing step-pyramid at Sakkara, the cemetery of Memphis. The pyramid stands about 200 feet tall, and it is basically six mastaba-like steps built of stone, one atop the other. A subterranean burial chamber lies beneath, and several burial shafts have been found that were for royal family members.

Just as extraordinary is the massive surrounding funerary complex that accompanied this pyramid, perhaps an eternal Memphis in stone, in an enclosure measuring approximately 850 by 1,700 feet.

The Third Dynasty Step Pyramid of Djoser at Sakkara.

A Lost Pyramid

Very little was known of Djoser's successor, Sekhemkhet, until the discovery of his unfinished pyramid in 1951 by Egyptian archaeologist Zakaria Goneim (1911–1959). The platform of what was likely to be a very large stepped structure was found with a ramp cut into the rock leading down to a blocked doorway. A dangerous passageway leading to a large unfinished burial chamber was cleared of loose debris. Some objects found during excavation bore the name of Sekhemkhet, thus attaching an ancient name to this intriguing find. In the center of the chamber stood a beautiful sealed sarcophagus cut from a single block of translucent alabaster. The tomb showed no indication of ancient robbery, but when it was opened in 1954, the sarcophagus was empty. It remains a mystery; perhaps the final resting place of Sekhemkhet is to be found elsewhere.

Collapsed and Bent Pyramids

The Fourth Dynasty ruler Snefru is given the credit for building the first true pyramid with a square base and four triangular sides, but dating just before this is a very odd pyramid at the site of Meydum near the Fayyum. It seems to have been built by Snefru's predecessor, Huni, and was probably finished by Snefru. It is quite an extraordinary sight today. Its sloping sides have disappeared, revealing a blocky inner core. Many Egyptologists believe that the pyramid's faces experienced a catastrophic collapse due to a weak foundation. Others argue that the sides were massively quarried for use in other building projects.

Snefru built two pyramids of his own at Dashur, south of Memphis. His so-called Bent Pyramid takes on a less steep angle of ascent about two-thirds of the way up. Not surprisingly, there are various explanations for the change in shape, including the need for a hasty completion upon the death of Snefru or that modifications were made in the aftermath of a disaster at the Meydum pyramid. Whatever the reason for the bend in the Bent Pyramid, Snefru got things right with his other Dashur construction, the Red Pyramid.

A standard plan for pyramids developed that included several components. An orientation toward the cardinal directions was typical and would allow the eastern side to face the rising sun. On the inside of the pyramid was a burial chamber, of course, and on the outside were two temples. A mortuary temple stood next to the pyramid itself, and a valley temple was located some distance away. The mortuary and valley temples were connected by a causeway.

> **Nile Notes**
>
> There is an old Arab saying: "Time fears no man, yet time fears the pyramids."

The pyramid itself was often surrounded by a walled enclosure.

It Doesn't Get Any Bigger

The Great Pyramid of Khufu at Giza is rightly celebrated for its sheer size and architectural sophistication. Some are surprised that such a monument appears so early in the 3,000-year course of Egyptian civilization, a singular monumental construction never to be surpassed in subsequent generations. It is a product of a well-organized and resource-rich Old Kingdom under a ruler with sufficient power and status to pull off such an incredible accomplishment. Let's take a look at some of the specifications:

- **Base dimensions**—Originally 754 feet on each side, now 745 feet due to quarrying of outer facing stones. Approximately 13 square acres and oriented to the four cardinal directions.
- **Height**—Originally 481 feet tall, now 449 feet due to quarrying of summit blocks.
- **Angle**—A little over 51°.
- **Amount of stone**—Perhaps more than 2.3 million blocks of stone, mostly limestone but also some immense granite blocks used in such features as the burial chamber.
- **Estimated time needed for construction**—Between 20 and 25 years.

Associated with the Great Pyramid are three subsidiary pyramids located on its east side for queens, and numerous mastabas and shaft tombs belonging to relatives and officials.

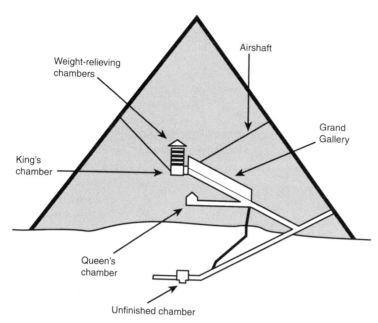

A cross-section of the Great Pyramid of Khufu at Giza showing its inner chambers.

(*After* The Pyramids of Egypt, *by I.E.S. Edwards.*)

Airshaft

Weight-relieving chambers

Grand Gallery

King's chamber

Queen's chamber

Unfinished chamber

The size is indeed imposing, but don't forget that there are very impressive structures within! An entrance on the north side leads to what is called the Ascending Passage, which is a tall vaulted corridor that ultimately leads up to the so-called King's Chamber containing a granite sarcophagus. The King's Chamber is walled and roofed with immense granite slabs, and a series of relieving chambers was above the chamber to take some of the weight off the room below. Lower down is a smaller chamber referred to as the Queen's Chamber. And elsewhere, a small, steep passageway leads to a large unfinished room carved into the very bedrock. Overall, it's a sophisticated design, and the exact function of its various features is still debated among Egyptologists.

Diggers

Napoleon was quite impressed with the pyramids, and before a battle that took place within view of the pyramids in 1798, he inspired his troops by announcing, "Soldiers! From the heights of these pyramids, 40 centuries look down upon us!" He is also said to have personally calculated that the volume of stone found in the Great Pyramid was sufficient to build a wall around France 10 feet tall and 1 foot wide.

A Most Amazing Discovery

While clearing away material along the south face of the Great Pyramid in 1954, an Egyptian antiquities inspector named Kamal el-Mallakh noticed a thin line of mortar running across the bedrock surface. Subsequent investigation revealed a pit carved into the rock covered by 41 giant limestone slabs. Inside this pit was one of the most remarkable discoveries in a land full of remarkable discoveries: a complete, dismantled boat dating to the reign of Khufu, c. 2575 B.C. There were 1,224 pieces of wood, much of it imported cedar, plus ropes and other associated materials. The airtight seal of the covering stone slabs allowed for the incredible preservation of the pit's contents.

Nile Notes

Khufu's reconstructed ship, often called "the Solar Boat," can be visited in a special museum built directly above the pit in which it was found on the south side of the Great Pyramid.

It took years to put this veritable jigsaw puzzle back together, but the results are magnificent. The reconstructed boat is 142 feet long and 19 feet across at its widest point. Both its bow and stern are upturned in papyriform fashion. The boat was equipped with six pairs of long oars and a cabin. It is generally believed that the boat played a role in the solar journey of the deceased ruler, and it's possible that it might have actually been used during Khufu's funerary procession.

The magnificent recon-
structed boat found in a pit
at the base of the Great
Pyramid.

(David Moyer collection.)

Another set of stone slabs was found nearby the first, and, in 1987, a camera was inserted though a small hole in one of the stones to examine its contents. Sure enough, another dismantled boat was found within. Unfortunately, it is in terrible shape and will require a great effort to conserve and reconstruct—an ambitious project for the future.

Khafra Tries to Outdo Dad

Looking at the neighboring pyramid of Khafra, it almost appears bigger than that of Khufu and, in size, comes pretty close. Khafra, however, built his pyramid on slightly higher ground than his father, thus giving the impression of greater height. The internal structure of Khafra's pyramid is not nearly as elaborate, but it was accompanied by a truly magnificent valley temple, which apparently held many fine sculptures of the ruler. Khafra's pyramid is especially interesting today because it still retains a good bit of its original limestone casing near its top. When intact, the white limestone exterior of this and many other pyramids must have been gleaming and spectacular!

Lost and Found

When a camera was inserted through a stone slab to investigate the second covered boat pit on the south side of the Great Pyramid, it quickly became obvious that this pit hadn't remained perfectly sealed as had the first: A beetle was found cavorting around the inside.

Diggers

The Italian explorer Giovanni Belzoni was the first to enter the Khafra's Giza pyramid in recent times (1818). In doing so, he wanted to be sure that he himself would receive the credit for this achievement, so he painted his name and the date in large black letters on the wall of its burial chamber, where they can be seen today.

The Great Sphinx

Next to Khafra's valley temple is another readily recognized symbol of ancient Egypt, the Great Sphinx. The Sphinx is a gigantic sculpture with the body of a crouching lion and the head of Khafra. It is 240 feet in length and about 60 feet in height to the top of its head. It was carved out of a natural limestone outcrop with the rear of the body excavated into the surface bedrock. At one time it was colorfully painted and sported a beard. This magnificent sculpture has suffered much through the years; its nose has been smashed, and its beard has fallen off. The whole monument has been subject to intensive preservation, and its conservation continues.

The Great Sphinx as it sits to the east of the pyramid of Khafra at Giza.

(David Moyer collection.)

Smaller but Classy

Menkaura's pyramid, the third giant structure at Giza, is significantly smaller than that of Khufu and Khafra. It measures only 355 feet across each side, with an original height of 215 feet (now 203 feet). Its lower third was faced in granite from Aswan. Despite the fact that its limestone casing blocks have been quarried and its north face is marred by the gashes of treasure hunters, it is still a beautiful little pyramid.

When Richard Vyse and John Perring entered Menkaura's pyramid in 1837, they found a badly damaged wooden coffin and a stone sarcophagus bearing the ruler's name. The style of each indicates that these were replacement items from a much later age, as if Menkaura's burial was being restored. Both items were shipped to London for the British Museum, but the ship bearing the sarcophagus sank at sea, where it remains.

The Later Pyramids

As noted in the last chapter, the Old Kingdom pyramids after the Fourth Dynasty became smaller and simpler. Pyramid building seems to have come to a halt during the tumultuous First Intermediate Period that followed, but it was resumed during the Middle Kingdom. The first ruler of that new era, Menthuhotep I, built a large tomb complex at Deir el-Bahri on the west bank of Thebes in Upper Egypt. It has been argued that it was crowned with a small pyramid.

The Twelfth Dynasty ruler Amenemhet I built a pyramid at Lisht near the Fayyum, liberally borrowing small blocks of limestone from some of his Old Kingdom predecessors. His was the last to be built with a core of stone blocks. Those who followed used stone rubble or mud brick for their fill. As a result, most of these pyramids haven't survived very well after their casing stones were removed.

> ### Nile Notes
>
> Pyramids were given names. Those at Giza were "Horizon of Khufu," "Khafra is Great," and "Menkaura is Divine."

It's possible that pyramid-like features were included on some of the tombs of the late Seventeenth Dynasty Theban rulers, but the evidence isn't extensive. During most of the New Kingdom, royal tombs were carved in a special place, the Valley of the Kings, which was situated below a huge pyramid-shape peak. During the same period, several private individuals in the Theban area incorporated a small, steep-sided pyramid feature into the design of their tombs.

The much deteriorated pyramid of Amenemhet III at Dashur, with its exposed mud brick core.

(David Moyer collection.)

Construction Controversy

The pyramids still hold several puzzles for Egyptologists and archaeologists, but one of the biggest is their very construction. Particularly for the great pyramids of the Fourth Dynasty, we are still trying to figure out how, without modern machinery, it was possible to quarry, transport, and install an enormous number of large blocks of stone while maintaining a high degree of geometric perfection. Such a task would be quite difficult to accomplish even today, and the costs would be astronomical. Most of the discussion on this subject revolves around the Great Pyramid itself, the biggest and most architecturally impressive of the lot.

Cutting That Stone

The Egyptians were adept at quarrying stones, and limestone is one of the easiest stones to cut. Most of the blocks for the Giza pyramids seem to have been quarried near the building site, and a limestone quarry at Tura, on the east bank of the Nile, was a favorite spot for obtaining brilliant white casing stones. Boats, rafts, or barges would have been needed for transport from quarries across the river, as well as for bringing down exceedingly heavy pieces of granite from such places as Aswan, several hundred miles upstream.

Moving Those Blocks

We are also not certain how they managed to get the massive stones to the building site. The annual flooding of the Nile during the inundation could greatly facilitate the bringing of materials closer to the construction zone. Ropes were no doubt used, but to what extent rollers and sledges were put to work isn't known. The Egyptians probably didn't have a lot of wood to build the huge quantities of these sorts of tools that would be needed. Enough men using brute strength to pull stone blocks along a lubricated runway or ramp might very well have been sufficient to do the job.

> **Nile Notes**
>
> Some scholars have questioned the identity of the builder of the Great Pyramid because Khufu's name does not appear formally carved anywhere within the huge structure. Ancient workmen's graffiti on some stone blocks such as those in the pyramid's relieving chambers, however, clearly indicate that they were working for their boss, Khufu.

> **Lost and Found**
>
> After a hiatus of hundreds of years, the practice of building royal stone pyramids was taken up by Nubian rulers beginning in the Twenty-fifth Dynasty (c. 747 B.C.). These relatively small and steep-sided Egyptian-inspired structures were constructed at such sites as Nuri and Meroe in what is today the country of Sudan.

Piling the Stones

There are two general theories explaining how the large stones were lifted and placed on the growing structure: ramps and levers. One version of the ramp theory involves a huge ramp running up the side of the pyramid or a series of ramps positioned at the corners. Such ramps, though, would be amazing constructions in and of themselves and would involve a tremendous volume of material. Ramps of this sort would need to grow with the pyramid to maintain a reasonable angle for transporting blocks. Another version of the ramp theory calls for a spiraling ramp winding its way around as the pyramid is built. Some experts question the stability of such a structure, but it would involve far less material than the first ramp idea.

Herodotus was the first to suggest the second theory for the construction of the pyramids. He wrote that the Great Pyramid was built using levers to lift the blocks from layer to layer. This, too, is controversial in terms of the amount of energy needed to transport blocks to higher levels and also because of the wood scarcity issue. It's possible that a combination of both ramp and levering methods was used very efficiently to produce the stunning final result.

Infrastructure

Because it is so utterly impressive, many of those interested in the pyramids tend to focus on the engineering and symbolic nature of the monuments. We must never forget, however, that these structures were built by people, and these people had their needs. A work crew of perhaps 20,000–35,000 or more people needed to be fed, housed, and provided with various other amenities to keep them healthy and hopefully content. How and where the work crews were housed was somewhat of a mystery at Giza until excavations on the plateau beginning in the 1980s revealed what appear to be some of the workmen's facilities, including a large bakery and cemeteries.

A Reasonable Scenario

One of the best ideas I've heard among the many "building the pyramids" schemes is that they were organized as great public works projects. There was probably a permanent crew of specialized workmen year round that was augmented by state-recruited labor, which was especially abundant during the time of the annual flooding of the Nile. In return, the workers were employed and did their national duty, plus reaped whatever extended spiritual value there was for participating in perpetuating the afterlife of a god-king.

The Seven Wonders

Khufu's Great Pyramid is usually considered to be one of the Seven Wonders of the Ancient World.

Pharaoh's Domain

The Greek name for Egypt's Old Kingdom capital, Memphis, is derived from the name of the pyramid of Pepi I (Men-nefer), which means "the beautiful establishment."

Diggers

Recent experiments in quarrying and moving stone blocks have demonstrated that many of the seemingly arduous tasks of building a large pyramid could be readily accomplished with a surprisingly few number of people. One study indicated that the Great Pyramid could be built in 20 to 40 years with a regular crew of about 5,000!

Nile Notes

There is no evidence that any significant number of slaves was used in building the pyramids, and certainly not Hebrew slaves. They apparently worked on other projects more than a thousand years later.

Seven was considered a special number in several ancient cultures, and it also was in the world of the Greeks. Lists of this and that might be composed in sevens—the seven greatest, worst, biggest, smallest, loudest, and so on. And thus we have a list of the Seven Wonders of the Ancient World. The elements of the list were debated in ancient times, but the definitive choices seem to have been established sometime during the European Renaissance. And here's the list of the other six:

◆ The Pharos Lighthouse at Alexandria in Egypt, which served as a beacon for ships at sea. It was built around 280 B.C. and was destroyed in earthquakes. (See Chapter 17, "Uninvited Visitors.")

◆ The Hanging Gardens of Babylon (in modern Iraq), built by Nebuchadnezzar around 600 B.C. to please his foreign wife.

◆ The Mausoleum at Halicarnassus in Turkey, built about 360 B.C. as a tomb for the Persian governor Mausolos.

◆ The Colossus of Rhodes, a massive bronze statue of the god Helios on the Greek island of Rhodes. It was built around 290 B.C., and an earthquake brought it down less than a century later.

◆ The beautiful Temple of Artemis at the Greek city of Ephesus (in modern Turkey), built by King Croesus around 560 B.C. It burned down, was rebuilt, and was finally destroyed by the Goths in A.D. 262.

◆ The giant Statue of Zeus at his temple in Olympia, Greece. It was sculpted from wood and sheated in gold, and it dates from about 430 B.C. It eventually ended up in a palace in Constantinople, which burned in A.D. 462.

Of the seven, only the Great Pyramid remains more or less intact, although pieces of the Mausoleum have been retrieved and can now be seen in the British Museum in London. Fragments of the Pharos Lighthouse also may have been recently found in the waters off Alexandria.

The Least You Need to Know

◆ The pyramids of Egypt were built as royal burial places.

◆ The shape of the pyramids evolved from rectangular mastabas to the step-pyramid, to structures with a square base and four triangular sides.

◆ The Great Pyramid at Giza was the largest ever built and is considered one of the Seven Wonders of the Ancient World.

◆ The Fourth Dynasty was the height of large and sophisticated pyramid building, although many more pyramids of smaller dimensions and lesser quality were constructed in the centuries that followed.

◆ Although we are not sure of all the details of Egyptian pyramid construction, it is clear that they were built by very skilled and well-organized Egyptians.

Chapter 12

Chaos and Stability

In This Chapter

- ◆ The Old Kingdom crumbles
- ◆ Civil chaos ensues
- ◆ Unity is restored
- ◆ The Middle Kingdom begins … and ends
- ◆ Foreigners take over

With its centralized authority under a divine ruler, the period called the Old Kingdom flourished for about 500 years. After the Fourth Dynasty, though, an increasing trend, in which provincial leaders exercised more power, ultimately had severe consequences for a unified Egypt. In this chapter, we're going to look at what's called the First Intermediate Period, which saw the temporary end of a cohesive nation. We'll see how order was restored for a good while during the prosperous era known as the Middle Kingdom, which also would disintegrate during the so-called Second Intermediate Period.

Bad Times Coming!

As we learned in the last chapter, the largest and most expensive pyramids ever constructed in Egypt were built during the Fourth Dynasty of the Old Kingdom. With such projects as a measure of wealth and control, the rulers of that

Glyphs _____

Nomarchs are the leaders or governors of **nomes,** the various provinces of Upper and Lower Egypt.

Pharaoh's Domain _____

Both Manetho and Herodotus mention a brief reign of an Egyptian queen named Nitocris not long after the death of Pepi II. Apparently, she was quite ruthless and, in one instance, murdered hundreds of people at a banquet by drowning them in river water. Unlike later queens, however, we have no actual statues or other contemporary evidence for this queen.

era were indeed powerful. When we start heading into the Fifth and Sixth Dynasties, the building continues, but the monuments get smaller. Some Egyptologists suggest that this is an indication of more austere, if not less motivated, times.

After the extremely long reign of the Sixth-Dynasty ruler Pepi II, signs of instability become evident. A few provincial rulers, or *nomarchs*, began to flex their muscles, and Egypt was soon thrown into civil disarray. Why did this happen? The subject is controversial and Egyptologists don't know for sure, but some have suggested that the disorder was due to the exceedingly lengthy reign of Pepi II. In power for perhaps as long as 94 years, Pepi II might have eventually become unable to keep a tight grasp on national affairs, leaving an opening for some of the wealthy and ambitious nomarchs to step in. By this time, many of the nomarchs were already building their own provincial bureaucracies and lavish tombs.

It is also a possibility that famine or other environmental factors contributed to the civil disarray. Scientists have discovered that around this time, there was a severe drop in rainfall, so that low Nile inundations and resulting famines may have been a factor, too.

Who's the Boss?

During the Seventh through the Eleventh Dynasties, there were power struggles between competing Egyptian rulers. According to Manetho, in the Seventh Dynasty, Egypt had 70 different kings in a period of 70 days, which is probably a kind of metaphor for some serious administrative chaos at Memphis, but Egyptologists don't know this for sure. The Eighth Dynasty is nearly as obscure as the Seventh, but we know that in the Ninth and Tenth Dynasties, rulers were based out of the city of Herakleopolis, which is about 45 miles south of Memphis. These rulers challenged the authority of a now politically weak Memphis and proclaimed themselves the rulers of Egypt.

In reality, these new rulers controlled only a portion of Egypt because the powerful southern district of Thebes wanted no part of it, and their own Eleventh-Dynasty line of rulers likewise competed for power. One of these early Theban rulers, Intef II, was so cocky that he self-assuredly called himself the King of Upper and Lower Egypt, although he, too, controlled but a fraction of the Two Lands. At one point, yet another entity, the nomarch of Hierakonpolis, entered the fray from south of Thebes, only to be defeated.

With the central authority of a unified Egypt utterly compromised, some scholars look upon this somewhat confusing so-called First Intermediate Period as a veritable Dark Age. A number of nomes no doubt thrived during this period, but the Old Kingdom's foreign policy and trade, along with national building projects, could not continue as before. Overall, the details of much of this historical interlude are rather meager.

Thebes Wins!

The Tenth Dynasty of Herakleopolitan rulers began fighting in earnest with those in Thebes. The Theban Eleventh-Dynasty line of rulers eventually prevailed under their leader, Mentuhotep I, and Egypt was once again united. With central authority restored, the chronological period known as the Middle Kingdom began, and, as in those other periods called "Kingdoms" by Egyptologists, Egypt exercised the benefits of its centralized authority. Great building projects resumed, and the arts once again flourished.

A Golden Age

With the victory of Mentuhotep I, Thebes became a prominent place and remained that way for many centuries. The Theban god Amun became popular at the national level, and what would become the massive temple complex of Karnak was regularly augmented. Mentuhotep built a massive funerary complex on the west bank of Thebes, and the role of the mighty pharaoh was reestablished.

The Eleventh-Dynasty rulers following Mentuhotep I continued the consolidation process, and a new dynastic line of rulers was begun with Amenemhet I. Dynasty 12 is often seen as a kind of golden age in Egyptian history. Egypt really thrived politically, economically, and culturally during this time, and its rulers were strong and

Lost and Found

While excavating on the west bank of Thebes in 1923, American archaeologist Herbert Winlock encountered a mass grave of 60 slain warriors. Some of the bodies had been shot with arrows, and others had serious head wounds. It is believed that these may have been Eleventh-Dynasty soldiers of Mentuhotep I, perhaps killed while battling the forces of the Herakleopolitans.

Glyphs

A **coregency** is a practice in which a royal successor is chosen and rules alongside the reigning king, taking over at the death of his mentor. It is intended to ensure a smooth and competent succession. Occasionally it can cause chronological headaches for Egyptologists when they discover that certain reigns did or did not overlap as previously thought.

A text from the Twelfth Dynasty is known as the *Instruction of Amenemhet*. The text is addressed to Senusret I as if written by his deceased father. It offers advice to Senusret, including the warning not to trust anyone.

active. The style of art and writing from this period would be regarded as "classical" and emulated throughout the remainder of Egyptian history.

One of Amenemhet I's many accomplishments was to establish a new administrative capital away from Thebes and closer to the juncture of the Two Lands at a place called Itj Tawy, about 20 miles south of Memphis. It was a pleasant location, strategically located so that Amenemhet could keep a close eye on activities to the north and the south. Amenemhet resumed the pyramid-building practice of his Old Kingdom predecessors and built a large one at the site of Lisht, not far from the new capital. He also initiated the practice of *coregency*, in which a royal successor is chosen and rules alongside the reigning king, taking over at the death of his mentor.

Lost and Found

In 1936, French archaeologists excavating at a Middle Kingdom temple dedicated to Montu at the site of Tod, south of Luxor, found a bronze box bearing the name of Senusret II. Inside were precious silver cups (perhaps from Crete), some gold ingots, a lion made of silver, and some lapis lazuli cylinder seals from Mesopotamia. Apart from its artistic value, this find, known as the "the Tod Treasure," indicates widespread relations between Egypt and other lands.

Capable Rulers

Amenemhet was apparently assassinated, but his son and coregent, Senusret I, ruled ably as a political stabilizer and great builder. Their successors, Amenemhet II and Senusret II, were also exceedingly capable. The latter is especially known for transforming the Fayyum region near the new capital into a greatly productive agricultural region.

The Twelfth Dynasty was also a time of great trade. Egypt occupied neighboring Nubia and maintained forts there, and it was also a presence in Palestine. Items from as far away as the Mediterranean island of Crete have been found in Egypt at this time, and a few Egyptian items have been found in Crete as well. The expeditions to quarries and gold mines continued, and each ruler continued to build structures for himself, the gods, and the people of Egypt.

Senusret III was a great warrior pharaoh, engaging in military campaigns in Nubia and Palestine. He also restructured the Egyptian government to curtail any ambitions for power that the provincial nomarchs might entertain. His successor, Amenemhet III, is considered to be the last great ruler of the Middle Kingdom. Very little is known about Amenemhet III's son and successor, Amenemhet IV, but when he died, his sister, Sobeknefru, took over.

A sculpture of Senusret III showing his distinct and stern royal look of concern and strength.

(David Moyer collection.)

Middle Kingdom Writing and Religion

Before continuing with history, let's take a brief look at a couple of the cultural aspects of the Middle Kingdom—namely, religion and literature.

Stylish Death for the Masses

With a single divine ruler no longer in control during the First Intermediate Period, some interesting cultural changes took place. As noted, when the nomarchs grew in power, they began building larger tombs for themselves, and this

Pharaoh's Domain

Most of the Middle Kingdom rulers held the names Mentuhotep, Amenemhet, and Senusret. The name Mentuhotep means, "[the Theban war-god] Monthu is satisfied." Amenemhet means "foremost of [the god] Amun," and Senusret means "man of the goddess Usret."

trend continued even after control was consolidated in the Middle Kingdom. Cemeteries of rock-cut tombs, such as that at Beni Hasan in Middle Egypt, feature beautifully decorated walls. Unlike the sculpted and painted walls typical of the Old Kingdom mastabas, the walls of these rock-cut tombs were usually covered with plaster and then painted. Wooden funerary figures of servants and little models were quite popular. These models are quite delightful to look at, but they also give us a miniature three-dimensional perspective of homes and other buildings, activities, and even plants and animals of the time.

Lost and Found

In 1920, an expedition team from the Metropolitan Museum of Art was working in the Twelfth-Dynasty tomb of Meketre on the west bank of Thebes when members discovered a well-hidden cache of beautiful funerary figures and little models. The nicely preserved models included several different kinds of boats, models of a butcher, a carpenter shop, a bakery, a brewery, and a granary, along with servants and offering bearers. Meketre, a high steward and royal chancellor, was very well equipped for the Egyptian afterlife!

Even more interesting, the funerary practices that were previously reserved for the divine ruler seem to have become democratized and available to the masses. Variations of the esoteric texts that were once found written solely on Old Kingdom funerary monuments, the "Pyramid Texts," began to appear on the coffins of ordinary mortals. (Mortals who could afford the more expensive coffins, that is.) Many of these "Coffin Texts" survive on the typical rectangular painted wooden coffins of the First Intermediate Period and the Middle Kingdom. In an even more radical change, it became common for the deceased to be identified with Osiris, the god of the dead, just as the divine ruler was. So now, even the lowliest peasant could become an Osiris when it was all over! The god Osiris really rose to prominence in this period, and his city of Abydos became a center of pilgrimage.

A Middle Kingdom coffin with funerary texts.

(David Moyer collection.)

For Your Reading Pleasure

The Middle Kingdom is also well known for its literature. Many copies of the more popular texts survive, as they were used as teaching exercises in scribal schools for many years to come. Those stories that involved advice, or morality stories, served the double purpose of teaching good behavior while helping students master the art of writing. Here are a few of the more popular tales from this time:

- ◆ *The Story of Sinuhe*—An official in the court of the Twelfth-Dynasty ruler Amenemhet I flees when he hears of the king's death. He is adopted by Bedouins and creates a good life for himself in West Asia, yet he dearly longs for Egypt. Eventually he is invited back to his beloved homeland, where he receives a hearty welcome.

- ◆ *The Tale of the Shipwrecked Sailor*—A man becomes a castaway on an exotic island which was home to a giant talking snake.

- ◆ *The Story of the Eloquent Peasant*—A peasant is abused by a higher-ranking man who confiscates his property. The peasant pleads his case, and his petitions are so articulate that he is invited back to repeat the performance. Eventually justice prevails.

These are wonderful stories, but when you read them in direct translation, don't expect the same style and flow as if they were originally written in English. Egyptian literature requires a little getting used to, but you'll eventually find that not only are the stories good, but there are loads of interesting cultural insights to be gained!

Losing Control ... Again!

Although the Thirteenth Dynasty is considered part of the Middle Kingdom, it increasingly bore little resemblance to the political strength of the Twelfth Dynasty. The Thirteenth Dynasty consisted of numerous rulers—obscure individuals with short reigns. Egypt's political stability was seriously in question and would in fact be rudely taken advantage of.

Even during the Middle Kingdom, groups of traders and herders from the area of Palestine had settled in the eastern Delta and elsewhere in Egypt. They must not have been considered much of a threat, because there seems to have been a sizeable population of these foreigners at the time. Sometime around the time of the Thirteenth Dynasty, the settlers got organized and established their own dynasty in the Delta and claimed rule over all of Egypt. They were known as the Hyksos, and it was the first time that Egypt was dominated by foreigners (it wouldn't be the last).

Egyptologists aren't certain who, exactly, the Hyksos were. The name actually comes from Greek historians, who probably derived it from the Egyptian word *hekau-khasut*, meaning "rulers of foreign lands." They appear to be of West Semitic origin, meaning probably from the Palestine region. They established a capital at Avaris in the eastern Delta, and a series of six Hyksos rulers reigned during the Fifteenth Dynasty. This period of Hyksos domination is known as the Second Intermediate Period (c. 1650—1550 B.C.).

As with the First Intermediate Period, Egypt was no longer strong and unified.

The Hyksos actually sacked Memphis, and, needless to say, the Egyptians weren't pleased. A rival group of Egyptian rulers based in Thebes emerged, the Seventeenth Dynasty, and they at first at least pretended to try to get along with the ruling foreigners. But as you'll see in Chapter 14, "An Empire Is Built," they ended up battling the Hyksos and eventually ran them right out of town!

The Hyksos weren't necessarily all bad for Egypt. They brought some new technology, and their cultural ties with western Asia would benefit Egypt in later years. In their own way, they made concessions to the culture of Egypt, incorporating the cult of the god Seth into their religious practices. Domination of Egypt by foreigners, though, would not be tolerated for long!

Diggers

American Egyptologist Herbert Eustis Winlock (1884–1950) was one of the most outstanding archaeologists working in Egypt during the twentieth century. Between 1906 and 1931, he investigated a variety of important ancient sites while working for New York's Metropolitan Museum of Art. His excavation of Middle Kingdom sites is especially notable, and he was the author of many excellent archaeological reports and articles.

The Least You Need to Know

- The disintegration of central authority at the end of the Old Kingdom led to a time known as the First Intermediate Period.

- A few nomarchs made claim to the authority of Egypt, including the nomarchs of Thebes, who ultimately prevailed.

- The reunification of Egypt brought about a prosperous and creative period known as the Middle Kingdom.

- Exploiting weaknesses at the end of the Middle Kingdom, a group of foreigners known as the Hyksos established themselves as rulers of Egypt, much to the humiliation of the native Egyptians.

Part 4

The Age of Empire

Some Egyptologists argue that the Old Kingdom or even the Middle Kingdom were Egypt's finest days. Others contend that the New Kingdom was unsurpassed in its political and cultural achievements. The New Kingdom was an age of empire during which Egypt's reach extended out in several directions, and it was a time of such fascinating individuals as Hatshepsut, Akhenaten, and Ramesses II.

Egypt's neighbors sometimes played starring roles in its past, particularly during the New Kingdom. We'll find out who Egypt's neighbors were and what kind of relationships they had with Egypt. With the neighborhood mapped out, we'll run through the history of the New Kingdom itself. No introductory book about Egypt would be complete without at least a few words about one of the most important archaeological sites of that era—the Valley of the Kings. Finally, we'll open the pages of the Bible to some of the action-packed scenes that took place in Egypt during this time. So welcome to the New Kingdom!

Chapter 13

Meet the Neighbors!

In This Chapter

- ◆ Borders on all sides
- ◆ Neighbors on all sides
- ◆ Powerful rival near-Eastern civilizations
- ◆ Minoans and Libyans
- ◆ The golden land of Nubia

By now, it's probably clear to you that Egypt did not exist in isolation in the ancient world, but it had a number of neighbors in the greater region of the Near East. A few of them have already been mentioned, especially Nubia. In this chapter, we're going to take a look at some of the other people living in the vicinity and their relationships with ancient Egypt. These interactions became increasingly complex through time, especially from the New Kingdom onward.

Borders

As we learned in Chapter 3, "Ancient Egypt in Space and Time," the land of ancient Egypt had natural borders that hindered movement. To the north of the Delta was the Mediterranean Sea. To the west and east were deserts, and to the south a series of cataracts (river rapids) in the Nile south of modern Aswan. There were people living outside of all these boundaries, and Egypt interacted with a good number of them—as friendly trading partners and as military enemies.

Nile Notes

Archaeologists and Egyptologists are very cautious when discussing commerce and foreign interactions. For example, a scientist could find foreign objects in Egyptian tombs and jump to the conclusion that some sort of contact had been made between Egypt and a distant land. The object, though, doesn't necessarily define the relationship in how it was obtained. It could have been purchased, traded, given as a gift, stolen, or captured as war booty. It also may have passed through many hands before reaching its final destination. In short, it can often be difficult to determine the nature of such relationships based on a limited number of artifacts and texts. Furthermore, relationships between foreign lands can change dramatically over time.

A View to the East

Let's first turn to Egypt's eastern border to meet its neighbors. The Eastern Desert was regularly exploited for mining and quarrying operations, but paths also provided access to the Red Sea. Egyptian expeditions to the Land of Punt (probably somewhere near Ethiopia) may have been launched somewhere from the Red Sea coast, and if visitors from the Persian Gulf region came by sea, this is where they'd end up. Just across the way was the Sinai Peninsula, another area that provided excellent mining opportunities.

Some of Egypt's neighbors.

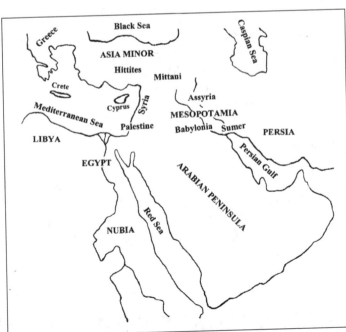

The northeastern Delta region provided access both into and out of Egypt, and it was used in times of peace and war. The region along the coast of the southeastern Mediterranean, referred to geographically as Palestine or Syro-Palestine, was home to diverse groups of people and has its own very complex history. As the crossroads between Egypt and West Asia, Palestine was the scene of great triumphs and tragedies through time, and it remains so today.

People generally known as Canaanites lived in Palestine during much of Egyptian history (through the New Kingdom) and were later joined by Philistines, the Hebrew tribes, and others. Many fortified cities existed in the region, which indicate its volatile nature. Nearly every major Near Eastern civilization pounced on Palestine at some time, and the people who lived there didn't necessarily always get along, either. There was interaction between Egypt and Palestine as early as the late Predynastic era, and items from each source have been found in both places.

To the north of Palestine is the Lebanon region, which was a great source of wood for the ancient Egyptians from early on. The port of Byblos was an especially notable center of commerce. A great trading and seafaring civilization known as the Phoenicians thrived there beginning around the time of the New Kingdom.

Land Between the Rivers

Even farther to the east was the homeland of one of the other great civilizations of the ancient world: Mesopotamia. Mesopotamia has often been called "the cradle of civilization," and its status as a complex society slightly predates that of ancient Egypt. In this area, which encompasses much of modern Iraq and stretches to the Persian Gulf, we have some of the earliest evidence of the domestication of plants and animals and the development of large towns and then cities. The word *Mesopotamia* means "the land between the rivers"—the Tigris and Euphrates Rivers, which flow south to drain into the Persian Gulf. Irrigation and the rich soil of the rivers' flood plains provided the basis for agriculture and population growth.

Pharaoh's Domain

The people to the east were often referred to as "Asiatics" and were typically depicted by the Egyptians as having beards, light skin, and foreign costumes.

Diggers

The study of ancient Mesopotamia is called Assyriology, practiced by scholars known as Assyriologists (after one of the dominant groups, the Assyrians). Like Egyptologists, they are interested in all aspects of civilization in the region and are usually trained in reading its ancient scripts.

Mesopotamia

The histories and cultures of Mesopotamia and Egypt were quite different. Whereas Egypt maintained civil stability for much of its 3,000-year existence, the dominant cultural group in Mesopotamia changed a number of times.

Those Creative Sumerians

By 3500 B.C., there were large towns in much of Mesopotamia. Not long after that time, we find the first evidence of the Sumerian civilization, which was the first major civilization in the area. The origins of these people remain a puzzle. Their language is like no other known, ancient or modern.

It's possible that the Sumerians might have had some sort of role in the development of Egypt's complex culture. This is a very controversial subject. Some Egyptologists argue that their beloved Egyptians by no means required any outside stimulation to develop as they did. Others, including myself, have no problem with the idea that Sumerians or others might have been in some way involved. The evidence is quite provocative. As I mentioned in Chapter 9, "The Earliest Egyptians," there is artistic, architectural, and artifactual evidence of contact between Egypt and Mesopotamia in the late Predynastic and Early Dynastic period. Archaeologists have found small, tubular, engraved stone cylinder seals (rolled across clay as official seals) and these objects are very characteristic of Mesopotamia. Furthermore, Mesopotamia didn't have very much stone, so its people developed interesting ways of building with mud brick, including the uses of niched facades, which were used in early Egypt as well.

Mesopotamian-like motifs have been found on the famous Narmer palette, which many believe celebrates and depicts the unification of Upper and Lower Egypt and which traditionally heralded the birth of Egyptian civilization. The palette depicts two very un-Egyptian mythological beasts with intertwined necks along with a niched fort or palace facade. The Narmer palette is not the only item from this era with unusual motifs.

Lost and Found

At the important early site of Buto in the Delta are walls decorated with clay cones that are similar to those found in early Mesopotamia. Could this be evidence of a foreign colony in Egypt during its formative years?

Questions also arise about the origins of Egyptian writing. Some Egyptologists have suggested that perhaps the very idea of Egyptian hieroglyphs was imported. Writing appeared in Mesopotamia before it did in Egypt, and in its earliest form it was pictographic in nature. Whether or not there was some sort of influence on Egypt, the writing systems in both areas developed in dramatically different ways. In Egypt, picture-like symbols remained, whereas in Mesopotamia, the wedge-shaped *cuneiform* script developed.

Contact with Mesopotamia might have been indirect, but some Egyptologists have pointed out that artistic depictions of possible foreign boats with high prows might indicate more direct contact. Egypt certainly had direct contact with Mesopotamia in later times. The New Kingdom pharaoh Tuthmosis III, for example, took his army to the edge of the Euphrates River. Of more serious consequence were Assyrian (one of the groups that dominated Mesopotamia for a time) attacks on Egypt during the Twenty-fifth Dynasty. And the Twenty-sixth Dynasty was even established with Assyrian-approved Egyptian rulers.

Glyphs

Cuneiform is a wedge-shaped script typically impressed into clay tablets and characteristic of Mesopotamia and other ancient cultures in the surrounding region.

Meet the Persians!

Another great empire appeared to the east of Mesopotamia: Persia. The Persians, who were centered in what is today Iran, tussled with the Greeks and anyone else in their way and eventually conquered the Land between the Two Rivers. The Persians made their way south and west, passing through Syria and Palestine and right into Egypt during the time of the last dynasties. (More about this can be found in Chapter 17, "Uninvited Visitors.") The Persians were kicked out of Egypt by the Macedonian Greeks under Alexander the Great.

A Couple More Players

Pharaoh's Domain

Several Eighteenth-Dynasty pharaohs, including Tuthmosis IV and Amenhotep III and IV, married princesses from Mitanni. These sorts of marriages were a way of securing a truce or alliance between the two competing powers.

The Hittites, who lived in the central region of modern Turkey, were one of the great powers to emerge in the Near East. The Egyptians were in contact with them beginning approximately 1700 B.C., and over the years the relationship between the two fluctuated wildly. The Hittites started playing a significant role in Egyptian affairs during the New Kingdom. Actual written correspondence exists between Hittite and Egyptian rulers, giving us an idea of attitudes toward one another and important events.

During the early New Kingdom, Egyptian warrior pharaohs had established dominance in several areas of Palestine and in Syria, which the Hittites wanted to include in their sphere of control. Things got tense. The great Nineteenth-Dynasty pharaoh Ramesses II fought the Hittites in northern Syria, and eventually the two rival powers signed a peace treaty. The Hittite empire was destroyed not long afterward, apparently by a group of wandering marauders and colonists from the northeast Mediterranean known as the Sea Peoples. These people also gave Egypt a good bit of trouble!

This remarkable profile of four foreign groups was sketched on the wall of the Eighteenth-Dynasty tomb of Ramose at Thebes.

(From Atlas de l'Histoire de l'Art Égyptien, *by Prisse d'Avennes.)*

Another group Egypt had to contend with was the kingdom of Mitanni in northern Mesopotamia. Most of our knowledge of these people comes from their neighbors, who had quite a bit to say about them. They competed with the Hittites for foreign territory, invaded Syria and Palestine, and battled it out with some of the Eighteenth-Dynasty pharaohs. This scrappy little entity was eventually absorbed by the neighboring Mesopotamian empire builders.

A View to the North

The Egyptians referred to the Mediterranean as "the Great Green," and although they don't have a reputation as being great roving seafarers, they certainly were able to import and export items to and from Egypt by sea. Egyptian items have been found on the islands of Crete and Cyprus in the Mediterranean, and items from those islands have been found in Egypt. Crete is especially noteworthy as home to a very unique and sophisticated sea-oriented civilization known as the Minoans. During the New Kingdom, visits by foreign emissaries, including those from Crete, are depicted on wall paintings.

In the last several years, some exciting finds have been made at Tel el-Daba, the site of the ancient Hyksos capital of Avaris in the eastern Delta. Fragments of distinct Minoan-style wall frescoes have been found, suggesting that there might have been a Minoan colony in Egypt. The dating is still uncertain, but the frescoes appear to date to the Second Intermediate Period or the early New Kingdom.

Pharaoh's Domain

Several Eighteenth-Dynasty pharaohs, including Tuthmosis IV and Amenhotep III and IV, married princesses from Mitanni. These sorts of marriages were a way of securing a truce or alliance between the two competing powers.

Lost and Found

One of the greatest archaeological shipwreck discoveries from ancient times was found at Ulu Burun in Turkey. The ship, which sank around 1306 B.C., contained many tons of diverse cargo, including ingots of copper (probably from Cyprus), tin and glass, and jars containing items such as olive oil. Hundreds of other items, such as ebony, elephant and hippo ivory, and precious objects from Egypt (including a golden scarab bearing the name of Queen Nefertiti), Palestine, and elsewhere indicate that this ship (whose home port is unknown) was really making the rounds in the Mediterranean!

A View to the West

The deserts to the west of the Nile Valley and Delta weren't of much interest to the Egyptians. If the agricultural areas in the Delta and Nile Valley themselves didn't form a kind of western border, certainly the north-to-south chain of oases to the west served as the outermost extremes; the oases were connected to the Nile Valley by overland routes.

The Egyptians referred to different ethnic groups living to their west as Libyans (with various tribal names), and these people seem to have been nomads and herders. They weren't a particularly literate people and they didn't leave any texts, so we don't know very much about them. They did, however, occasionally make the Egyptian enemies list. They became a bit threatening in the New Kingdom, and some forts were built in the western Delta to keep them away. And joining a coalition with the Sea Peoples to attack Egypt didn't enhance their popularity, either! Some of these people settled in Egypt and actually ruled parts of the land during the Third Intermediate Period.

A View to the South

The northern border of the land of Nubia, Egypt's southern neighbor, begins at the Nile's first cataract, near the modern Egyptian city of Aswan, and extends north of modern

Khartoum in Sudan. Nubia played host to major civilizations and figures prominently in much of Egyptian history.

Map of Nubia.

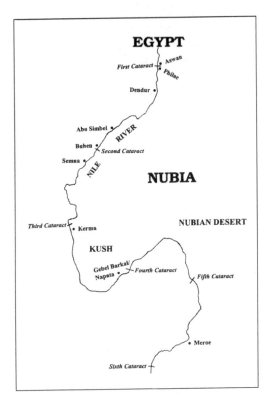

Nubia connected Egypt to the African continent, and all kinds of desirable and exotic goods made their way north to Egyptian territory from and through Nubia. Such products included ivory, ebony, ostrich feathers, leopard and panther skins, exotic oils and resins, and even monkeys. Nubia was especially known for its gold, which was of particular interest to the Egyptians.

Nubia can be divided into two geographical territories: Lower Nubia between the first and second cataracts of the Nile, and Upper Nubia to the south. Lower Nubia enjoyed a situation similar to that of the Nile Valley, in which agriculture was sustained along the great river's banks. The Upper Nubian climate was somewhat more harsh, yet ancient people nonetheless were able to thrive there.

Pharaoh's Domain

The Sixth-Dynasty tomb biography of Harkhuf tells of a dancing pygmy from "the land of the horizon-dwellers" in Nubia who was transported down the Nile to the delight of a very young king, Pepi II. Harkhuf was given orders to keep the little guy safe from falling overboard or experiencing other calamities.

Early Nubians

Like the Egyptians to the north, the people of Nubia participated in the development of agriculture and the various accompanying Neolithic phenomena, including the establishment of permanent settlements. These settlements were in full swing during Egypt's late Predynastic times. As in the case with Predynastic Egypt, archaeologists obtained most of their knowledge about these early Nubian cultures by excavating their graves.

Give Me an "A"!

Lacking indigenous names for the Nubian cultures, archaeologists have supplied some of their own. In Lower Nubia, two major cultures are referred to as the A-Group and the C-Group. In Upper Nubia, the Kerma culture is named after a major representative site.

The A-Group people were farmers and herders, and they seem to have existed between at least 3900 B.C. until roughly 2900 B.C. In looking at their grave goods through time, it is possible to see some of the similar developments in cultural complexity noticeable in early Egypt, including the emergence of powerful leaders. There is also evidence of trade between the Egyptians and these Nubians, and they are mentioned many times in Old Kingdom texts. Something happened to the A-Group folks around 2900 B.C. Perhaps the Egyptians destroyed them or, more likely, pushed them south.

> ### Nile Notes
>
> With the identification of an A-Group and a C-Group in Lower Nubia, you are probably wondering where the B-group is. It apparently doesn't exist. What had been identified as B-group graves are now understood to be poorer or plundered A-group graves.

Give Me a "C"!

The so-called C-Group appeared in Lower Nubia about 400 years later and persisted from about 2500 to 1500 B.C. They likely had their cultural origins in Upper Nubia, and many of the artifacts that they left are quite different from those of their A-Group predecessors in the area. The C-Groupers traded with the Egyptians, but the Egyptians themselves wanted to exert more control over their southern neighbors. During the Middle Kingdom, they built forts near the second cataract of the Nile. During Dynasty 13, Egypt lost control of Nubia, and Nubians occupied the Egyptian forts. And toward the end of Dynasty 17,

> ### Nile Notes
>
> Much of the archaeological work in Lower Nubia took place in response to dam-building projects in the vicinity of Aswan. The dams threatened to flood and destroy a huge quantity of Nubian archaeological sites, and they eventually did. (See more about this dam business in Chapter 20, "Facing the Future.")

the rulers of Nubia and the Hyksos rulers were treating one another as equals. This situation would change, of course, when the Hyksos were expelled from Egypt.

Give Me a "K"!

In Upper Nubia, the so-called Kerma culture thrived about the same time as the more northern C-Group. The Egyptians referred to the land occupied by the Kerma as Kush. The Kerma developed into a powerful entity with rulers whose burials were accompanied by the deaths of a large number of sacrificed humans. The Kerma people began working their way north into Lower Nubia during some of the weaker moments in Egyptian history, but when power was consolidated again, the Egyptians worked hard to control both Upper and Lower Nubia. It took a lot of effort and fierce fighting, but during the New Kingdom, Nubia was incorporated as a territory of Egypt and was ruled by a special viceroy.

Egyptianizing the South

With Nubia under Egyptian control, it seems that the C-Group people had been absorbed into Egyptian culture. The Egyptians spread their culture south, and a number of impressive temples were constructed south of the first cataract. The largest temple was built at Abu Simbel by the Nineteenth-Dynasty pharaoh Ramesses II. Egyptian influence is notable in the adoption of Egyptian writing, art styles, and religious practices—including a special preference for the worship of the god Amun, for whom Ramesses built a temple at Gebel Barkal.

Mighty Kush!

As you'll see in the following history chapters, Egypt once again lost its grip during the Third Intermediate Period, and when Egypt was weak, those under its dominance grew strong. This is certainly the case in Nubia, where the Kingdom of Kush grew into a substantial power. During the Twenty-fifth Dynasty, the kings of Kush actually were the rulers of Egypt! The culture that they maintained is a very interesting coalescence of both Nubian and Egyptian characteristics.

The history of the civilization of Kush is divided into two periods, named after the capital city at each time: the Napatan Period (c. 900–295 B.C.), after the city of Napata, and the Meroitic Period (c. 295 B.C.–A.D. 320), after Meroe. Napata is located near the fourth cataract of the Nile, and the city of Meroe is found south of the

> **Nile Notes**
>
> During the Meroitic Period, symbols ultimately derived from Egyptian script were used to write the Nubian language. Although inscriptions survive, we're really not quite sure what that ancient language is, or what all the grammatical details are. So, in a sense, it remains only partially deciphered.

fifth. One of the most interesting characteristics of both periods is the building of little stone pyramid superstructures for their royal tombs. Fields of these steep-side structures can be found at such sites as Nuri, Kurru, Gebel Barkal, and Meroe.

The steep-sided royal Nubian pyramids at Gebel Barkal show obvious Egyptian influence.

(David Moyer collection.)

Nubia was home to a truly great ancient African civilization. It's a fascinating subject all its own. It played a great role, indeed, in the history and economy of its northern neighbor, Egypt.

The Least You Need to Know

- ◆ Egypt had natural borders on all sides and neighbors on most.
- ◆ Foreign goods could have been obtained in many ways, and archaeologists need to be careful in reconstructing such things as trade relationships.
- ◆ Egypt was actively involved in trade and other interactions with neighboring cultures from the earliest time of its civilization.
- ◆ During ancient Egypt's long history, other great powers in the Near East came and went, and they interacted with—and sometimes conquered—Egypt.
- ◆ The land of Nubia was host to a vibrant African civilization, which played an important role throughout much of Egyptian history.

14

An Empire Is Built

In This Chapter

- ◆ The expulsion of the Hyksos
- ◆ A new era begins
- ◆ The emergence of warrior pharaohs
- ◆ A royal heretic takes over
- ◆ The New Kingdom declines

The time period known as the New Kingdom (c. 1550–1069 B.C.) is certainly one of the most interesting to historians of Egypt. It was a time of great wealth, political and military zeal, unusual and powerful rulers, and religious fervor. While some might argue that the Old Kingdom, with its pyramids, best epitomizes ancient Egypt, others see the New Kingdom as the pinnacle of Egyptian civilization. It is comprised of the Eighteenth, Nineteenth, and Twentieth Dynasties.

Kicking Out the Hyksos

As stated earlier, the term "kingdom," as applied to Egyptian history, refers to a time when Egypt was unified and strong. When we last left off with our historical summary, Egypt was not in a kingdom period. The Hyksos controlled Lower Egypt and ruled from their capital of Avaris. In the south, Theban rulers held power, and resentment toward the northern occupiers grew. For Egypt to be once again united, the Hyksos would have to go!

During the latter part of the Theban Seventeenth Dynasty, serious attempts to oust the Hyksos began. A ruler/warrior by the name of Seqenenre Tao made a mighty effort and was apparently killed in battle. His successor, Kamose, resumed the struggle, but it would be the next Theban ruler, Ahmose, who would be successful in sacking Avaris, kicking out the Hyksos, and reuniting Egypt. Ahmose was so successful that he took some of the fighting into Palestine, perhaps to pursue any remaining Hyksos support to be found there. Ironically, the Egyptians were aided by new military technology that seems to have been introduced by the Hyksos, including the horse and chariot.

Lost and Found

A big axe wound was found on the skull of the mummy of Seqenenre Tao. This nasty gash was likely the result of a direct blow from a Hyksos battle weapon.

Back in Business

With Ahmose's victory, a new era began in Egypt, and a new dynasty, the Eighteenth (c. 1550–1295 B.C.), commenced. It would be the age of the warrior pharaoh, and Egypt would exercise its might to the south in Nubia and far to the northeast in Palestine and Syria. Ahmose's successor, Amenhotep I, continued with the reconsolidation efforts begun by his predecessor.

The name Amenhotep (literally, "the god Amun is satisfied") is representative of the New Kingdom. The cult of the god Amun was dominant for much of that time period, with huge temples dedicated to him maintained by a large priesthood. Amenhotep I initiated major building at the temple of Karnak at Thebes, an activity that was actively continued by many who followed. Also during this time, the god Amun became even more popular in its coalescence with the sun god Ra in the form of Amun-Ra.

Pharaoh's Domain

Amenhotep I and his queen, Ahmose-Nefertari, became deified cult figures after their deaths, perhaps due to their association with the restoration of Egypt.

The pharaoh Tuthmosis I expanded Egypt's dominance into Nubia and Syria during his short reign. Not very much is known about his short-lived successor, Tuthmosis II, but we do know quite a bit about his stepsister/wife. Known as Hatshepsut, she is one of the most fascinating women in all of ancient history.

Hatshepsut: The Female Pharaoh

The male heir to the throne on the death of Tuthmosis II was the very young Tuthmosis III, Hatshepsut's stepson. Apparently, Hatshepsut took advantage of the situation and established herself as co-regent with the young Tuthmosis III, eventually presenting herself as the *de facto* ruler.

Builder and Adventurer

Hatshepsut ruled for about 20 years and presided over a period of relative peace and prosperity. Her reign is noted for her great building projects and a notable foreign expedition. Her mortuary temple, built on the west bank of Thebes, is truly a marvel. It features three terraces on which are carved some of the highlights of her rule. Her expedition to Punt, a region far south along the Red Sea, is wonderfully depicted with ships being loaded with exotic products. The obese queen of Punt, too, can be seen in her hefty glory. There is also a depiction of the transport of two obelisks, which were erected at Karnak.

Clever Queen of Controversy

Hatshepsut's reign is somewhat controversial among Egyptologists today. Females generally did not rule in Egypt, and this matter of essentially usurping the throne from its rightful, albeit youthful, owner was a bold act. Hatshepsut's political skills must have been extraordinary. In adapting herself to the role of ruler, she is often depicted wearing the symbolic beard of kingship, yet her feminine features are often not hidden. And in inscriptions, a feminine pronoun is frequently used to describe her activities, thus indicating that she was not a female pretending to be a man, but was actually a woman acting as the ruler of Egypt.

Lost and Found

The exact location of the land of Punt has been the subject of much debate. Many scholars believe that it was located in the region of Ethiopia and was thus accessible by boat via the Red Sea.

Nile Notes

Hatshepsut did not have a male consort as ruler, but it has long been suggested that she had a boyfriend: her architect, Senenmut. Senenmut was sufficiently favored to have one of his two tombs situated in the area of Hatshepsut's mortuary temple.

The beautiful terraced mortuary temple of Hatshepsut at Deir el-Bahri on the west bank of Thebes.

(David Moyer collection.)

Building the Empire

We do not know how Hatshepsut died. Her tomb in the Valley of the Kings is in horrible shape, and her mummy has never been positively identified. We do know that Tuthmosis III, Hatshepsut's stepson, was next to come to power, and at least in the latter parts of his more than 30 years as sole ruler, he seems to have engaged in the defacement of his stepmom's monuments.

Tuthmosis III was a real warrior, and he is sometimes referred to as the "Napoleon of Egypt." Among his actions were 17 years of military campaigns in Palestine and Syria, taking his battling far east—all the way to the Euphrates River. During one incident, he laid siege for seven months to the city of Megiddo in Palestine, obtaining a huge amount of booty in the process.

There are many advantages to empire building, and the Egyptians reaped the rewards. Military adventures abroad resulted in the capture of great resources of all kinds. And those towns and regions that wanted to avoid the harsher side of the Egyptian military regularly paid tribute to them. Rather importantly,

Nile Notes

A tale from the time of Tuthmosis III records the Egyptians' capture of the Palestinian town of Joppa. In this story, 200 soldiers are smuggled into the town in baskets, from which they emerge once inside the city walls. This story is very reminiscent, of course, of the famous Greek tale of the Trojan Horse and the Arabian tale of Ali Baba.

expanding Egyptian domination to the south and northeast helped to maintain security for Egypt itself.

More Tough Guys

The son of Tuthmosis III, Amenhotep II, was considered to be quite a fighter and athlete and followed in his father's footsteps. Curiously, his successor, Tuthmosis IV, seems to have been unrelated, and his right to be ruler was legitimized in some odd ways. The so-called "Dream Stele," found between the paws of the Great Sphinx at Giza, tells a story of how the sphinx spoke to Tuthmosis IV while he slept at its base and promised him the throne of Egypt if he removed the sand that encumbered his body. However it happened, Tuthmosis IV became pharaoh, although his rule was relatively short.

The Golden Rule of Amenhotep III

If Tuthmosis III was the Napoleon of Egypt, then Amenhotep III might have been the Louis XIVth of the Two Lands. During his reign, Egypt was very wealthy, and the cult of Amun-Ra was in full swing. Although there were military campaigns as necessary, Amenhotep III seems to have been quite the diplomat, making peace (or at least truces) with competitors, including the kingdom of Mitanni. Along with his greatly honored principal wife, Tiye, Amenhotep included two Mitannian princesses and one from Babylonia in his household.

Amenhotep III was a great builder. He constructed a magnificent palace for himself on the Theban west bank at a place now called Malkatta. Located well inland, this palace featured an artificial harbor fed by the Nile. Amenhotep III also built a huge mortuary temple for himself, of which little remains except two colossal statues.

> **Pharaoh's Domain**
>
> The athletic abilities of Amenhotep II have been well noted. It was claimed that he was able to shoot arrows through thick copper targets from a moving chariot.

> **Lost and Found**
>
> The two seated statues at Amenhotep III's temple are called the Colossi of Memnon. Records indicate that after an earthquake in 27 B.C., one of the statues emitted a moaning sound every morning, perhaps due to a natural process of heat and air. Later repairs to the statue in the third century A.D. seem to have curtailed the phenomenon.

The two colossal seated statues of Amenhotep III, the "Colossi of Memnon," are mostly what remains of his now vanished (quarried) mortuary temple.

(From Description de L'Égypte.*)*

Disrupting the System

What happened after the death of Amenhotep III is one of the most interesting and bizarre episodes in ancient history. The throne of Egypt was left to the great pharaoh's son, a fellow also named Amenhotep. The rule of Amenhotep IV, however, traumatized Egypt, and the country required a number of years to recover from the damage.

The Heretic King

For reasons not well understood, Amenhotep IV became obsessed with the development of a religious cult centered on the worship of a manifestation of the sun referred to as Aten. The Aten was typically depicted as a solar disk with outreached hands, and Amenhotep soon changed his name to "Akhenaten" (spirit of the sun-disk), to reflect his devotion to this deity. This, of course, was a major and devastating affront to the status quo of the wealthy priesthood of Amun, especially when Akhenaten cut off their funds and many of the operating temples were shut down.

To top things off, Akhenaten moved the Egyptian political and religious capital to a new site in Middle Egypt. This new city, called Akhetaten—"horizon of the sun-disk"—was located at the site known today as Tel el-Amarna (thus the term *Amarna Period*, which is used as a name for this unique time period and cultural phenomenon during the Eighteenth Dynasty). Far away from the normal centers of power, Akhenaten pursued his obsession.

Temples to Aten were built at Akhetaten and elsewhere. Unlike the traditional temples of the time, which contained dark and mysterious inner chambers and cult statues, the Aten temples were open to the sky, allowing the sun-disk to display itself in person.

There are plenty of depictions of Akhenaten and his principal wife, Nefertiti, along with their daughters, engaged in worship. It has often been suggested that Akhenaten was practicing some sort of primitive monotheism—that is, a belief in one supreme god. Even though Akhenaten promoted the sun-disk as superior, he was hardly a monotheist, though: He, himself, was also considered to be divine offspring as the ruler of Egypt.

Glyphs

The **Amarna Period** refers to the time during the Egyptian Eighteenth Dynasty that was characterized by Akhenaten and his immediate successor's religious and cultural devotion to Aten and the relocation of the political and religious capital to Amarna.

Nice Art!

Apart from the unusual religious and political situation, the Amarna Period was a time of distinct and innovative art. In contrast to the typical stoic and idealized official art forms, Amarna art tends to be lively and more expressionistic. Perhaps the most interesting manifestation of this trend are the artistic depictions of Akhenaten with his family. The royal family is often shown with peculiarly shaped heads and pot bellies. Several examples of royal statuary depicting Akhenaten show him with an elongated face, broad hips, and feminine features. Some claim that several of these odd and almost androgynous-looking sculptures actually depict Nefertiti. The artistic style is nonetheless unusual and has led to all kinds of speculation about the physical condition of the Amarna royal family.

Pharaoh's Domain

There has been speculation that Akhenaten might have suffered from some sort of disease or physical abnormality, such as the endocrine disorder known as Froehlich's Syndrome, hydrocephaly or the genetic disease known as Marfan's Syndrome.

As you might imagine, Akhenaten made many enemies. He died of unknown causes in the seventeenth year of his reign. A royal cemetery was constructed near Amarna, but there is little left of the royal burial. It's likely that his body was destroyed soon after it was buried, but at least a couple of scholars have suggested that his remains were later removed from Amarna and cached in the New Kingdom royal cemetery at Thebes, the Valley of the Kings.

*This colossal statue of
Akhenaten, one of a number
of such statues unearthed at
Karnak, shows the peculiar
physical features often depicted
in Amarna Period art.*

(David Moyer collection.)

Akhenaten's queen, Nefertiti, seems to have played a very important role, perhaps even serving as co-regent. At Akhenaten's death, an obscure individual known as Smenkhkare became the ruler for about two years. Some have suggested that this successor might have actually been Nefertiti.

Famous Because He's Dead!

Whoever Smenkhkare was, he was quickly succeeded by a young boy of about eight years old by the name of Tutankhaten, meaning "living image of the sun-disk." The young pharaoh soon changed his name to Tutankhamun, "living image of the god Amun," thus ushering out the Amarna Period and returning things to some semblance of the way they were before the heretic pharaoh.

Tutankhamun was apparently the offspring of Akhenaten, but the identity of his mother is not known for certain. As a young man, he was probably manipulated by those familiar with the way things had been before Akhenaten, and "the boy king" served as a post-Amarna transition figure. Tutankhamun would have likely been a passing character in Egyptian history, had it not been for the discovery of his virtually intact tomb in the Valley of the Kings in 1922 (see the next chapter, "King Tut's Valley").

Cleaning Up the Mess

Tutankhamun died at age 18 from unknown, and perhaps suspicious, causes. An older Amarna official by the name of Aye married Tut's widow and took over the throne for a few years, and he was followed by a powerful general named Horemheb. These two rulers began the difficult process of restoring order in Egypt, including reopening the old temples and regaining military and diplomatic lost ground. While Akhenaten was busy with his sun cult, Egyptian dominion in territories to the east was threatened by another great regional power, the Hittites.

Setting Things Straight

Horemheb was actively involved in tearing down the remnants of the Amarna Period and reinstating the cult of Amun. A later formal list of kings didn't even mention Akhenaten, Smenkhare, Tutankhamun, and Aye, instead adding those years to the rule of Horemheb!

Horemheb chose as his successor a close friend, vizier, and military leader who took the throne name of Ramesses I. From him, a new dynasty, the Nineteenth (c. 1295–1186 B.C.), ensued. Ramesses I ruled for about a year, and the restoration of Egypt's wealth and power continued under his son, Seti I. Seti was a great builder and warrior who reasserted Egypt's might in Nubia, Palestine, and Syria, battling the Hittites as necessary. Among his restoration projects was the building of a symbolic tomb for the god Osiris at Abydos.

Ramesses Is Great

Ramesses II continued where his father, Seti, left off, fighting the Hittites and building extensively. He is often referred to as Ramesses the Great because of his long and energetic career, although some suggest that his bloated ego was his greatest legacy. Temples and statues commissioned by and

Nile Notes

A letter has been found in Hittite archives in which a late Eighteenth Dynasty royal widow requests that a Hittite prince be sent to Egypt for the purpose of a marriage alliance. Apparently the prince died in transit, and thus this intriguing arrangement fell through. Some scholars believe that this woman was none other than Ankhesenamun, the widow of Tutankhamun!

Lost and Found

In his attack on Amarna-era monuments, Horemheb dismantled a temple to Aten at Karnak and used the decorated blocks as filler for a pylon in the great temple complex. Ironically, this served to preserve the blocks through time, much to the delight of modern Egyptologists who have been able to reconstruct portions of Akhenaten's building.

dedicated to Ramesses II can be found all over Egypt. His cartouche is seemingly every-where, and he was not above the practice of usurping his predecessors' monuments and adding his own name. Still, he was quite the dynamo. He built a new capital for himself up in the Delta and named it Pi-Ramesses and continued to battle the Hittites. Ramesses II ruled for about 67 years. He maintained several wives, the most notable being Nefer-tari, and was also married to a Hittite princess. He fathered perhaps 40 daughters and approximately 45 sons.

Ramesses II. Portrait by Winifred Brunton.

One of the most famous battles in ancient history pitted Ramesses II against the Hittites at the Syrian site of Kadesh. Ramesses barely escaped in what seems to have been ulti-mately a stalemate. We sure know a lot about the battle because Ramesses advertised his own bravery in several major inscriptions. Royal propaganda was not unusual in his time, and Ramesses was a master. It reinforced his position as a god-king and probably made his people proud.

Ramesses II eventually entered into a peace treaty with the Hittites, which allowed both parties to concentrate on other problems. For the Egyptians, trouble was appearing on the northwest borders as groups of Libyans were beginning to attack.

Raiders from the Sea

Ramesses II's successor was named Merneptah, and he aggressively fought battles in Palestine and Nubia and against the Libyans. Other groups also began to give Egypt trouble. Referred to as the "Sea Peoples," they seem to have been large, migrating groups of refugees from famine or conflict in the north Mediterranean. The rich land of Egypt was tempting, and Merneptah had to fight them off in the Delta.

After Merneptah died there was some odd political maneuvering, but eventually a new dynasty, the Twentieth (c. 1186–1069 B.C.), was established under Setnakht, whose son, Ramesses III, was the last great pharaoh of the New Kingdom. Like his predecessors, he continued to battle it out with the encroaching Libyans and others. His beautiful and well-preserved temple at Medinet Habu, on the west bank of Thebes, survives as a spectacular monument to his reign.

> **Nile Notes**
>
> One of the largest freestanding statues of Ramesses II can be found at Memphis. For years, it lay face down, but it can now be viewed on its back in a protective shed.

The Beginning of the End

A string of pharaohs, all of them named Ramesses, followed Ramesses III. It seems to have been a sort of cultural, economic, and political downhill slide. Very little monumental building took place, and there is evidence of increasing corruption. The power of the priesthood of Amun was growing to such an extent that by the time of the last pharaoh of the New Kingdom, Ramesses XI, it was debatable who was really in charge of Egypt. A little more about that comes in Chapter 17, "Uninvited Visitors."

The Least You Need to Know

- The expulsion of the Hyksos initiated a new and prosperous era in Egypt: the New Kingdom.
- Egypt regularly benefited from its impressive military might.
- The Eighteenth-Dynasty female pharaoh Hatshepsut was one of the most extraordinary women known in ancient history.
- The heretic pharaoh Akhenaten attempted to radically alter Egyptian society during the so-called Amarna Period.
- Ramesses II was one of the greatest builders and warriors of ancient Egypt.
- Near the end of the New Kingdom, the might of Egypt was challenged by the likes of encroaching Libyans and Sea Peoples.

15

King Tut's Valley

In This Chapter

- ◆ A secret cemetery
- ◆ Rich discoveries and mystery tombs
- ◆ King Tut!
- ◆ The village of tomb builders
- ◆ Hidden mummies

As impressive as the pyramids built during the Old and Middle Kingdom were, they failed to protect the remains of the divine rulers that they were built to hold. The great monuments stood out against the skyline for all to see. To robbers, they must have been irresistible, seemingly begging to be violated.

During the New Kingdom, a different strategy was begun. The dead were no longer buried in large structures visible to anyone in the area; an isolated desert valley in southern Egypt was selected in which tombs could be constructed and then protected. Known to us today as the Valley of the Kings, this royal cemetery is overshadowed by a large pyramid-shape peak, which might have served as a symbolic pyramid for all of the tombs found below.

The Secret Valley

Located in the desert mountains across the Nile from the ancient capital of Thebes, the Valley contains about 30 royal tombs carved into the limestone bedrock and about an equal number of smaller tombs belonging to family members or special friends. Most of the royal tombs had walls that were beautifully painted with religious and funerary motifs; a heavy stone sarcophagus in a lower chamber held the mummy. Despite its relatively remote location, the Valley of the Kings ultimately failed to protect most of the mummies of the rulers of Egypt from tomb robbers and others. A virtually intact burial of one king, however, that of Tutankhamun, was discovered by archaeologists in 1922, and the Valley of the Kings will be forever linked with his name. More on him later.

> **Pharaoh's Domain**
>
> The Arabic name for the Valley of the Kings is *Wadi Biban al Moluk,* "the valley of the gates (or doors) of the kings." Although it did serve as the burial place of New Kingdom pharaohs, a lot of other people were interred in there as well.

Thutmosis I was the first ruler to have a tomb in the Valley. Like several of the earlier Eighteenth Dynasty tombs that would be constructed there, his tomb was cut into an unobvious place in a limestone cliff. This tomb seems to have been expanded by his daughter, Hatshepsut, and penetrates deep down through the solid rock into a loose layer of crumbly shale. The tomb builders must have learned a lesson from building Thutmosis's and Hatshepsut's tomb, because the later tombs are more solid structures.

A view of the Valley of the Kings.

Nile Notes

There are actually two Valleys of the Kings. The easternmost is the most famous and contains the vast majority of the tombs. The westernmost consists of two huge branches and has not been completely explored. It holds just a few known tombs, including those of Amenhotep III and Aye. The local name for this valley is *Wadi al-Garoud,* or "Valley of the Monkeys," named after the paintings of baboons found in Aye's tomb.

As more tombs were constructed, they began to vary in design, a few with cartouche-shape burial chambers, and many incorporating a series of corridors and halls. One feature became common: a deep shaft or well, which some say had a symbolic function but could likewise serve very practically as a sump for the waters of flash floods or as an obstacle to robbers.

The builders of the tombs of the later New Kingdom didn't seem to make any attempts to hide the tombs' locations. Some were apparently fitted with cedar doors and their entrance lintels were bedecked with red solar disks. Some of these tombs run long and straight into the rock, with no turns. And there doesn't seem to have been any general plan for the Valley of the Kings. Several tombs ran into others during construction. Along with esoteric funerary texts, in some tombs are found Greek, Latin, and Coptic graffiti—evidence of the tombs' later visitors.

Nile Notes

The tomb of Tuthmosis I and Hatshepsut (Tomb 20) in the Valley of the Kings is one of the deepest and most treacherous to be found in Egypt. The tomb descends steeply into the mountainside, through a layer of rotten, crumbling shale that expands when wet. As a result of flooding, the lower portion of the tomb is nearly destroyed. The tomb was home to thousands of bats, and the air down deep is vile. Fortunately for Tuthmosis I, his burial was later removed to a smaller, less fragile tomb in the Valley.

Tourists and Diggers

Although the Valley of the Kings had been visited sporadically by tourists and travelers for thousands of years, the first known excavator was Giovanni Belzoni in 1817. Belzoni discovered several major tombs, including those of Ramesses I and Seti I. The latter is considered by some to be the most grandly decorated tomb in all of Egypt. It has suffered greatly (see Chapter 20, "Facing the Future").

In 1827, early British Egyptologist John Gardner Wilkinson (1797–1875) began a numbering system for tombs in the Valley that continues to be used to refer to these tombs today. Back then, there were 21 known tombs. The last new tomb discovered, that of Tutankhamun, bears the number 62.

Nile Notes

Egyptologists use the prefix "KV" to designate tombs located in the Valley of the Kings. Thus Tomb 21, which is in the Valley of the Kings, is typically referred to as "KV 21." The system is not perfect. Some tombs in the same numbering scheme aren't found in the Valley itself, and a couple aren't even really tombs.

Other excavators to follow included the Frenchman Victor Loret (1859–1946) and American millionaire Theodore Davis (1837–1915), who both successfully located numerous tombs. The excavating techniques used by the likes of Loret and Davis can be likened to a human bulldozer. Hundreds of local workmen with hoes and baskets were employed to plow the Valley down to the bedrock in search of tomb entrances. And many were found. For Davis, it was more of a hobby, and he employed several professional archaeologists to supervise the digging.

Three Incredible Discoveries You've Probably Never Heard Of

Some very interesting tombs were discovered in the Valley of the Kings even before the discovery of Tut. Surprisingly, they did not seem to cause much of a stir, although, in my opinion, they are very worthy of attention.

Royal Best Friend?

In 1899, Victor Loret uncovered a very small, undecorated one-room tomb, KV 36, that was absolutely packed with a nearly intact burial of a dark-skinned, apparently Nubian man named Maiherpri who himself was found remarkably well-preserved. Robbers had searched for jewelry and made off with linens and such, but much of the tomb's contents remained intact. The titles of Maiherpri indicate that he was raised in the royal nursery and was a royal fan bearer. Such high privileges and the fact that he was buried in the royal valley suggest that he was a close companion to the ruler. Some Egyptologists have suggested that the ruler was Amenhotep II, whose tomb lies nearby, but this remains uncertain.

Respect for the In-Laws

In 1905, James Quibell, working for Theodore Davis, discovered KV 46, the tomb of Yuya and Thuya, the in-laws of Amenhotep III. Stairs and corridors led to a single large, undecorated chamber. Not surprisingly, there was evidence of robbery, yet the tomb was remarkably intact. The mummies were found in multiple coffins, and their faces were covered with gilded masks. They are two of the best-preserved mummies from ancient Egypt. The tomb contained a huge collection of burial equipment, including the couple's canopic jars, chairs, chests, beds, many ushabtis, a chariot, food provisions, and a spectacular funerary papyrus.

Pharaoh's Domain

In American culture, at least, much is made, often humorously, of strained relationships with parents-in-law. Apparently such was not the case with the privileged burial of those of Amenhotep III. On the other hand, Amenhotep's tomb does not lie nearby but is found in the adjacent West Valley!

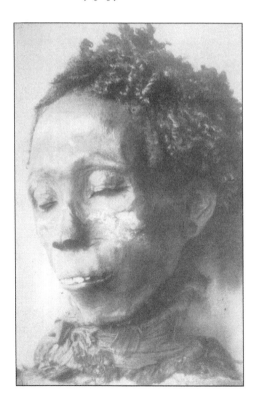 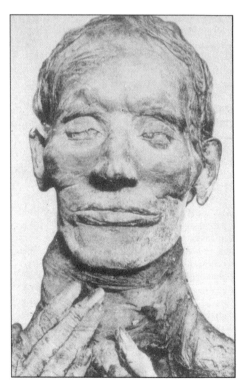

The faces of two well-preserved mummies from the Valley of the Kings: Maiherpri (left) and Yuya (right).

(From Fouilles de la Vallée des Rois, *by G. Daressy, and* Tomb of the Yuaa and Thuiu, *by J.E. Quibell.)*

A Genuine Mystery Tomb!

One of the most controversial tombs in all of Egypt is KV 55. Another excavator for Davis, Edward Ayrton, found this tomb in 1907. Its door showed evidence of having been breached and reclosed on at least a couple of occasions. The gilded wall of a large shrine lay across rubble in the entrance corridor, and the tomb's undecorated single room contained more damaged shrine pieces. On the floor was a coffin that contained a much-decayed mummy. Some beautifully carved Amarna-style canopic jars sat in a niche along one wall. The shrine belonged to Queen Tiye, the wife of Amenhotep III and the mother of Akhenaten. Cartouches and an image of the latter were hacked off the shrine's wall.

Whose tomb was this? Some have suggested that it is the cached body of Akhenaten himself, brought from Amarna and stowed in the royal valley. The body, which was initially described as that of a woman, seems to be of a young man in his twenties. The undecorated walls provide no clues, and even the cartouche on the coffin has been hacked out. Could it be the short-term successor of Akhenaten, Smenkhkare? With such a mix of materials, could this be some sort of burial cache of Amarna-era royal personnel brought south to the Valley from the tombs near Akhetaten?

The Biggest Discovery of Them All!

In 1912, Davis gave up digging in the Valley of the Kings. In his own words: "I feel that the Valley … is now exhausted." A few years later, the English Lord Carnarvon obtained permission to dig there, and the work was supervised by Howard Carter, an experienced archaeologist who had spent much of his life in Egypt. After several unsuccessful seasons of digging, Carnarvon was ready to give up. Carter urged his sponsor to give it one last try, and this persistence paid off. On November 4, 1922, the first of 18 steps was uncovered, leading down to a sealed door. It was the tomb of the obscure late Eighteenth Dynasty pharaoh Tutankhamun!

> **Diggers**
>
> Howard Carter (1874–1939) began his career in Egypt as a very talented artist, copying the decorations of tombs and temples for archaeological publications. He eventually became an inspector of antiquities in Egypt and a freelance archaeologist. His professional association with Lord Carnarvon resulted in the discovery of the tomb of Tutankhamun in 1922.

The plastered and sealed door led to a rubble-filled corridor that ended in another sealed door. What Carter and Carnarvon found was utterly spectacular: a virtually intact royal tomb! The first chamber contained chariots, chests, gilded beds and other furniture, and food provisions, with a side chamber holding even more.

Another sealed door was flanked by two guardian statues. When opened, the chamber beyond was almost completely filled by four nesting golden shrines. Within was a stone sarcophagus containing three nesting coffins, the innermost of solid gold. The mummy inside wore a gold mask, and exquisite jewelry was found in the wrappings and on the mummy itself. Another room attached to the burial chamber contained yet another trove of incredibly preserved objects.

The world was entranced by the discovery (see Chapter 18, "Egyptomania!").

Nile Notes

Carter's description of his first peek through a small hole in the door is one of the most entrancing moments in all of archaeology:

"At first I could see nothing, the hot air escaping from the chamber causing the candle to flicker, but presently, as my eyes grew accustomed to the light, details of the room within emerged slowly from the mist, strange animals, statues, and gold—everywhere the glint of gold. For the moment ... I was struck dumb with amazement, and when Lord Carnarvon, unable to stand the suspense any longer, inquired anxiously, 'Can you see anything?' it was all I could do to get out the words, 'Yes, wonderful things'."

It took nearly 10 years to empty the tomb of its contents. Most of the material is on display in the Egyptian Museum in Cairo, although the mummy itself remains in its tomb, KV 62, resting in the outermost of its three coffins.

Tut Trivia

The details surrounding the tomb, its contents, and Tutankhamun himself could fill volumes—and they do—but here are a few bits of information that you might find fascinating:

♦ There is evidence that the tomb was probably broken into by robbers twice. They obviously didn't get much, which suggests that they were caught!

♦ Tut's tomb probably was saved from subsequent robbing because the large tomb of Ramesses VI was later built above, and the debris from its construction served to deeply bury KV 62.

♦ KV 62 was probably not originally intended as Tut's tomb. Because of his early death, a typical big royal tomb was probably not finished, so he was put into a smaller tomb intended for lesser royalty and private individuals.

Diggers

George Edward Stanhope Molyneux Herbert, a.k.a. Lord Carnarvon (1866–1923), became a collector of Egyptian antiquities. He sponsored excavations in Egypt beginning in 1906 and culminating with the discovery of the tomb of Tutankhamun. His untimely death shortly thereafter was the inspiration for a lot of silly rumors about curses (see Chapter 19, "Alternative Theories").

◆ No one is sure what caused the death of "the boy-king" Tutankhamun, but theories suggest everything from murder to a chariot accident.

◆ Although Carter wrote a three-volume popular description, he never published a complete scientific report on the tomb and its contents. Reports on individual groups of objects are being written by various scholars, but even 75 years after the discovery, we are still many years off from having a complete record.

More Surprises

Very little archaeological work took place in the Valley of the Kings after the discovery of Tutankhamun. Then, in the late 1970s, activity began to resume. Conservation studies were conducted, tombs were mapped, and the tomb of Ramesses XI was excavated. Eventually, several expeditions were mounted that focused on individual tombs, sometimes with surprising results.

It's Huge!

In 1987, as part of an archaeological mapping project, American Egyptologist Kent Weeks relocated the tomb known as KV 5. The tomb was explored in the early nineteenth century and was found to be poorly preserved and of marginal interest, with its known chambers choked with flood debris. After a few years of carefully removing some of the debris, Weeks further explored the tomb by crawling through narrow spaces. The tomb did not end where others had previously thought. In fact, more than a hundred additional rooms have thus far been discovered, making it one of the largest and most complex tombs in Egypt, and certainly in the Valley. The tomb belongs to the sons of Ramesses II, whose tomb lies nearby. It will be years before its complete extent is known.

> **Lost and Found**
>
> There are a few royal individuals for whom neither a tomb nor a mummy has been found, thus leaving open the possibility that both may have escaped the ravages of robbers. For example, anybody seen Ramesses VIII around here lately?

Boring? *Au Contraire!*

Although the Valley of the Kings is known for its numerous big royal tombs, most people are unaware that about half of the tombs there are typically small and undecorated. Many such tombs were considered to be boring or of little interest when originally discovered a hundred years ago by explorers on the hunt for big game: large, decorated, and hopefully intact royal tombs.

Beginning in 1989, I began a project to investigate a series of these tombs. One of these tombs, KV 60, was long-lost but quickly rediscovered. Inside, on the floor of the burial chamber, lay what appears to be a royal female mummy! Another tomb, deeply buried beneath flood debris, contained the remains of what might be two more royal female mummies! The other tombs investigated were found to contain multiple burials.

Pharaoh's Domain

South of the Valley of the Kings is another royal cemetery known as the Valley of the Queens. It contains the painted tombs of several New Kingdom royalty, including the spectacularly decorated tomb of Nefertari, a chief wife of Ramesses II.

The fact that these individuals were buried in the Valley of the Kings indicates that they were very special. It's possible that these tombs contain some of the queens and other royal individuals whose tombs have never been found. Perhaps they have been under everyone's noses all along in those "boring" little undecorated tombs in the Valley!

The steps leading down to the rediscovered undecorated tomb KV 60.

Village of the Royal Tomb-Builders

Building royal tombs required many skilled laborers and the resources to support them and their families. To facilitate the construction of tombs in the Valley of the Kings, a special village was built in the general vicinity to house the workers and their families. This famous village is called today by its Arabic name, Deir el-Medineh, and is one of the most important archaeological sites in all of Egypt. Located against the western cliffs across the river from the ancient capital of Thebes, it was a relatively short walk up and over the cliffs to the royal cemetery.

The workmen's community of Deir el-Medineh is one of the best preserved village sites surviving from ancient Egypt.

(Courtesy of Paul Leroy.)

The village was apparently begun during the reign of Tuthmosis I, in the early part of the New Kingdom. When in full force, Deir el-Medineh probably housed about 100 adults, plus children. A wall surrounded much of the settlement, and dozens of houses were located on either side of a central street running north/south. The houses were typically one-story mud-brick–and–stone structures with four rooms. A sort of living room was found in the front, and the other rooms served as storage or sleeping areas. The kitchen was usually found in an open space in the back. Because they were situated in a somewhat remote location, the workers' village required regular supplies of just about everything, including food and water.

Moonlighting for the Afterlife

When not working on tombs in the Valley, some of the workers built tombs nearby for themselves and their families. Some of these tombs consisted of a small chapel with a mud-brick pyramid on top. A shaft concealed in the floor of the chapel, or in a courtyard in front, led to underground tomb chambers, which were sometimes beautifully decorated.

Lost and Found

The first major scientific excavations at Deir el-Medineh were conducted by an Italian archaeologist named Ernesto Schiapparelli (1856–1928) during the years 1905, 1906, and 1909. Perhaps the crowning achievement of his work there was the discovery in 1906 of the intact tomb of the architect Kha and his wife, Merit. The tomb contained many things that must have come from their home, including different kinds of furniture, clothing, chests, and cosmetics—even a wig and hair-care products! There was also quite a bit of food left in the tomb, quite dry but still identifiable.

During the reign of Ramesses XI, the last king of the New Kingdom, the village was apparently abandoned due to political unrest, and the work in the Valley of the Kings was organized by supervisors based at a nearby temple. The tomb of Ramesses XI was the last to be built in the Valley, and it's doubtful that it was even used for that ruler's burial. No longer in use, some of the houses in Deir el-Medineh were likely reused on occasion, and its tombs and deserted homes were occasionally pilfered for goods.

During the reign of one of the later Greek rulers of Egypt, Ptolemy IV, a temple dedicated to the goddesses Hathor and Maat was built nearby. In later years, when Christianity spread through Egypt, the temple was converted into a monastery and church. In fact, the modern Arabic name for the site, Deir el-Medineh, refers to this monastery: It literally means "monastery of the city." Eventually, the entire area of Deir el-Medineh was essentially abandoned. The ancient village disappeared under the blowing dust of ages; it eventually was rediscovered just a couple of hundred years ago.

Not only have a large number of houses been excavated in the workmen's village, but thousands of documents have been found, which allows us to learn the details of the daily lives of the occupants of Deir el-Medineh. Many of the workers' names and their relatives, occupations, manner of working, and even personal business and problems were written on papyrus or ostraca.

Because of its great state of preservation and thorough excavation, Deir el-Medineh has provided scholars with perhaps the best information we have about actual daily life in ancient Egypt. Skeptics might ask, however, if we should look at

Diggers

A French Egyptologist by the name of Bernard Bruyère (1879–1971) excavated the site of Deir el-Medineh over a period of about 30 years, beginning in 1921, and essentially revealed the remains of the village in its surviving entirety.

the information retrieved from the Village as typical of ancient Egyptian life in general. After all, this is a very specialized group of people living in an atypical location. Although this is true, the workers at Deir el-Medineh were people like everyone else, requiring food, clothing, and housing. And apart from the details of their specialized work in the Valley of the Kings, the wealth of surviving written material shows that these were people whose concerns and problems were not particularly unusual, but recognizable everywhere in societies today, including our own.

Moving the Mummies

After the Valley of the Kings had ceased to be used for royal burials at the end of the Twentieth Dynasty, most of the royal mummies were collected by priests from their pilfered tombs, rewrapped, and placed in special hiding places. Two such caches of these royal mummies have been found containing most of the great pharaohs of Egypt's New Kingdom, plus some other interesting folk. One was the tomb of Amenhotep II, where that great king was joined by 14 other mummies, including Tuthmosis IV, Amenhotep III, Ramesses IV-VI, and Seti II.

One of the most famous discoveries of all times in Egypt was a cache of mummies discovered by local villagers around 1878 near the site of Deir el-Bahri in the cliffs on the Nile side of the Valley of the Kings. DB 320, as it is officially designated (or, just call it the Deir el-Bahri royal mummy cache), is a very long tomb at the bottom of a deep shaft, very well hidden near the base of a towering limestone precipice. The cache contained 40 mummies, including many of the New Kingdom's most prominent rulers (Amenhotep I, Tuthmosis I-III, Seti I, and Ramesses II), along with coffins and assorted funerary equipment.

Pharaoh's Domain

Some of the coffins and mummies in the Deir el-Bahri royal mummy cache had ancient notes written on them that indicate when the mummies had been rewrapped and moved. A few had been cached more than once before joining their peers in the big collection! And to confuse matters, x-ray studies of the mummies suggest that several of them might have been mislabeled!

The villagers who found the cache secretly looted it, and the quality of objects reaching the antiquities market tipped off government officials that something very special had been found. After some investigation and intrigue, the location of this remarkable mummy hoard was revealed. The cache was cleared out in a period of 48 hours, and the mummies and their coffins were shipped to Cairo, where many are on display today.

Mummies on Display

Many of the royal mummies are on public display in the Egyptian Museum in Cairo. Special nitrogen-filled cases have been provided in the last few years to aid in their preservation. Some people think that such public display of dead royalty is in very poor taste. Former Egyptian President Anwar Sadat even went as far as to close the mummy room for some time, yet it has been reopened and remains a popular tourist attraction.

The Least You Need to Know

- The Valley of the Kings was the royal burial ground for most of the New Kingdom rulers.

- There have been many fascinating discoveries in the Valley.

- The tomb of Tutankhamun remains one of the most spectacular archaeological discoveries of all time.

- Construction work in the Valley of the Kings was supported by a special village of workers known as Deir el-Medineh.

- All known tombs in the Valley of the Kings were visited by robbers, to some extent, and many of the royal mummies were later collected and hidden in caches.

Chapter 16

Egypt and the Holy Book

In This Chapter

- ◆ Egypt as featured in the Bible
- ◆ The life and times of Joseph, son of Jacob
- ◆ Moses confronts the Pharaoh
- ◆ Horrible plagues and magnificent miracles
- ◆ Seeking physical clues to biblical stories
- ◆ Baby Jesus visits the Nile

The Bible remains one of the most influential books ever written. Billions of copies have been printed in thousands of languages, and its contents are revered as holy by three of the world's great religions: Judaism, Christianity, and Islam. It is a book of origins and laws, and morals and values. It is a book of inspiration, history, and literature; and it is one of the foundational documents of Western Civilization. And Egypt plays an important role in it, garnering hundreds of mentions! It would take at least a book in itself to cover all the stories and insights, so we're just going to look at a few of the most interesting examples.

Nile Notes

To learn more about the Bible, take a look at *The Complete Idiot's Guide to the Bible*, by Stan Campbell and James S. Bell.

The Bible is actually a library of books. The books of the Old Testament, or the Hebrew Bible, tell the story of the Jewish people and their relationship with God and fellow humans. The Christian addition to the Bible, the New Testament, contains the teachings of Jesus and some of his followers. Muslims consider both the Old and New Testaments—the entire Bible—to be sacred Scripture and add an additional volume of holy revelations, the Koran, to their scriptural canon.

Floods, Famines, and Pharaohs

Egypt is mentioned in the very first book of the Bible, Genesis. After the great flood that Noah and his family (along with a notoriously large collection of animals) survived in Noah's famous ark, the sons of Noah and their wives begin to repopulate the land. Genesis 10:6 names Noah's son Ham as the great ancestor of the Egyptian people.

The great biblical patriarch, Abraham from Ur, ventured into Egypt during a time of famine. The Pharaoh became attracted to Abraham's beautiful wife, Sarah, and fearing for his life, Abraham passed her off as his sister. The ruse was exposed, and Abraham and Sarah were deported.

Glyphs

The Hebrew word for Egypt is **Mitzraim.** The "aim" part of the word is a dual ending, thus noting the traditional division of ancient Egypt into two lands, Upper and Lower Egypt.

Lost and Found

The biblical story of Joseph has interesting parallels in the Egyptian *Tale of the Two Brothers*, in which a man who rejects the advances of his brother's wife is turned upon by the wife and her angry husband.

Jacob and Sons

Abraham's central role in the Bible was his acceptance of a covenant with God: In exchange for their devotion, God would look after Abraham and his descendents. Abraham had a son named Isaac, and it's through Isaac that the Jewish people trace their ancestry. (Another son of Abraham, Ishmael, was born to a maid-servant named Hagar. The Arabs trace their ancestry to him.)

Isaac's son, Jacob (who would also be known by the name "Israel"), was quite an interesting fellow himself. He had 12 sons, and he favored one, Joseph, in particular. This, of course, was bound to promote sibling rivalry, and one day his brothers sold him as a slave, and Joseph ended up in Egypt.

Joseph's sparkling personality got him a nice job with an Egyptian official, but when he turned down the naughty advances of his employer's scheming wife, he ended up in jail. There, he was brought to the attention of the ruler of Egypt, due to his ability to interpret dreams as predictions of the future. Joseph was rewarded with a job as one of the highest officials in Egypt.

Joseph interpreting Pharaoh's dream.

(Illustration c. 1866 by Gustave Doré.)

Meanwhile, there was a dry spell in Palestine, and Joseph's brothers traveled to Egypt to stock up on food. After a few dramatic encounters with his clueless brothers, Joseph revealed himself, and it was happy reunion time. The whole family, including Jacob, immigrated to Egypt.

Abused by the Pharaoh

One of the greatest stories in the Bible is told in the second biblical book, Exodus. The story is of immense importance for the Jewish people and others who follow the God of Abraham because it shows God making good on His promise to look after His people. The Exodus story begins in Egypt 400 years after Joseph. The situation was not so nice for the numerous descendants of Jacob and his 12 sons, whom we can now refer to as the 12 Hebrew tribes, or the Israelites. They had been enslaved by the Egyptians, and

Glyphs

The name Moses is not an uncommon one in Egypt. Several kings had the name, including Tuthmosis and Ramesses. The *mosis/moses* part means "born of"—in these cases, the Egyptian gods Thoth and Ra, respectively.

there were so many of them that the Egyptians feared a slave revolt. An order was given to exterminate all newborn Hebrew boys. One mother saved her son by putting him in a waterproof basket, where he was discovered by a bathing princess. The boy was given the name Moses and was raised in the royal household.

Pharaoh's Domain

Hebrews refers to the descendants of Jacob's 12 sons, who themselves became the patriarchs of 12 tribes. These people are often referred to as the 12 tribes of Israel, with Israel being a name for Jacob, or the Israelites. Today they' re called "Jews," after the tribe of Judah.

According to Exodus, Moses later killed a brutal foreman over some slave abuse and went into exile. At the age of 80, God contacted him through an amazing talking burning bush. God ordered the fugitive to go back to Egypt to save his people, who were still enslaved. Moses was understandably reluctant, but with assurances that God would help, he set out and confronted the Pharaoh. There was a new pharaoh in place since he had left, but the memory of Moses was still alive in Egypt. The Pharaoh scoffed at Moses's insistence that he set free the Hebrew slaves, and then the miracles began ....

Pain and Suffering

Moses, along with his brother, Aaron, confronted the Pharaoh with their outrageous demands to free the Hebrew slaves. As a demonstration of the might of his God, Moses, occasionally with Aaron, attempted to bend the will of the Pharaoh with a series of 10 miserable plagues:

1. First, the water of the Nile River was turned to blood, making the water undrinkable and killing all the fish. The royal magicians were able to duplicate this effect, so Pharaoh remained unimpressed.

2. The second plague involved frogs—frogs everywhere, even in the Pharaoh's own bed and in the bread ovens. Interestingly, the king's own magicians were likewise able to convince some frogs to come out of the water as well. Pharaoh promised to release the Hebrews if Moses could ask God to destroy the frogs at a given hour. The masses of frogs died the next day—"croaked," so to speak—and were piled into stinking heaps. Afterward, the Pharaoh changed his mind and God inflicted another plague.

3. Gnats! This must have been incredibly disgusting! The king's magicians were unable to duplicate this feat. However, Pharaoh was unconvinced.

4. Flies! Swarms of flies infested all the houses of the Egyptians, again including the royal household, but not in those of the Hebrews. Moses asked God to deal with the flies, and He did. Again, that was ineffectual. Next!

5. An affliction killed the Egyptians' livestock, but not those of the Hebrews.

6. The next plague, boils on Egyptian men and beasts, required that Moses throw a handful of kiln ashes into the air. Pharaoh remained stubborn, so perhaps a little frozen precipitation would do the job ....

7. Hail! Moses warned Pharaoh of this one, and those who heeded the warning took shelter, while exposed people, animals, and crops were destroyed in a fearsome display of hail, thunder, and lightning, although not where the slaves lived.

8. Not impressed? How about some locusts then? The locusts were so thick that they darkened the surface of the land, and they ate anything edible that might have survived the hailstorm.

9. Would three days of darkness do the job? Nope!

> **Nile Notes**
>
> Just a reminder: The pyramids of Egypt were not built by Hebrew slaves. The Great Pyramid at Giza, for example, was probably already a thousand years old at the time of Moses.

The book of Exodus makes it clear that God was offering an awesome demonstration of power over the Egyptian gods, to the point of ridicule.

Saving the Worst for Last

Egypt's Pharaoh was proving very stubborn, despite nine utterly nasty plagues. One more would be needed to sway the king to release the Hebrew slaves:

10. The first-born sons of all the Egyptians would die. The Hebrews were instructed to kill an unblemished lamb and smear its blood on the doorposts and lintels of their homes. This would serve as a sign to pass over the homes of the Hebrews when the Angel of Death was on his way to deal with the Egyptians.

This final horrible plague had the proper effect. The Hebrews quickly packed up and left, with Pharaoh's permission. The Israelites were miraculously guided in their journey by a cloud during the day and by a pillar of fire at night.

All was going well until Pharaoh decided to give chase while the Hebrews approached a body of water known as the Sea of Reeds. Here, one of the most magnificent miracles of Exodus occurs. Trapped between the water and the marauding Egyptian army complete with chariots, God caused the waters to part, allowing the Hebrews to safely cross before crashing down again and drowning the Egyptians. From there, they wandered for 40 years in the wilderness of Sinai. There Moses climbed a mountain and received the laws of God to present to his people. Thereafter, the Hebrews engaged in a campaign of conquest to settle themselves in the promised land of Canaan in the Palestine region.

The opening phrases of the
Book of Exodus in Hebrew.

EXODUS

שמות

א

וְאֵלֶּה שְׁמוֹת בְּנֵי יִשְׂרָאֵל הַבָּאִים מִצְרָיְמָה אֵת יַעֲקֹב אִישׁ
וּבֵיתוֹ בָּאוּ: רְאוּבֵן שִׁמְעוֹן לֵוִי וִיהוּדָה: יִשָּׂשׁכָר זְבוּלֻן
וּבִנְיָמִן: דָּן וְנַפְתָּלִי גָּד וְאָשֵׁר: וַיְהִי כָּל־נֶפֶשׁ יֹצְאֵי יֶרֶךְ־
יַעֲקֹב שִׁבְעִים נָפֶשׁ וְיוֹסֵף הָיָה בְמִצְרָיִם: וַיָּמָת יוֹסֵף וְכָל־
אֶחָיו וְכֹל הַדּוֹר הַהוּא: וּבְנֵי יִשְׂרָאֵל פָּרוּ וַיִּשְׁרְצוּ וַיִּרְבּוּ
וַיַּעַצְמוּ בִּמְאֹד מְאֹד וַתִּמָּלֵא הָאָרֶץ אֹתָם:

Natural Explanations

There has been a lot of speculation about the many interesting events in the Exodus story, particularly because most of these incidents seem to be the kind of things that can occur on their own in nature. Some have suggested that the Nile turning "to blood" and becoming undrinkable could be a result of algae infestation or an occurrence of reddish mud or silt flowing downstream from a southern source. The magicians of pharaohs were able to create a similar effect although probably in a jar or a pool because the Nile was already red according to the story. It's a common magic trick still performed today, and it usually involves the use of chemicals.

It has even been suggested that many of the plagues that followed might have been a chain reaction to a temporarily polluted Nile. Frogs get out and die, flies abound, and animals and humans get sick. Hail is known to be very damaging, and every year Egypt has a "khamseen" season, which is a time when sandstorms are prevalent. And some of these storms can radically affect visibility and perhaps explain the darkness.

Defenders of the Bible, of course, will point out that the timing and the intensity of these events are a demonstration of God's power. The story also tells how the Hebrew slaves were spared all of these things. The last plague, the death of the first-born Egyptians, does not follow any known natural phenomenon.

> **Nile Notes**
>
> To explore the Bible's many miracles and mysteries, check out *The Complete Idiot's Guide to Biblical Mysteries,* by the author of this book, Donald P. Ryan.

Miracles? Or Volcanos and Tidal Waves?

There have been attempts in recent years to explain the guiding cloud and pillar of fire, along with the parting of the waters as effects of the eruption of a Mediterranean volcano.

This volcano, named Thera, exploded violently and had a severe, although not clearly defined, impact on some of the cultures of the region. Although there are some difficulties in dating, the eruption seems to have taken place around 1629 B.C.

If Thera did erupt at the time the Hebrews escaped Egypt, it is possible that the cloud that guided them by day was the smoke from the massive plume of the erupting volcano, and the pillar of fire guiding them at night could have been the fiery lava, which would have been visible against the dark night sky. Furthermore, the parting of the sea might have been caused by a huge tidal wave or tsunami. Then again, these just might be miracles! Many, however, think the eruption's date is a few centuries too early to fit with other information related to the possible date of the Exodus.

Red Sea or Sea of Reeds?

Although the body of water that parted allowing the Hebrews to cross has often been called the "Red Sea," the words in the Hebrew Bible are actually "yam suf," or Sea of Reeds. This suggests a marshy area such as those found in the northeastern Delta region of Egypt. It would be a lot shallower and perhaps a shorter distance, depending upon where the crossing took place. On the other hand, there are those who insist that, indeed, the yam suf is the great body of water known as the Red Sea, and the Hebrews might have crossed it in the narrows of its westernmost arm before entering the Sinai peninsula.

Lost and Found

There's not much left of Thera. The rim of part of its blown-out crater forms the present island of Santorini, where archaeologists have discovered incredibly well-preserved ancient remains under a blanket of old volcanic ash.

Pharaoh's Domain

When the Hebrews exited Egypt, they also took with them a mummy: the bones of Joseph.

Who's That Bad Man?

The Exodus tale involves two pharaohs: One is popularly referred to as "the Pharaoh of the Oppression," and the other is known as "the Pharaoh of the Exodus." The Pharaoh of the Oppression was king when the book of Exodus begins, and the Pharaoh of the Exodus was the ruler who dealt with Moses and the 10 plagues. Egyptologists and biblical scholars have devoted a lot of energy to trying to figure out who these pharaohs might have been, to tie the Exodus firmly into historical chronology.

Ramesses the Great

After years and years of discussion, there is still no consensus, but here are a couple of clues:

The Bible mentions that the Hebrew slaves were working on the twin store-cities of Pithom and Pi-Ramses, both of which have been located up in the Nile Delta area of Egypt in the vicinity where the Hebrews were likely settled. The name Ramses is the big tip-off because there were several kings by that name in the Egyptian Nineteenth and Twentieth Dynasties (c. 1295–1069 B.C.). As a great builder and a formidable military leader, Ramesses II is a favorite candidate for the Pharaoh of the Exodus.

Read the Fine Print

There is but one mention of the Israelite people in Egyptian texts. It is found on a large inscribed stone table, or stele, dating to the reign of the successor of Ramesses II, Merneptah. Merneptah's stele gives a list of names of cities conquered by the Egyptians in Palestine. Along with these cities is the name Israel, and it is written differently than the other names. Rather than using the special hieroglyph at the end of the word, which would indicate that it is the name of a foreign country, the word Israel uses the glyphs that indicate a people rather than some sort of settlement. This is fascinating, but it indicates that the Hebrews were already established by that time in the region of Palestine; for some, this causes some serious timing problems.

The name of Israel as it appears on Merneptah's stele.

Very interestingly, in the last few years it has been noted that there might also be a picture of the Israelites on an Egyptian temple! The picture is part of a damaged inscription of Merneptah that seems to report the conquests recorded on his stele, and it is accompanied by illustrations. There's a good argument for this being the case, but it's hard to prove. Even so, it's the closest thing to a picture of the ancient Hebrews that we have.

A Lack of Evidence

In an attempt to dismiss the historical reality of the Exodus, critics might point to a lack of Egyptian evidence for the details; but, then again, the Egyptians were not known for admitting their mistakes. Would a grandiose pharaoh such as Ramesses II brag anywhere that his army was defeated by a ragged group of slaves? Hardly. Even when the Egyptians won a battle, they tended to exaggerate their success in very boastful terms.

Lost and Found

A few expeditions have sought to prove the accuracy of the biblical Exodus story by searching for the remains of the drowned Egyptians and their chariots in the Red Sea. I have seen pictures of what are claimed to be coral-encrusted chariot wheels, and I'm not impressed.

The location of the Red Sea crossing is a big question, and the preservation of such objects is also questionable.

Passover

The miraculous and wonderful story of the Exodus is precious to Jews. It tells how God indeed looked after His people and delivered them from slavery. The story is commemorated every year in the Jewish observance of *Pesach*, or *Passover*. Passover is observed for just over a week in the spring, but the most notable event is a meal called a seder, which is held on the first night. During the seder, Jews retell the Exodus story and eat symbolic food. This annual dinner, shared among family and friends, ensures that the story of the Exodus will not be forgotten!

Glyphs

Pesach, or **Passover,** is one of the most celebrated Jewish holidays, and it commemorates the Exodus story. It is celebrated each year in the spring.

The Promised Land

The Bible tells of Moses receiving the laws of God on Mt. Sinai and eventually leading his people to the edge of the Promised Land— essentially, the geographical territory of Palestine, which today includes the modern state of Israel, the West Bank of the Jordan, and some adjacent regions. The Israelites attacked and conquered much of the area—which was inhabited by Canaanites, Philistines, and a number of other groups—and eventually established a capital at Jerusalem.

Pharaoh's Domain

Although the Sinai Peninsula, home to the traditional site of Mt. Sinai, falls within the borders of modern Egypt, it really wasn't a part of the Egyptian homeland. It's northern part, though, served as a busy crossroads between Egypt and parts east.

It's not the purpose of this book to go into detail about the complex archaeological and historical issues surrounding the Israelites' conquest and settlement of Palestine, but a few additional points can be made. Palestine was in the path of all sorts of marauders and empire-builders, including the Babylonians, Assyrians, Persians, Greeks, Romans, and, of course, the Egyptians. The Egyptians passed through the area many times, subjugating towns, demanding tribute, and fighting battles against their enemies on foreign turf. But it wasn't all mayhem: One of the early Jewish kings, Solomon, was said to have had a pharaoh as a father-in-law in a marriage alliance!

Raiding the Temple

The Bible tells of the attack by an Egyptian pharaoh on Jerusalem during which the Holy Temple and the palace were looted:

> In the fifth year of [the Jewish] King Rehoboam, Shishak king of Egypt came up against Jerusalem; he took away the treasure of the house of the Lord and treasures of the king's house; he took away everything. He also took away all of the shields of gold which Solomon made.

> —II Kings 14:25–26 Revised Standard Version

"Shishak" is usually identified with the Twenty-second Dynasty pharaoh Sheshonq I. Second Chronicles, Chapter 12, provides more details, including some military details such as the employment of "... twelve hundred chariots and sixty thousand horsemen. And the people were without number who came with him from Egypt—Libyans, Sku-ki-im, and Ethiopians." And God, through a prophet, explained to the Jewish rulers why this was allowed to happen to His people: "You abandoned me, so I have abandoned you to the hand of Shishak."

Egypt Be Cursed!

Elsewhere in the Old Testament, Egypt, along with other pagan lands, are offered dire futures because of their pagan and wicked ways. Here is a small sample, courtesy of the prophet Isaiah [Chapter 19]:

> An oracle concerning Egypt. Behold, the Lord is riding on a swift cloud and comes to Egypt; and the idols of Egypt will tremble at his presence, and the heart of the Egyptians will melt within them. And I will stir up Egyptians against Egyptians, and they will fight, every man against his brother and every man against his neighbor .... And the waters of the Nile will be dried up, and the river will be parched and dry; and its canals will become foul, and the branches of Egypt's Nile will diminish and dry up, reeds and rushes will rot away ....

Given the disintegration of the ancient Egyptian civilization and the environmental changes that have occurred since, you can't help but wonder if some of these things indeed came to pass!

Lost and Found

The Bible notes that the wisdom of the Jewish King Solomon surpassed that of "all the people of the east, and all the wisdom of Egypt" (I Kings 4:30). There are several examples of surviving Egyptian "wisdom texts," and some scholars have pointed out amazing parallels between these and such biblical works as the Book of Proverbs. Are they somehow related? Did one group borrow wise advice from another, or was this sort of information part of the great Near Eastern culture?

Hiding Out in Egypt with Jesus

Egypt also appears in some of the Christian books of the Bible, the New Testament. The first four books, known as the Gospels, portray the often miraculous life and teachings of Jesus of Nazareth. According to the Gospel of Matthew, three wise men from the east set out in the direction of Palestine in search of a special baby. The wise men approached Herod, a Jewish king ruling under the permission and bidding of the Romans, and asked him where they might locate the newborn king of the Jews. This, of course, immediately riled the egotistical and homicidal Herod, who decided to locate the baby Jesus and have him killed. He asked the wise men to let him know where this baby would be found. Warned in a dream, they presented their gifts to Jesus and left without informing Herod. Herod, determined to have the baby destroyed, went on a killing rampage of all male children 2 years of age or younger in the vicinity of Bethlehem.

But Jesus was spared: An angel appeared to Joseph, the husband of Mary, the mother of Jesus, in a dream telling him to take his family and escape to Egypt. The details of their travels are not described in the Bible. In Egypt, however, there are rich traditions that trace the path of the Holy Family on a journey that may have lasted up to three years. There are lots of interesting stories about the baby performing a variety of miracles, including healing people, calming wild animals, and producing springs of fresh water. On at least a couple of occasions, the legends say, he was able to cause trees to bend over so that their delicious fruit could be picked. Today, churches are located up and down the Nile and elsewhere, built at places where Jesus and his family were thought to have spent time or where miracles occurred.

The Least You Need to Know

◆ Egypt plays an important role in the Bible where it is mentioned many times.

◆ The story of the Exodus, in which God delivers His people from Egyptian servitude, plays a key role in Judaism.

◆ Egyptian archaeology is relatively silent regarding many of the biblical stories.

◆ Egypt continued to play a role in the lives of the Hebrew people even after they established themselves in the Promised Land.

◆ Jesus journeyed to Egypt as an infant, and the memory of this visit persists today among Egyptian Christians.

Part 5

Changing Times, Ideas, and Influences

The might and grandeur of the New Kingdom didn't last forever. Internal disputes and the designs of foreign powers began to whittle away—and eventually dismantle or transform—much of Egypt's ancient culture. Even before its light was fully extinguished, though, a fascination with the old culture arose—an allure that continues today. This fascination takes many forms, from mainstream scholarly Egyptology to various bizarre and esoteric interpretations, some of which are very controversial. Hang on as we examine the end of ancient Egyptian civilization and how it continues to persist in the present.

Chapter 17

Uninvited Visitors

In This Chapter

- ◆ Wild political competition ensues
- ◆ Fighting off the Libyans, Nubians, and Persians
- ◆ Alexander the Great collects Egypt
- ◆ Cleopatra seduces the Romans
- ◆ The Copts and Muslims move in

It's evident that there was a major change in Egypt's power structure during the reign of Ramesses XI, the last ruler of the New Kingdom. While Ramesses ruled from the north, the powerful priesthood of Amun began to assert itself as an authority in the South. One high priest, in particular, Herihor, was a prime instigator in the power play. After the death of Ramesses XI, it seems as if Egypt's glory days as a mighty unified state were seriously on the decline.

Who's the Boss?

The time known as the Third Intermediate Period (1069–747 B.C.) can be a confusing historical puzzle. It begins with the Twenty-first Dynasty, when essentially there were two cooperating sets of rulers: a king ruling from Tanis in the Delta and a line of high priests in the south. This odd situation seemed to work out fairly well, with marriage alliances providing bonds between the two rulers.

Dazed and Confused

The last ruler of the Twenty-first Dynasty didn't leave a successor, but a son-in-law named Sheshonq became the first ruler of the Twenty-second Dynasty. This new line is known as the Libyan Dynasty because Sheshonq's family were descendents of Libyans who had settled in the Delta. Their capital was based in Tanis. Sheshonq united Egypt, and, as mentioned in Chapter 16, "Egypt and the Holy Book," was the "Shishak" mentioned in the Bible. After a while, the country began to split up into rival power centers. Both the Twenty-third and the Twenty-fourth Dynasties are fairly obscure, and both actually are contemporaneous with the time span of the Twenty-second! The Twenty-third was a rival group of rulers based in the Delta town of Leontopolis, and the Twenty-fourth consists of but two rulers operating out of Sais, another Delta town. Yes, this is a confusing situation and it demonstrates that no one line of rulers controlled all of Egypt. Egypt was once again disunited.

Royal Discoveries

While the world was enraptured with the discovery of Tutankhamun's tomb in 1922, very few people are aware that other rich royal tombs were later found, and not in the Valley of the Kings. And while even Tut's was lightly robbed, one of these tombs was actually intact! These tombs belonged to some of the rulers of Egypt during the Twenty-first and Twenty-second Dynasties. They were discovered at the site of Tanis in 1939 and 1940 by the French Egyptologist Pierre Montet. As the world concentrated on the unfolding events of the Second World War, these discoveries unfortunately did not receive the attention they deserved.

Lost and Found

Surprisingly, the stone sarcophagus found in the intact burial of Psusennes I at Tanis originally belonged to the New Kingdom pharaoh Merneptah. The sarcophagus had been removed from the Valley of the Kings and reused!

One burial complex in the form of a series of chambers, contained remains of Shoshenq III, Takelot II, and Orsokon II. A second set of tombs in the vicinity belonged to Psusennes I and included burials of Shoshenq II, Siamun, and Psusennes II. These burials seemed to have been disturbed to one extent or another in ancient times, yet Psusennes himself lay unmolested in a hidden adjacent chamber as did Amenemope. Although these graves were mere small chambers compared to the typical grandiose tombs of the New Kingdom pharaohs, they are equally significant. Many of the dazzling objects found therein, including outstanding examples of artistry in gold, silver, and jewelry, are worthy of admiration.

Nubians, Assyrians, and Saites, Oh My!

The Twenty-fifth Dynasty was ruled by Nubians from their capital at Napata. The Nubians initially controlled Upper Egypt but eventually ruled over the whole land. This dynasty marks the beginning of what Egyptologists refer to as the Late Period (747–332 B.C.). In the east, the Assyrians of Mesopotamia were becoming an ever greater threat, and the Nubian rulers had to deal with this. In 671 B.C., the Assyrian king Esarhaddon entered Egypt and sacked Memphis. His successor, Ashurbanipal, paid another violent visit to Egypt in 662 B.C. Apart from battling the Assyrians, the Twenty-fifth dynasty was characterized by building projects, especially those dedicated to perpetuating the cult of Amun.

The Twenty-sixth Dynasty was established with Egyptian rulers who were selected by the Assyrians for their perceived loyalty. This is certainly one of the more interesting of the Late Period dynasties. Reigning from the Delta city of Sais, these rulers employed Greek mercenaries to help secure their power. They also encouraged foreign immigration of Greeks and others and a Greek city named Naukratis was established in the Delta. The Twenty-sixth Dynasty was also characterized by a cultural revival, in which the art and other practices of the Old and Middle Kingdom were emulated.

The Assyrian empire was succeeded by that of the Babylonians, who set out to maintain Assyria's former holdings. The Babylonians never made it to Egypt, although they managed to conquer some of Egypt's foreign territories. Egypt's freedom from outside domination, however, would be very short-lived.

Pharaoh's Domain

The Assyrians from the Mesopotamian region maintained an awesome and well-organized military force. They were often quite brutal in their tactics and were highly feared. A raid by the Assyrians usually meant great destruction and the carrying away of both booty and captives to Assyria.

Lost and Found

Herodotus reported that a large group of Cambyses's Persian soldiers were overwhelmed in a sandstorm and lost in the desert. Modern searches for this "lost army of Cambyses" have not yet located the bodies.

Persia Takes Its Turn

Dynasty 27 began with the invasion of Egypt by the Persian King Cambyses in 525 B.C. The Persians, having conquered the Babylonians, became the new superpower in the region. Egypt then became a province of Persia and was ruled by a governor known as a *satrap*, while the Persian king himself ruled from his own capital back at home. The Twenty-seventh Dynasty kings were, in fact, the kings of Persia.

The Slippery Slope

We know little about the Twenty-eighth, Twenty-ninth, and Thirtieth Dynasties. The Twenty-eighth consisted of a single ruler, a prince of Sais, who declared himself king when the Persian King Darius II died. Taking advantage of temporary Persian weakness, another line (the Twenty-ninth Dynasty) based in Mendes ruled for a while. The rulers of the Thirtieth Dynasty were temporarily able to rebuff the return of the Persians and initiated another cultural revival, but the Persians returned in force in 343 B.C. and once again held dominion over Egypt (Dynasty 31).

Here Come the Greeks!

Meanwhile, elsewhere in the Mediterranean, other civilizations were flourishing and soon turned covetous eyes to the rich bounty of Egypt. During the fifth century B.C., Greece was primarily composed of numerous more or less independent city-states, and Athens was experiencing its so-called Golden Age, a time when art and architecture, philosophy, literature, and science were flourishing. The Greeks had been successful in routing the powerful Persian forces that sought to subjugate them. Unfortunately, classical Greece would suffer from strife between the city-states themselves, which, along with such distracting factors as the plague, served to weaken the region as a whole.

In the north, the weakening of the city-states was being carefully observed by a large Greek kingdom known as Macedonia. And when the opportunity seemed ripe, King Phillip II of Macedonia launched an impressive campaign to conquer his southern brethren. Phillip was assassinated, but his efforts were continued by his young son, Alexander III.

Nile Notes

In spreading their culture, the Greeks introduced a dialect of their language known as *koine*, which was used as a common tongue in the vast territory conquered by Alexander the Great.

Alexander Flexes His Muscles

During the next 13 years, Alexander, or "Alexander the Great," as he is regularly referred to, conquered an immense area that comprised the largest empire in ancient times. Persia was added to Greece as was Asia Minor, Syria/Palestine, and lands extending all the way to the Indus River! Everywhere the conquering Greeks went, they instilled their Greek culture in a process that we might call "Hellenization." Greek religion, thought, and science were passed along; most importantly, the Greek language was instituted as the official means of communication. Numerous vestiges of this process still exist. Old Greek towns, temples, amphitheaters, and other remains of Alexander's conquest can be found throughout his vast empire.

Egypt was conquered in 332 B.C., and Alexander was proclaimed pharaoh and welcomed as one who liberated the Egyptians from Persian rule. Alexander contributed to the Egyptian's perception of him as a living god by being crowned in Memphis. More importantly, he established a new city on the site of a small fishing village on the Mediterranean Coast. The city came to be named Alexandria, after the great conqueror himself.

Alexander died in Babylon in 323 B.C., and it was up to his generals to sort out who would rule which territories.

Within a few years, a general named Ptolemy established a dynasty that would rule Egypt for close to 300 years. These were Greek, not Egyptian, rulers of Egypt. Yet they retained most of the roles and obligations of their pharaonic predecessors, albeit with a distinctly Hellenistic flavor. All of Ptolemy's male successors bore his name, and altogether there would be fifteen Greek rulers of Egypt with the name Ptolemy. This is why this era of Greek rule is often referred to as the "Ptolemaic Period."

Ptolemy II was a clever and creative leader. He made real efforts to integrate Greek rulership into Egyptian culture. He adopted the Egyptian practice of brother/sister royal marriage. New temples were built to the Egyptian gods, and a religious cult was initiated around a new god. This god, known as Serapis, was a hybrid deity incorporating aspects of both Egyptian gods such as Osiris and those of Greece. Serapis became quite popular and had temples dedicated to him and his own priesthood.

Much of the history of Ptolemaic Egypt reads like the most contrived of soap operas. There is plenty of family intrigue, betrayals, and worse. In short, there's lots of bad behavior. Yet several of the Ptolemies were great rulers and left lasting legacies.

Lost and Found

Alexander the Great is said to have been buried in Egypt. A variety of tales speculate about when, where, and how, but the most likely location of his burial seems to be in the city of Alexandria itself. Despite many attempts, neither the tomb nor the body of Alexander has been located.

Diggers

Two Oxford gentlemen, Bernard Grenfell (1869–1926) and Arthur Hunt (1871–1934), were perhaps the most successful of the "papyri hunters," archaeologists who dug in ancient Egyptian town sites in search of documents. The two retrieved a huge number of scraps of Greek manuscripts, and because the old towns were often occupied for centuries, the town dumps also sometimes contained Roman and Christian documents of equal interest.

Egypt Is Colonized

With a Hellenistic ruler in place, large numbers of Greek colonists began to flow into Egypt. Greek farming estates and commercial enterprises began to pop up all over, especially in the broad and agriculturally rich Nile Delta and Fayyum regions. Local Egyptian labor was typically employed. Greeks were generally appointed as government officials in a bureaucracy headquartered in Alexandria.

The sites of many of these towns can still be identified today. They survive in various stages of preservation—from a few mud bricks to large, standing walls far out in the desert. Surprisingly, much of what we know about this time period comes from garbage! During the late nineteenth century, a few enterprising archaeologists discovered that large quantities of Greek documents written on papyrus could be recovered from ancient refuse dumps on the outskirts of these old towns. Dozens of local workmen were hired to plow through the dumps, pulling out bits and pieces of written material by the thousands. The documents cover a wide range of subjects, from personal letters to inventories, contracts, and receipts.

A cartouche bearing the name of Alexander the Great in hieroglyphs.

The City of Alexandria

Alexandria was one of the great intellectual, cultural, and commercial centers of the ancient world. The boundaries and layout of the city were intentionally planned.

Library and Museum

Among the highlights of the city was an institute or "museum" that played host to professional scholars in a variety of fields. Numerous Greek philosophers, mathematicians, and scientists thrived in the city, including Euclid, Erastosthenes, and Archimedes. Attached to the museum was an amazing library that held perhaps more than 400,000 manuscripts. Legend has it that the library represented an attempt to collect and preserve the accumulated knowledge of the (now) ancient world.

The museum and library no longer exist. The contents of the library are said to have been burnt, a tragedy of epic proportions for human knowledge. Several people have been accused of starting the fire, including Julius Caesar (c. 47 B.C.); Theophilus, the Christian patriarch of Alexandria (A.D. 391); and the Muslim Caliph Omar, around the time of the Arab conquest of Egypt (A.D. 642). The fact remains that we really don't know who torched the library.

A Beacon of Light

Egypt was home to two of the classical Seven Wonders of the Ancient World. The Great Pyramid at Giza, which was discussed in an earlier chapter, was one of the Wonders; the second was a great lighthouse built on a small island named Pharos, located just off the coast from Alexandria. The lighthouse was commissioned by Ptolemy I, and, when completed, it stood around 384 feet tall and was covered in white marble. During the day,

Glyphs

The study of (primarily Greek) papyrus documents, typically from Egypt, is known as **papyrology.**

Nile Notes

One of the projects undertaken at the museum and the library was to translate the Hebrew Bible into Greek. Seventy-two rabbis were gathered for the task, and the result is known as the *Septuagint*.

Lost and Found

In 1990, an international commission met at Aswan and agreed to build another great library at Alexandria. Millions of dollars were contributed to the cause, and a Norwegian firm is completing the construction of this large and sophisticated new building. The library is planned to open in the next year or two.

the lighthouse beacon was produced using a mirror to reflect the sun's light; at night, fires were reflected in the mirror to guide the ships. It must have been a magnificent sight, and it no doubt saved many a sailor's life. The lighthouse was in operation for several centuries until it was demolished by a series of earthquakes in the 1300s A.D.

Cleopatra Meets the Romans

After King Tut, Cleopatra VII is probably the most recognized name from ancient Egypt. This is perhaps a bit unusual, I suppose, because she wasn't even an Egyptian, and the greatest days of native Egyptian civilization were arguably long over when she lived. Nonetheless, quite a bit of information has survived through the writings of her fellow Greeks, and the dramatic stories about her are full of romantic and political intrigue.

Cleopatra presided over the end of Greek rule in Egypt, and some say that her death closed the curtain on what we might consider ancient Egypt.

Cleopatra was apparently quite beautiful, very articulate, and well educated. Her story takes place during a time of the rapid expansion of the Roman Empire. Ptolemaic Egypt had made several concessions to the Romans, who eventually acted as their "guardians." During Cleopatra's lifetime, Egypt played a very significant role in the power struggle among the leaders of Rome itself, including such big names as Julius Caesar, Pompey, Mark Antony, and Octavian.

Are you ready for the soap opera? Cleopatra shared the rule of Egypt with her brother/husband, Ptolemy XIII, with whom she was a political rival. The Roman leader Julius Caesar visited Egypt in 48 B.C. and met the young queen. After Ptolemy XIII died in battle, Cleopatra married her younger brother (Ptolemy XIV), but she gave birth to Caesar's child. In 44 B.C., her Roman boyfriend, Caesar, was murdered by a Senate conspiracy. A new power struggle broke out, this time primarily between Roman leaders Antony and Octavian.

Antony, too, became romantically involved with Cleopatra, and some Romans, including Octavian, thought that she was actively manipulating him at the expense of the Roman Empire (he was apparently giving her gifts of Roman territory). Rome declared war

Pharaoh's Domain

Cleopatra was not an Egyptian queen; instead, she was a Greek queen of Egypt.

Lost and Found

Cleopatra and Mark Antony were said to have been buried together in Alexandria, but their remains have never been found.

Glyphs

The term **Graeco-Roman Period,** or **Graeco-Roman Egypt,** refers to the time period during which the Greeks and Romans ruled Egypt, beginning in 332 B.C. with the invasion of Alexander the Great through the period of the Roman emperors.

on Cleopatra in 32 B.C. and in a great sea battle at Actium off the coast of Greece, Octavian defeated Antony, who was accompanied by the naval forces of Cleopatra. Antony retreated to Egypt with Cleopatra, where he killed himself. Octavian arrived in Alexandria in 30 B.C. and had little interest in playing games with Cleopatra. Egypt was declared a Roman province, and Cleopatra committed suicide (with a poisonous snake, so the story goes).

A marble portrait of Cleopatra VII.

(David Moyer collection.)

Octavian went on to become Rome's first emperor, better known as Augustus Caesar, and he considered Egypt his own personal property. Governors were appointed, and Roman law was introduced. Egypt became a source of resources for Rome, especially grain and tax revenues. Like most of the previous foreign rulers, the emperors of Rome adopted the role of divine ruler.

Nile Notes

Would you like to learn more about the Romans? Take a look at *The Complete Idiot's Guide to the Roman Empire*, by Eric Nelson.

Missionaries

The Christian religion appeared during the first century A.D. in neighboring Palestine, which, like Egypt, was under Roman rule. It is not surprising that the new religion appeared quite early in Egypt, where its message was appreciated by many. Tradition says that it was introduced around A.D. 40 by St. Mark, the author of the Gospel by that name.

Christianity did have quite a bit of competition with the Egyptian, Greek, and other cults. Various Roman emperors were notorious for their brutal treatment of the nonconformist Christians, and many people were martyred, especially in the third century. Eventually, Christianity became the official religion under the emperor Constantine in the fourth century, and it thrived in Egypt, where it developed as the *Coptic* Church.

> **Glyphs**
>
> **Coptic,** the last vestige of the Ancient Egyptian language, is no longer actively spoken, but it remains the liturgical language of the Christian orthodox Coptic church of Egypt. **Coptology** is the study of that language and the history and theology of the Coptic church.

Among the contributions of the church in Egypt is the development of the monastic tradition. Egypt was home to hermits who lived in harsh contemplative isolation and to devout monastic communities. The Coptic church, with its own patriarch, hierarchy of priests, churches, and monasteries, still survives in Egypt today, and Coptics comprise approximately 10 percent of the Egyptian population.

Changing Times

With the age of the Roman Empire, we have reached the end of our chronology for ancient Egypt, but one more essential event needs to noted. In the year A.D. 570, the prophet Mohammed was born in the city of Mecca in Arabia, and the Islamic religion was born. The new universalistic religion spread quickly by way of conquering Arab armies, and within a few centuries it reached to the Far East and all the way to Spain in the west. Egypt was conquered in A.D. 642; Islam became the majority religion and the Arabic language became the status quo. Egypt developed into an important and powerful intellectual and cultural center of the Arab world, and it remains so today.

The Least You Need to Know

- ◆ After the New Kingdom, power and control in various parts of Egypt passed through many hands.

- ◆ Foreign entities such as the Nubians, Assyrians, and Persians were at times able to hold sway over Egypt.

- ◆ Alexander the Great conquered Egypt in 332 B.C. and established Greek rule for the next 300 years.

- ◆ Egypt was incorporated into the Roman Empire in 30 B.C.

- ◆ Both Christianity and Islam came to Egypt in the first several centuries A.D. and had lasting effects.

Chapter **18**

Egyptomania!

In This Chapter

- ◆ Egyptian style goes global
- ◆ King Tut mania
- ◆ Moses for the masses
- ◆ Mummies come to life

You're reading this book, so you no doubt have some interest in ancient Egypt. You aren't alone. People have been fascinated by all things Egyptian for a long time, at least as a cultural undercurrent, with occasional widespread outbursts of public enthusiasm. In this chapter, we'll take a look at Egyptomania, as this phenomenon is called. Let's first take a peek at the origins of the allure of Egypt.

Early Egyptomaniacs

Although the Greeks were interested in Egyptian art and culture, if anyone should be credited with seriously starting *Egyptomania*, it would be the Romans. Not only did they collect Egyptian sculptures, obelisks, and other objects when they ruled Egypt, but they began to imitate Egyptian styles themselves. They even built a few little pyramids in Italy as tombs. The

Glyphs

Egyptomania is the fascination with the culture of ancient Egypt.

Nile Notes

Wolfgang Mozart's 1791 popular opera, *Die Zauberflöte* (*The Magic Flute*), incorporated mystical Egyptian/Masonic themes, and some of the sets produced for its production emphasized such notions.

Roman Emperor Hadrian (ruled A.D. 117–138) was very much an Egyptomaniac: In his villa near Rome, he maintained a garden full of Egyptian-inspired statuary and other faux pharaonic features.

Renaissance Revival

With the spread of Christianity and Islam, the perception of ancient Egypt as a pagan land put a bit of a damper on Egyptomania, but it later was revived during the Renaissance and has been going strong since then. With the Renaissance's renewed and vibrant interest in the arts and the world itself, the wonders of the now-mysterious Egypt once again became attractive. Poking around in the ancient Roman ruins occasionally turned up some authentic Egyptian sculptures along with some of the imitations.

As old Greek and Latin texts were studied and published, knowledge and speculation about the ancient Egyptians increased, including guesses about the true meaning of the hieroglyphs. Groups such as the Rosicrucians and the Freemasons traced with pride their arcane roots to ancient Egypt, complete with mystical symbolism. A couple of the popes—Pius II (1458–1464) and Sixtus V (1585–1590)—got into the act by resurrecting some of the Egyptian obelisks that that had been collected by the Romans nearly 1,500 years previously.

Reports from the Field

Accurate information about Egypt itself was considerably lacking until Richard Pococke's and Frederik Norden's visits to the area in the 1730s (see Chapter 2, "Rediscovering the Past"). The published descriptions of their trips fueled further interest.

Napoleon's expedition, of course, produced a major wave of enthusiasm. Before the publication of the famed *Description*, which published the findings from Napoleon's expedition, one of the expedition members, Baron Dominique-Vivant Denon, published his own illustrated account in 1802 that dazzled and inspired people. Egyptian-themed arts continued to flourish in Europe, with items produced ranging from small pieces of jewelry to furniture, to grand and imaginative architecture.

On his return from his adventures in Egypt, Giovanni Belzoni published his *Narratives* (1820) accompanied by color plates which also generated excitement (see Chapter 2 for more on Belzoni). Appropriately, his popular exhibition of drawings and antiquities was held in London in a pharaonic-inspired building called the Egyptian Hall.

Published scholarly expeditions to Egypt offered even more material, with the side benefit of providing ideas for artistic designs. The tombs and temples of Egypt were becoming increasingly accessible both by tourists and in print and publications such as Prisse d'Avennes' *Atlas de Histoire de l'Art Égyptien* (1878–1879), which served as veritable design handbooks for Egyptomaniacal artists and artisans.

Pharaoh's Domain

Even William Shakespeare wrote about Egypt, as featured in his play *Antony and Cleopatra*. In Act III, Scene 9, he writes: "Egypt, thou knew'st too well, My heart was to thy rudder tied by th' strings, And thou shouldst tow me after."

Egypt Goes to the Opera

In 1869, the Suez Canal was opened, and the Cairo Opera House was inaugurated not long thereafter. The opera opened with what is now one of the most beloved and spectacular operas ever written and produced, *Aida*. The music was written by the Italian composer Giuseppi Verdi, with the story line by Auguste Mariette, the French Egyptologist who served as the director of the antiquities service. The opera was a crescendo of Egyptomania, with carefully designed costumes, props, and grandiose sets. It is often still performed on this grand scale, as it should be.

Pharaoh's Poetry Corner

Do you like poetry? Egypt has inspired its fair share over the century. Literary luminaries such as John Milton, Lord Byron, John Keats, Robert Browning, and Alexander Pope all made poetic references to Egypt. There are poems dedicated *To A Pair of Egyptian Slippers* (Sir Edwin Arnold), *To The Obelisk During the Great Frost* (Mathilde Blind), and *To the Nile* (John Keats). Others have been inspired by [*On*] *Seeing an Egyptian Mummy in Berlin, 1932* (Richard Eberhart), *An Egyptian Tomb* (William Bowles), and *Cleopatra* (numerous poets).

Percy Shelley's *Ozymandias* (1818) is an oft-quoted favorite and is an ode to a mammoth fallen statue of Ramesses II (referred to as Ozymandias) at his mortuary temple in Thebes as viewed in the early nineteenth century. So that you're not left out of the poetic Egyptomania, I've included it here:

Diggers

Some modern poets have dedicated whole volumes to the theme of ancient Egypt, including John Greening, *The Tutankhamun Essays* (1984), and Clark Coolridge, *At Egypt* (1988).

> *I met a traveller from an antique land*
> *Who said: Two vast and trunkless legs of stone*

Stand in the desert. Near them, on the sand,
Half sunk, a shattered visage lies, whose frown,
And wrinkled lip, and sneer of cold command,
Tell that its sculptor well those passions read
Which yet survive, stamped on these lifeless things,

The hand that mocked them, and the heart that fed;
And on the pedestal these words appear:
"My name is Ozymandias, king of kings:
Look on my works, ye Mighty, and despair!"
Nothing beside remains. Round the decay
Of that colossal wreck, boundless and bare
The lone and level sands stretch far away.

The Twentieth Century

Architectural styles with Egyptian themes continued to be popular in Europe and America during the late nineteenth century and can be found on a variety of structures, including libraries, museums, and even prisons! After the turn of the century, Egypt became more popular as a tourist site, and a steady stream of archaeological discoveries was made. Pyramids, camels, and the romance of the Nile were successful commercial images and were prominently used to sell products ranging from cigarettes to soap and beauty products. Meanwhile, in the Valley of the Kings, Egyptomania was about to receive a power-boost!

> **Pharaoh's Domain**
>
> The Palmolive Company once advertised its soap with an Egyptian theme and a slogan promoting the "reincarnation of beauty."

Murad "Turkish" cigarettes used the charm and mystery of ancient Egypt to promote the product in the first decade of the twentieth century.

(David Moyer collection.)

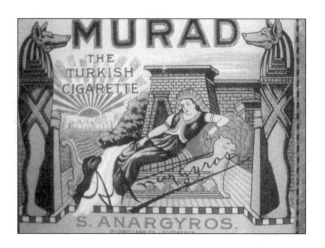

Boy King Fuels an Industry

The discovery of the tomb of Tutankhamun in 1922 was an utter sensation, as it still is decades later. Tutmania was epidemic and spawned all manner of cultural phenomena. There were songs about Egypt and "Old King Tut," Egyptian-inspired clothing styles became the rage, and the once obscure "boy-king" was the trendiest thing in town! The public was now regularly exposed to ancient Egypt, and this popularity has endured.

In 1972, the treasures of King Tut went on tour to the British Museum, which fueled the fire of public enthusiasm for all things Egyptian. Large numbers of people flocked to see a sample of the objects from Tut's tomb. Huge crowds turned out again in 1977–1979 when a similar exhibition was presented at several venues in the United States. Loads of manufacturers exploited the craze to produce hundreds of Egyptian souvenirs and other goods. American comedian Steve Martin had a big hit with his song, "King Tut," which was a satire on the whole phenomenon.

Museum curators learned an important, if not predictable lesson: The public loves ancient Egypt, and any exhibition on the subject will probably do well. Another traveling exhibit with objects related to Ramesses II visited several museums in the 1980s and was likewise quite successful.

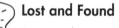

Lost and Found

Because they create a sense of permanence and eternity, Egyptian themes, including pyramids, obelisks, sphinxes, and pylons, have been popular in American and European cemeteries for several hundred years.

Yet Even More ...

During the last couple decades, Egypt has continued to inspire people. One of the more dramatic examples is the huge glass pyramid erected at the entrance to the Musée du Louvre in Paris, designed by famed architect I. M. Pei. With a completely different function altogether, the Luxor Casino and Hotel in Las Vegas, which opened in 1993, proudly boasts that it is the only 30-story pyramid-shaped hotel and casino in the world. It is decorated with an Egyptian theme and is even graced with a gigantic sphinx.

On a more musical note, the dynamic British duo of Andrew Lloyd Webber and Tim Rice wrote a musical based on the biblical story of Joseph, entitled *Joseph and the Amazing Technicolor Dream Coat* (1968). Much of the story takes place in Egypt, of course, but its modern spin features an Elvis-like pharaoh. For more avant-garde tastes, Philip

Nile Notes

And who could forget the musical group known as The Bangles, with their big 1986 hit, "Walk Like an Egyptian"?

Glass produced an opera based on Amarna themes, called *Akhenaten* (1984). More recently, a contemporary version of *Aida* has been produced by Elton John and Tim Rice.

The Luxor Hotel and Casino in Las Vegas is Egyptianized throughout.

(David Moyer collection.)

Read All About It!

During the nineteenth century, more books on Egypt were published, including interesting travel narratives and Egyptian histories. The numbers of these tomes increased greatly during the last hundred years, with both nonfiction and fiction titles selling well. Several prominent late–twentieth-century authors, such as Robin Cook (*Sphinx*, 1979), Allen Drury (*A God Against the Gods*, 1976), and Norman Mailer (*Ancient Evenings*, 1983) have even dabbled in ancient Egyptian fiction. Mika Waltari's novel *The Egyptian* (1949) was roughly based on the ancient story of Sinuhe and was made into a major motion picture. Some recent authors writing ancient Egypt-based series include Lauren Haney, Pauline Gedge, Lynda S. Robinson, and Wilbur A. Smith.

> **Nile Notes**
>
> Egypt is also the subject of many children's books. My favorites are *The World of the Pharaohs* (1960), by Hans Baumann, and *The Golden Pharaoh* (1959), by Karl Bruckner. Dozens more have been published in the decades since these titles were published.

In my humble opinion, the most entertaining and Egyptologically accurate fiction today are the Amelia Peabody mystery tales, set in Victorian England and colonial Egypt and written by Elizabeth Peters. Peters is a pen name of Egyptologist Barbara Mertz. The several titles in this wonderful series include *The Curse of the Pharaohs, Lion in the Valley, The Deeds of the Disturber, The Mummy Case, The Hippopotamus Pool, Lord of the*

Silent, and *The Golden One*. Another mystery by Mertz (this time using the pen name Barbara Michaels), *Search the Shadows*, also offers fictional Egyptological intrigue.

This gas station in San Diego, California, demonstrates some conspicuous ancient Egyptian influence.

(David Moyer collection.)

Egypt on the Big Screen

When movies became popular during the early twentieth century, ancient Egyptian subjects were well represented, even in silent movies. Most attention seems to have been directed toward three primary themes: Cleopatra, the Bible, and mummies.

Cleo Goes Hollywood

The story of Cleopatra, Julius Caesar, and Marc Antony is a screenwriter's dream, with plenty of romance and intrigue. More than two dozen films have been made on the subject. The most famous to date is the 1963 version starring Elizabeth Taylor, Richard Burton, and Rex Harrison. It was one of the most expensive movies ever made, costing perhaps the equivalent of $300 million in today's economy. The film is a long one and is a notorious financial disaster, but it certainly attempted to show the grandeur of Egypt at the very end of its Greek rule.

The Good Book on the Silver Screen

Several movies have been made about the biblical exodus. The three most famous are two versions of *The Ten Commandments*, produced by Cecil B. DeMille, and the recent animated film *Prince of Egypt*. DeMille had a penchant for doing things in a big way, which is clear even in his first *Ten Commandments*, a black-and-white silent film released in 1929. A lot of effort was put into building huge sets, including palace facades and an avenue of sphinxes. The 1959 color version, starring Charlton Heston and Yul Brynner, was even more spectacular and involved a cast of many thousands.

Diggers

Would you like to be mummified in ancient Egyptian style when your time is up? Corky Ra can do it. Corky operates a business named *Summum* in Utah that offers Egyptian-style mummification, complete with a bronze coffin. Needless to say, it's not cheap. Corky will also mummify your pets.

In an odd twist of archaeology-meets-fantasy-meets-modern-times, a group of archaeologists set out to locate the remains of the old 1929 set for *The Ten Commandments*, which had been buried in sand at Guadalupe Dunes in California. Using sophisticated equipment that can locate things underground, they have found major pieces of the set and are beginning to excavate it as valuable relics of early filmmaking. Some might think that this is truly bizarre, but it sounds like a lot of fun to me!

Staggering Stiffs

Some of the most fun and scary expressions of Egyptomania are the movies featuring animated mummies, and there are many of them. The all-time classic film of this sort is *The Mummy*, starring Boris Karloff, released by Universal Pictures in 1932.

Several more mummy movies followed, including these:

◆ *The Mummy's Hand* (1940)

◆ *The Mummy's Tomb* (1942)

◆ *The Mummy's Ghost* (1944)

◆ *The Mummy's Curse* (1945)

◆ *Abbott and Costello Meet the Mummy* (1955), a comedy

One of the inspirations for Universal's mummies was none other than Ramesses III, whose well-preserved mummy has that special look the producers were looking for. Universal Pictures produced a new version of *The Mummy*, which came out in 1999. Its plot vaguely resembles the original, and its special effects are amazing. The film made a lot of money, and its sequel, *The Mummy Returns* (2001), was also quite spectacular—both visually and at the box office.

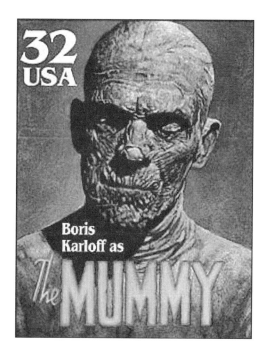

Universal Picture's The Mummy, *as played by Boris Karloff in 1932, is featured on this 1997 U.S. postage stamp. The mummy of Ramesses III, pictured, served as a role model for the look of several movie mummies.*

(Ramesses III picture from The Royal Mummies, *by G.E. Smith.)*

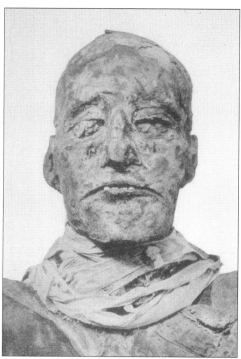

Bitten by the Bug

Over the last 2,000 years, ancient Egyptian culture has attracted a large following and continues to do so. There will be more books, movies, exhibitions, and television documentaries. If you think you've been bitten by the bug, don't forget to check out Appendix B, "Exploring on Your Own: A Select Bibliography"; Appendix C, "Resources for Further Exploration"; and Appendix D, "Egypt Abroad: Museums with Egyptian Collections." They'll help you feed your own personal Egyptomania!

The Least You Need to Know

◆ Interest in Egypt began with the Greeks and Romans, who presided over some of the last days of the great ancient civilization.

◆ Ancient Egypt was popular during the Renaissance, when it was thought to be an intriguing and mystical civilization.

◆ The cultural effects of Napoleon's invasion of Egypt, the opening of the Suez Canal, and discovery of the Tomb of Tutankhamun all served to boost an interest in ancient Egypt.

◆ Touring exhibits of King Tut's treasure and other Egyptian artifacts have fueled a public interest in Egyptology.

◆ Egyptomania continues unabated in many different forms.

Alternative Theories

In This Chapter

- ◆ Unusual theories
- ◆ Ancient astronauts
- ◆ Reincarnated Egyptians
- ◆ Mummy curses

This book has been written from the standpoint of traditional Egyptology. The information is based on 200 years of scholarly inquiry. Egyptology generally likes to portray itself as a scholarly, if not a purely scientific, endeavor. It borrows from the best of various disciplines in an attempt to achieve reasonable perspectives about the lives and times of the ancient Egyptians. Egyptologists like to deal with materials that can be measured or reassessed by others—and, if they speculate, they usually (or at least *should*) qualify it with words such as *perhaps, maybe,* or *it seems.* Such words can be very unsatisfying to those who want concrete answers to sometimes difficult questions; however, this is what a careful, scholarly approach demands.

There are others, though, who deal with the past in unusual and sometimes interesting ways, playing by a different set of rules—and ancient Egypt is a veritable magnet for such people. In this chapter, we'll take a look at some of the more popular fringe ideas, things like ancient astronauts, pyramid theories, ancient Egyptians in the Americas, and mummy curses.

The Other Side of the Fence

For centuries, people have been impressed by the accomplishments of the ancient Egyptians and have put forth many ideas about what it all means, from the stone-cold analytical to the outright silly. While there are a fair number of academic Egyptologists, the number of untraditional Egyptological notions and their promoters is perhaps even larger. Their theories are based on ideas that mainstream Egyptologists find to be only superficially credible, at best.

Egyptologists are often annoyed by these sorts of theories and their proponents and followers because their claims typically are outlandishly attractive and often detract from the mainstream—and generally more sober—academic discipline of Egyptology. In fact, mainstream Egyptologists are often painted as the bad guys in all this, perceived to be too stuck up to consider what's presented as the hidden "real truth," or they're accused of being part of the great conspiracy to cover it up.

They Came from Outer Space

We academic scholars got it all wrong, according to some folks. If we want to know how civilizations were created and how our ancestors accomplished their amazing engineering feats, we need to look to the sky. According to this view, aliens visited our planet in the past and taught the ancient Egyptians sophisticated things like stone carving and pyramid building. Perhaps they are even responsible for the human race itself, having mated with simple-minded hominids.

Lost and Found

An inscription in the temple of Seti I at Abydos has garnered a lot of attention because it seems to show a jet aircraft or UFO. In reality, the curious depiction is the result of the recarving of a new inscription over an old one. To an Egyptologist who knows hieroglyphs, this is obvious. To those who don't, it appears to be rather extraordinary!

According to Erich von Daniken, the godfather of this sort of speculation, evidence of alien mentors is everywhere. Illustrations and descriptions of these extraterrestrials can be seen in everything from drawings in caves to intricately carved Maya art, to ancient myths and the Bible. And how else can you explain the complex engineering that appears in ancient Egypt and elsewhere? Visits from superior beings, according to von Daniken, explain how complex cultures appear seemingly out of nowhere. His best-selling book, *Chariots of the Gods?* was first published in 1968 and has been followed by many sequels.

Who's Driving the Chariot?

It doesn't take a professional archaeologist to find a myriad of holes in such books as *Chariots of the Gods?* I first read the book when I was 14 years old, and it was clear to me even then that something was amiss. von Daniken seems to start with a conclusion and finds evidence for it everywhere he looks. One scholar compared it to the old psychologist's inkblot test. One person sees a spider, and someone else sees the Statue of Liberty. von Daniken sees ancient astronauts.

This sort of thinking assumes that ancient humans were neither particularly bright nor creative. There is no reason to believe that people 5,000 or more years ago were any less intelligent than we think we are today, even though they lacked computers and such. Knowing what we know about the intelligence and mobility of early people, why call on strange and otherworldly forces to account for human achievements?

Pharaoh's Domain

There is no evidence to suggest that the people living 5,000 years ago in Egypt, or elsewhere, were any less intelligent than we are now.

The Pyramids

The pyramids, especially the Great Pyramid of Khufu at Giza, have attracted an extraordinary amount of attention. Indeed, they are exceedingly impressive and have been a marvel to people for thousands of years. Egyptologists believe that pyramids were the graves of the rulers who were considered to be god-kings (see Chapter 10, "Age of Pyramids"), and, so far, very little has convinced them to believe otherwise. But to some speculators, the pyramids had additional functions or were unrelated to burial practices altogether. The ideas are numerous and include the notions that they channeled energy, that they were factories or machines, that mystical secrets or calendars are embodied in their measurements or design, and that secret chambers await discovery within. Some argue that they are aligned to constellations or are located on some sort of energy grids. Others claim that levitation was used to lift the stone blocks or that many of the blocks were created from a kind of cement.

It would take volumes to present the points and counterpoints of all the various theories, but, again, there is no need to appeal to extraordinary forces to account for the pyramids. They didn't appear instantaneously out of nowhere, and several hundred years of evolving funerary monuments before the Great Pyramid attest to their indigenous development. Furthermore, experiments have shown that building such monuments was certainly within the abilities of well-organized and motivated humans. As far as secret chambers or mystical concepts, such things are theoretically possible and are—and will be—subject to continuing assessment.

It seems that the more technological we become, the more difficult it is to believe that ancient people were capable of doing much of anything, lacking all our modern gadgetry. The Egyptians didn't require dump trucks, backhoes, walkie-talkies, or computer-assisted design programs to build the pyramids. They were masters of the clever and efficient use of simple tools. As I remind my students, I'm not that old (I was born in the late 1950s), but when I was a kid, there were no VCRs, cell phones, video cameras, home microwave ovens, CD players, or other items that are so much a part of current life and technology. And in my grandfather's day ....

Glyphs

Some Egyptologists have used the word **pyramidiots** to describe those who have offered untraditional viewpoints about the pyramids or their builders. Perhaps this is a bit unkind.

Nile Notes

It might be argued that many of the theories presented about the past are a reflection of the theorist, and this tells us as much about their philosophy as the idea that they address. In the case of ancient astronauts, for example, the underlying belief seems to be the lack of human ability.

Pyramid Power

In the 1970s, there was quite a pyramid fad, and there were all sorts of ideas about the alleged power of that shape. Pyramidal structures oriented to the cardinal directions were said to perform such feats as keep fruits and flowers fresh and sharpen dull razor blades. And as an added bonus, of course, the pyramid shape contributes to the preservation of Egyptian mummies.

Some people constructed pyramids over their beds or made special pyramid-shaped solariums in their homes, providing places to experience these mysterious curative and rejuvenating powers. If it really works, then the pyramids must shut themselves down occasionally because scientific experiments have not been able to show any extraordinary effects.

Some people believe that pyramids have special powers.

Chronological Revisionists

Recently, some people have argued that the Great Sphinx at Giza was carved between 5000 and 7000 B.C., several millennia earlier than Egyptologists generally believe it was created. A promoter of ancient Egyptian mysticism, backed up by a geologist from an American university, put forth the idea. The geologist claimed that the area around the Sphinx was far more eroded than the surrounding monuments known to date to the Old Kingdom (2575–2134 B.C.).

The Sphinx belongs to an earlier age, so goes the claim, and was created by an early advanced civilization. The head of the Sphinx was probably originally that of a lion, and during the Old Kingdom it was recarved to the likeness of King Khafra, with whose pyramid the statue is traditionally associated. Other geologists are not convinced, and archaeologists point to the fact that there are no related artifacts or other physical evidence of this so-called advanced civilization.

The Mummy's Curse

And while we're at it, we might as well talk about the so-called mummy's curse. According to some people, curses were placed on Egyptian tombs long ago, and anyone—tomb raiders and Egyptologists alike—who violates the cursed tombs will die or suffer other misfortunes. The most famous curse story surrounds the tomb of Tutankhamun, discovered in November 1922. It was reported that a tablet or inscription was found stating, "death will come on swift wings" to whomever violated the tomb. In April 1923, Lord Carnarvon, the sponsor of the Tut excavation, died in Cairo, and several visitors to the tomb likewise died in short order.

Let's look at the facts. No written curse was ever found on or in Tut's tomb. The story seems to have been the fabrication of bored newspaper reporters posted at the tomb and looking for an angle. Lord Carnarvon died of blood poisoning derived from an infected mosquito bite in the days before effective antibiotics.

Pharaoh's Domain —————

After the death of Lord Carnarvon, the newspapers went wild with mysterious stories. At the moment of his death, the lights in Cairo were said to have gone out, and his beloved dog, Suzy, back in England yelped and keeled over.

Pharaoh's Domain —————

One of the magical means by which the Egyptians could curse their enemies was through what are called "execration texts." Names of enemies could be written on clay figurines or pots that were then smashed.

But many people associated with Tut's tomb went on to live long lives. Howard Carter, who discovered the tomb and spent 10 years working there, died in 1939 of Hodgkin's disease, almost 17 years after the discovery. Dr. Douglas Derry (1874–1961), who performed the autopsy on the mummy in 1925, lived to a ripe old age. And so did many others involved with the excavation.

The Egyptians did believe in magic, however, and there are actual examples of written curses associated with ancient tombs. They basically threaten death to those who enter the tomb's chapel in an impure state or rob, vandalize, or otherwise violate the tomb. Such curses might serve to scare away a few believers, but in the long run, they were mostly ineffective. Some have suggested that the ancient Egyptians might have intentionally placed poison in some of the tombs to thwart robbers. If so, it was completely ineffective because the overwhelming majority of high-status Egyptian tombs were robbed. If curses or poisons are to be effective deterrents, they have to work before—or, at least, during—the fact. If someone dies a year later, well, the tomb has already been robbed!

There may be some basis in fact for the idea of illness associated with tombs. It's possible that some people may have died from contracting infections from mold, dust, or other material naturally produced in tombs. I, for instance, became seriously ill on a couple occasions while sifting fine particles of tomb dust that was mixed with old dried bat guano.

Inscriptions Everywhere

Everyone knows the story of Columbus and his 1492 encounter with the "New World." He was the first documented European to visit the Americas, until a single Viking site dating to around 500 years earlier was discovered way up north in Newfoundland in 1960. There are those who claim that not only did the Vikings visit America before Columbus, but so did just about anyone else in the Old World who ever owned a boat, including the Carthaginians, Phoenicians, Irish, Africans, Romans, Palestinian Jews, and—you guessed it!—the ancient Egyptians. Although these advocates may be sincere in their efforts, their enthusiasm often gets the better of them.

Some individuals have claimed to have found Egyptian inscriptions on a few North American stones here and there, including petroglyphs at sites in Colorado and Nevada. Similarly, people claim to have found evidence of an ancient Egyptian presence in Australia and elsewhere. Having reviewed much of the evidence, I remain wholly unconvinced.

> **Diggers**
>
> Norwegian archaeologist and author Thor Heyerdahl sailed two experimental reed boats, Ra I and II, into the Atlantic in 1969 and 1970. Because of their names and Egyptian-inspired design, many people have misinterpreted the voyages as attempts to prove that the Egyptians reached the Americas in ancient times and inspired the complex cultures that developed there. In reality, the voyages had little to do specifically with the Egyptians but were meant to test the seaworthiness of a type of craft that a number of ancient cultures seemed to have.

The idea of ancient Egyptians traveling far and wide has a certain appeal, but currently is unsubstantiated. Although the possibility (if not good probability) exists for people traversing the oceans to the Americas before Columbus, the Egyptians would be on the bottom of the list of candidates. They just don't seem to have been all that interested in ocean activities, nor is there much evidence of them having traversed very far even into the western Mediterranean.

The fact is, most of the discoveries involving that script and language appear to be either imaginative interpretations or outright hoaxes.

Lost and Found _____

Traces of nicotine and cocaine have been found in several Egyptian mummies, causing plenty of controversy. Were they actually smoking and snorting these things, or were they using other plants that contain similar residues that might be detected in a laboratory test? If they had tobacco and cocaine, which are both known as New World plants, where did they get it? The mystery is still unresolved.

Been Here Before

As you know by now, people have espoused many strange beliefs about ancient Egypt, but one of the most unusual is about reincarnation. Several people have claimed that in a former life they were a citizen of the Nile and that they perhaps retain vestiges of memory. Rarely can such claims be substantiated to scientific specifications. For the most part, if you claim to be a reincarnated priestess in a Hathor temple, I would simply have to believe you or not believe you. A skeptic would at least require that you demonstrate some sort of intimate, verifiable knowledge of your ancient life that could add credibility to your story.

Woman of Abydos

Dorothy Eady (1904–1981) is probably the most famous person to have claimed to have once been an ancient Egyptian. Dorothy displayed an unusual attraction to the subject of ancient Egypt as a child, eventually coming to believe that in a previous life she had been a priestess in a temple of the pharaoh Seti I at Abydos. She claimed to have had a clandestine fling with the pharaoh, and rather than disparage her boyfriend's reputation, she committed suicide. Dorothy believed that Seti himself came back to visit her on numerous occasions.

> **Nile Notes**
>
> I have met a number of people who claim to be reincarnated ancient Egyptians. Most assert that they are royalty or other high-status individuals and I have yet to meet a "reincarnated" farmer, pot-maker, or palace floor-scrubber. There are also duplicate reincarnated Nefertitis and King Tuts. No wonder I'm skeptical!

Dorothy had a son with her real-life Egyptian husband, and she named the child Seti, thus the name by which she became well known, Umm Seti, Arabic for "mother of Seti." She worked for the Egyptian antiquities service and settled in Abydos, where she was a true expert on the site. Umm Seti seemed to have detailed knowledge of ancient Egypt, but it's unclear whether there was anything authentically original in her stories that she couldn't have picked up in the course of her lifetime.

She had many friends and admirers, including professional Egyptologists, and her name is forever linked with Abydos and the pharaoh that she claimed to have loved in ancient times.

The Sleeping Prophet

Edgar Cayce (1877–1945) was another famous mystic associated with ancient Egypt. He would go into a trance and then give recitations about various individual's former lives. He believed in the existence of an early highly sophisticated civilization called Atlantis, whose citizens fled from destruction as their continental home sank into the ocean. Some traveled to Egypt where they sparked the civilization that we now know, and they left their library in a "Hall of Records" buried beneath the Sphinx at Giza.

I'd be interested in this "Hall of Records" myself if it weren't for the dubious notion of Atlantis and the prophetic credibility of Mr. Cayce. He predicted that Atlantis would rise from the ocean depths in the 1960s. I haven't seen any new continents appear on the map since then, have you?

Fulfilling a Need

Examples of "fringe" Egyptology are seemingly endless. Although some of the suggestions are theoretically possible, others don't conform to known laws of nature or to geological or archaeological evidence. Why do people believe in this sort of stuff? There are several possible reasons:

- Belief in supernatural phenomena provides a psychologically satisfying explanation for things that are not readily explainable.
- Calling on outside superior forces reinforces our belief that no one before us could have been as intelligent as we are.
- Some individuals have inexplicable personal experiences that suggest to them that there are mystical realms outside scientific observation.
- Lack of information regarding other possible explanations.
- People have a lack of trust in, or suspicion of, authority.
- It's fun!

> **Pharaoh's Domain**
>
> In some cases individuals who claimed to be the reincarnation of ancient Egyptians also claimed to speak the ancient language while in a trance or otherwise. Upon examination, their babblings tend to show little resemblance to what we know about Egyptian vocabulary and grammar.

> **Nile Notes**
>
> Skeptics who examine unusual phenomena have a saying: Extraordinary claims require extraordinary proof. It is rarely forthcoming.

Dealing with the Unusual

The way I look at it, basically two kinds of people are involved in promoting offbeat ideas: true believers and frauds. True believers are those with a sincere belief in a given idea, who usually want to share it with others. Frauds are those who knowingly promote false information to make a buck from the public or to exploit the true believers. Unfortunately, it is very difficult to tell the two groups apart. You should be very careful before calling anyone a fraud, but anyone knowingly taking advantage of others in such a way should be held accountable.

Although I remain unconvinced by most of the untraditional views, I don't condemn those who choose to believe this stuff. They are entitled to their beliefs, and berating them and calling them names (as some Egyptologists do) certainly doesn't help. In fact, it often hardens their opinions and adds fuel to the idea that scientists are closed-minded or conspiratorial. As a rule, an insult greatly lessens the chance that people will listen to and consider traditional perspectives on their subjects.

Pharaoh's Domain

More modern published editions of the ancient Egyptian Book of the Dead are probably bought by individuals seeking mystical wisdom than by Egyptologists. Readers looking for cosmic truth might be disappointed to find that this is a guidebook to assist the deceased in safely traversing the underworld and surviving judgment. Removed from its cultural environment, the book has little practical meaning, but if someone today can somehow find something inspirational in it, what the heck!

An Open Mind

I have read some of what Egyptologists consider to be fringe literature. Why? I want to be exposed to the range of ideas floating around, and I want to have a polite and informed response when people ask me about something. Once in a while these people, in their great enthusiasm, also dig up something (usually in a library or museum) or point out something that is genuinely valuable for mainstream investigation.

But if you're going to read the alternative theories, I also encourage you to read the responses to them by archaeologists and other experts. Then think for yourself, and if the odd theory still convinces you, then at least you have considered both sides of the debate. A lot of Egyptologists could benefit from doing the same. Clearly there are many ways of looking at the world, and I hope for at least a degree of respect for others who hold contrary opinions.

Revealing the Big Secret

As a final word on this subject, I would like to reveal to you the big secret regarding the grand Egyptological conspiracy to suppress a lot of the untraditional perspectives: *There is no big conspiracy.* Sure, there are certain constraints in the academic world that might hinder unfettered speculation, but a well-presented case for one thing or another will invite debate, and many things get sorted out—for better or worse—in the end.

The Least You Need to Know

- The ancient sophistication of the Egyptians has attracted a wealth of unorthodox ideas.

- Egyptologists believe that the Egyptians were fully capable of creating pyramids and other monuments. They were masters of the clever and efficient use of simple tools.

- There is no good evidence for a super-sophisticated civilization in Egypt that predates the traditional dynasties by thousands of years.

- There is no good evidence for effective mummy curses or an ancient Egyptian presence in the Americas.

- From a scientific viewpoint, claims for having lived past lives are considered questionable.

- People believe in unconventional ideas for many reasons, but the right to hold them should be respected.

Part  6

Ancient Egypt in the Modern World

We might be studying the past, but we are living in the present, with a responsibility to the future. In this section, we're going to look at some difficult issues that Egyptians—and all people concerned with preserving Egypt's past—must confront.

And if you would like to pursue your interest in ancient Egypt, you will find the last two chapters quite useful. You'll find valuable information about visiting the wonderful land of modern Egypt. And if you're toying with the idea of becoming an amateur or professional Egyptologist, the last chapter will give you some frank insights and some hot tips.

Chapter 20

Facing the Future

In This Chapter

- ◆ The inevitable decay of the past
- ◆ Hard choices
- ◆ A huge dam
- ◆ Some very difficult questions

So far in this book, we've explored many of the interesting facets of ancient Egyptian history and culture. In this chapter, however, it's time to consider the future. Some of the issues covered in this chapter are controversial, and almost all the decisions that need to be made about Egypt's future are difficult ones. So if you're not interested in controversy or unpleasant decisions, you might choose to move on to the next chapter, which is much cheerier—I promise!

That's All There Is!

The remains of ancient Egypt are a finite commodity. Our ancient friends are long gone, and we're left with whatever has survived. However, we live in a modern world, and serious and difficult choices need to be made about how we deal with such remains and to what extent it is reasonable to preserve them to satisfy our interests.

Nature Doesn't Care

Erosion and decay are natural processes, and when it comes to Egypt's monuments, a number of forces are at work. Heat and cold, wind and rain, along with chemical and organic processes, are all working to make the remains of the past disappear. Depending upon the material and the environment, artifacts can survive a few hours to many thousands of years. In many cases, things long buried remained intact until exposed by archaeologists, only to seemingly dissolve. The decay of other things, such as stone temples, takes much longer, but they are decaying nonetheless.

A Serious Matter

The Egyptian government is very concerned about the conservation and preservation of its precious monuments. Archaeologists today are required to care for the things they dig up. In fact, the general consensus now is that archaeology and conservation should work hand in hand. People who are skilled in conserving artifacts and monuments are highly desired on digs, as are the epigraphers who specialize in making permanent records of inscriptions and art.

The Needs of People

Egypt's population is expanding at a rapid rate. As a result, there is an increasing need for new housing and support facilities, factories, commercial centers, and the rest of the infrastructure to support the growing population and to expand agricultural production. Given that Egypt is essentially one big archaeological site, there will be conflicts of interest between saving the remains of the past and serving the needs of the people. It is a difficult balancing act. Protecting all the past is very likely an unreasonable, if not impossible proposition.

So what should be saved? Only the big or important stuff? Should a mound full of broken pottery and other ancient debris be preserved while living people don't have their needs met? These are difficult questions that have to be addressed by the antiquities authorities and other government officials. Ideally, an investigation and assessment of the nature of an archaeological site can take place to identify its significance before bringing in the bulldozers, but then you're faced with the difficult definition of the word *significance*.

> **Nile Notes**
>
> In the year 2000, Egypt's population was close to 70 million people, and growth is expected to continue.

Taming the Nile

For thousands of years, people living along the Egyptian Nile have been concerned about the annual flooding of the river that is so vital to the maintenance of agriculture. Too little water and famine could ensue, and too much could cause other disastrous problems. A dam on the Nile to control fluctuations has long been considered a way of keeping things steady.

In 1902, a dam was finished just south of Aswan and was raised even higher on two subsequent occasions. As a result, a number of monuments located behind this structure were flooded during the inundation or were even submerged most of the year. This dam was eventually deemed to be barely sufficient, so in the 1950s, a decision was made to build a much more massive one just south of Aswan to control the mighty Nile and at the same time produce a large quantity of hydroelectric power to service a modern and growing Egypt.

The dam, called the Aswan High Dam, was finished in 1971 and is one of the largest in the world. The huge lake created behind the dam is called Lake Nasser, after Egypt's formidable nationalist president Gamal Abdel Nasser.

The dam has been a real mixed blessing. Here are some of the benefits:

◆ With plenty of water in the lake, Egypt doesn't have to worry as much about the effects of drought.

◆ With the regulation of water output, crops can be grown year round.

◆ Hydroelectric power provides much needed energy for the growing country.

◆ Navigation is improved on the river.

And now, some of the adverse effects:

◆ The natural cycle of the Nile has been disrupted, and the rich alluvial silt no longer annually renews the soil as it has done for eons. Although crop yields have been increased, artificial fertilizers have been needed, and they tend to exhaust the soil.

◆ In its natural flow, the Nile carries millions of tons of sediment, which used to be deposited into the Mediterranean Sea. Much of this is now trapped behind the dam; without the annual accumulation near the river's mouth, the Egyptian Mediterranean coastline is eroding.

◆ When the dam was created, Lake Nasser flooded an immense territory. Tens of thousands of Nubian residents in Egypt and Sudan were relocated, and hundreds of archaeological sites were threatened and many lost.

As you can see, there are some serious advantages and disadvantages to such a radical alteration of nature's course.

Because we are concentrating primarily on the ancient past in this book, I'd like to share a remarkable story of how the present had to come to terms with the past. With the new dam, more than a dozen temples, thousands of prehistoric sites, several ancient fortresses, old Coptic churches, and many other remains of all ages were threatened with destruction by the massive reservoir that would extend from Egypt well into Sudan.

> ### Nile Notes
>
> The Aswan High Dam contains 17 times the mass of the Great Pyramid at Giza, and its construction required the effort of about 30,000 workers operating day and night for 10 years.

In 1959, both Egypt and Sudan petitioned the United Nations UNESCO committee for assistance in saving the monuments. The following year, a plea was put out for international help. During the next 20 years, about 40 missions from 25 countries working with Egypt and Sudan responded to help salvage threatened sites and monuments. It was an outstanding example of international cooperation, and although it was impossible to save all that was threatened, a splendid attempt was made and much was successfully recovered.

The Biggest Project of Them All

Among the monuments threatened by the dam were two huge temples built by Ramesses II for himself and his queen, Nefertari, carved into sandstone mountainsides at Abu Simbel. These magnificent monuments certainly would have been submerged and destroyed if drastic action was not taken. The result was an amazing international engineering project that sawed the temples and their mountains into pieces and re-erected them on higher ground.

The project began in 1964 and took around four years to complete. A small temporary dam held back the rising lake while a crew of nearly 2,000 people worked around the clock. A great concrete dome and support framework support the reconstructed temples, which now reside safely near the edge of the water, similar to ancient times. And a shaft of sunlight still penetrates to illuminate the statues in the innermost chambers on certain days of the year, just as before!

> ### Diggers
>
> A variety of proposals were offered on how to deal with the massive threatened temples of Abu Simbel. It was suggested, for example, that the temples could be lifted to higher ground on big hydraulic jacks, that a huge special dam could be built just for the temples, or that they could be protected by a huge dome that would allow visitors access to the temple by elevators from above. The dismantling project proved effective and was actually completed 20 months ahead of schedule.

The relocated temples of Abu Simbel along the shores of Lake Nasser.

(David Moyer collection.)

More Temples

Although Abu Simbel is the most famous example of the great Nubian rescue projects, other temples were saved as well. A small temple at Amada was moved on rails to a site about a mile and a half away from its original location. The great temple of Kalabsha, consisting of 16,000 blocks, was taken apart with cranes and then was moved and reassembled. One of the most beautiful temples of all, the temple at Philae, was removed in pieces by cranes and divers and was reconstructed on higher ground in the 1970s. Although it had lost most of its surviving colors from being submerged, it now stands majestically in its new location near Aswan.

Saving the Small Things

Many things couldn't be saved, including some of the large mud-brick forts. Prehistoric burials had to be excavated and recorded rapidly. But some whole decorated tombs were removed, as were

Pharaoh's Domain

The Graeco-Roman temple of Philae was referred to as "The Pearl of Egypt" by the French poet Pierre Loti. After the first Aswan dam was finished in 1902, it was submerged for much of the year, and at times its interior could be visited by boat!

Lost and Found

The Temple of Dendur now stands in the Metropolitan Museum of Art in New York City. It resides in a special glass-enclosed addition to the Museum that nicely offers a sense of its ancient beauty in natural light.

ancient rock art and inscriptions and some priceless church frescoes. Some of the saved material can be found at the National Museum of the Sudan in Khartoum and the Nubian Museum at Aswan. Remarkably, four small temples were given as gifts to Spain, the Netherlands, Italy, and the United States.

Loving the Monuments to Death

Egypt is visited by millions of tourists every year, and they contribute billions of dollars worth of much needed foreign currency to the Egyptian economy. And why not? It's a great place to go (see Chapter 21, "Exploring Egypt Today"). Unfortunately, the impact of tourists on ancient Egyptian artifacts isn't always positive. Most of Egypt's monuments were not designed to be visited by masses of people. The interiors of the tombs were never intended to be visited by anyone, yet millions of people travel thousands of miles to marvel at the tombs of the Valley of the Kings and elsewhere. Tour buses cause vibrations and spew pollutants. In some places, the accumulated moisture of tourists' very breathing can cause damage! A few unscrupulous folks occasionally leave graffiti and garbage, touch walls that they are asked not to, use flash photography in forbidden places, or commit other damaging acts.

> **Pharaoh's Domain**
>
> Several years were spent conserving the beautifully decorated tomb of Nefertari in the Valley of the Queens, and it was concluded that it could withstand only a very limited number of tourists per day. Get your ticket early, if you can—and don't touch the walls!

It is a difficult problem. How can we balance the need and desire for tourism with conserving the monuments? Area management plans have been designed to deal with some of these issues. Rotating which places may be visited has been tried as one possible solution. Limiting the numbers of tourists allowed in special sites has also been enacted.

Who Owns the Past?

Who owns the past? It's such a profound question! There are major museums all over the world (particularly in North America and Europe) full of antiquities from other parts of the globe. Fragments of the marble frieze from ancient Athens's beautiful Parthenon (the "Elgin Marbles") are in London; the stele with the Law Code of Hammurabi is in Paris; and museums in New York, Boston, and elsewhere in America are loaded with Egyptian antiquities.

On many occasions, I have heard off-the-cuff remarks by people regarding all the items from Egypt in the British Museum or elsewhere "stolen" by the likes of Belzoni and others. Shouldn't these objects be returned to Egypt? That's a serious question indeed. Are they not part of the Egyptian ancient cultural heritage?

Yes, there have been occasional calls to give artifacts back. On the other hand, you might be surprised to learn that the overwhelming majority of the stuff you see in museums was not technically stolen. Most of the treasures of the British Museum, for example, were obtained at a time when it was permitted to do so. Belzoni had permission from the government in charge during his era to remove what he liked from Egypt, as did his rivals.

The removal for export of a huge statue fragment of Ramesses II, as directed by Giovanni Belzoni in 1816.

Certainly in Egypt during much of the nineteenth century, there was not much national interest in a long-distant past among a generally poor population. The relics of pharaonic times had long been scorned as pagan by both Christians and Muslims. It probably came as quite a surprise when enterprising Egyptians living near sites of antiquities learned that visiting Europeans were interested in this old debris and were willing to pay for it! In antiquities shops, a visitor could readily buy many of the more common items, from amulets to fish mummies.

The freestyle digging and export of Egyptian antiquities was somewhat curtailed with the establishment of the antiquities service and a national museum in the mid-nineteenth century. Thereafter, the rules required that excavators split their finds fifty-fifty with Egypt, thus rewarding foreign museums for their efforts. And until just a couple of decades ago, there were government-licensed antiquities dealers in Egypt who were allowed to sell unremarkable run-of-the-mill objects.

Bring It on Home

You can be sure of one thing—Egypt isn't letting such things happen now. The days of the fifty-fifty split are long gone. Now archaeologists are no longer allowed to remove antiquities from Egypt, not even small samples for analysis, unless very special permission is granted by an antiquities committee. And the antiquities shops are no longer operating. After the 1952 revolution, the Egyptians were fully in charge of governing their country. Schools now teach about the grandeur of ancient Egypt and promote a national pride in the past.

Others argue that Egyptian artifacts permanently housed in foreign museums are the best advertisement there is for tourism, which plays a large role in Egypt's economy. Not only do museum-goers leave with an appreciation of the ancient culture, but many of them are inspired to visit Egypt to see the antiquities *in-situ*. And few dispute that the objects in such museums are well cared for. Moreover, from a practical point of view, museums fear that to return objects would establish a precedent that could result in the shrinking or decimation of their collections.

International treaties and conventions now in place provide rules for the return of various objects under certain circumstances. Many objects have been returned to their country of origin on a case-by-case basis. Certainly, objects that were actually stolen are covered by these agreements, and some organizations now circulate information about recent thefts to alert museums and collectors.

> **Nile Notes**
>
> In some recent incidents, Egypt has curtailed even traveling exhibits of its antiquities, fearing that they might be damaged. The country would also like to encourage foreigners to come to Egypt if they want to see some of its treasures.

Grave Robbers?

Here's a question that makes some people uncomfortable. Are archaeologists and Egyptologists merely another kind of grave robber, but with a more sophisticated philosophy and more refined excavation methods? Who are we to be digging up someone's ancient relatives? That's a fair question, I think. Maybe the following scenarios will help to resolve the issue:

Scenario 1:

Let's drift back in time a few thousand years. King Tut, the boy king, has just met his untimely demise by a means not clearly understood. His wife and family are probably terribly upset. The body is carefully mummified, and a procession to the Valley of the Kings carries tons of gilded objects to a small tomb. The jewelry-clad mummy of Tut, with its exquisite gold mask, encased in three splendid coffins, is placed in its sarcophagus; the tomb is sealed.

It's nearly miraculous that greedy robbers didn't effectively loot the tomb, and archaeologist Howard Carter then finds it in 1922. "Ooooh! Aaaah!" says everyone when the news comes out, and Tut becomes a celebrity! The mummy is removed from its coffin and examined, and the objects from his tomb make their way to Cairo for exhibition. So what's the big deal? Keep reading.

Scenario 2:

A poor Egyptian farmer goes secretly out at night with a shovel to illegally excavate an ancient grave. He's successful in uncovering several interesting artifacts, which he sells to enhance his meager income.

Aren't both scenarios similar, although different in the matter of scale, sophistication, and intent? Isn't the end result essentially the same—a grave is disrupted and its contents are dispersed?

Bones of Contention

Do we have any right to excavate the remains of ancient people, many of them lovingly interred in their final resting places by grieving friends and relatives? Should they be dug up and measured, with their bones or mummies and their grave possessions put on display or stored in boxes or shelves in a museum storeroom? Have we no respect?

Or, do we say, who cares because they're dead anyway and nobody alive knows them? Should the dead be used to satisfy the curiosity of the living? You can bet that neither King Tut nor any other of the great pharaohs ever expected that their bodies would be put on public display and their sacred tombs would be visited by millions of tourists.

> **Pharaoh's Domain**
>
> It has been proposed that tourists be directed to replicas of some of the more at-risk tombs, such as that of Seti I in the Valley of the Kings. This approach has been used to preserve Stone-Age cave paintings at Lascaux in France. Such an idea is controversial among both Egyptologists and tourists who might want to see the real thing.

> **Lost and Found**
>
> King Tut's mummy really took a beating. Many of his body parts were snapped off in the process of removing jewelry, and his head became detached from his body. He's even missing a part of his anatomy that I'd prefer not to name. It was there when they found him ....

National Treasure or World Heritage?

So, back to the question of who owns the past. There are Maya temples in the jungle that are slowly deteriorating. In Asia, heads are being removed from ancient statues of the Buddha for sale on the art market. Some extremists in Egypt have expressed a desire to blow up pharaonic antiquities because they are the remains of an undesirable pagan past and an attraction to pagan Westerners.

Should we care? Is it any of our darn business what goes on with the antiquities within the borders of another nation? Are we in any way personally related or connected to these things that belong to other cultures in other lands?

Diggers _____

On April 7, 1961, U.S. President John F. Kennedy addressed Congress on the topic of Egypt's threatened monuments:

"The United States, one of the newest of civilizations, has long had a deep regard for the study of past cultures, and a concern for the preservation of man's greatest achievements of art and thoughts; we have also had a special interest in the civilization of ancient Egypt from which many of our own cultural traditions have sprung—and a deep friendship for the people who live in the Valley of the Nile. In keeping with this tradition, and this friendship, I recommend that we now join with other nations through UNESCO in preventing what would otherwise be an irreparable loss to science and the cultural history of mankind .... By thus contributing to the preservation of past civilizations, we will strengthen and enrich our own."

Some people argue that although they themselves might not be Iraqi or Sudanese, they are nonetheless tied to the Sumerians or Nubians as fellow members of the human race. Are we all not ultimately genetically connected? And although our histories are dispersed, does not the human cultural heritage belong to all of us? That's something to think about.

A Little Something for Me?

How about owning antiquities yourself? There are numerous private collectors in this world. Some people collect Roman coins, while others might specialize in classical Greek vases or Mexican ceramic figurines. And some specialize in ancient Egypt. Is there anything wrong with this? Some Egyptologists and archaeologists think so. They contend that the existence of antiquities dealers and the private ownership of antiquities encourage the looting of archaeological sites. And as you know, when an artifact appears without its archaeological context (from where and with what was it found, etc.), much of its meaning is lost!

On the other hand, collectors will argue that owning a piece of the past develops a sincere appreciation for it. Should everything belong in a museum? Only a fraction of a museum's collection is on display, while the rest is warehoused and not immediately accessible to the public at large. Then again, if something is really different, unique, or exquisite, shouldn't the public be able to enjoy it as well? This is a very controversial subject;

> **Nile Notes**
>
> It has been suggested that perhaps archaeologists should stop digging up new things until the monuments already exposed are properly conserved. It has also been proposed that maybe archaeologists wanting to work in Egypt should concentrate on areas under immediate threat of destruction, such as in the Nile Delta, rather than in the drier areas to the south.

some Egyptologists are vehemently against selling antiquities, while a few are employed as experts by the dealers themselves.

Few Easy Solutions

As you can see, there are many practical and ethical problems to consider in dealing with the remains of Egypt's past. Fortunately, an increasing number of projects in Egypt are solely devoted to conservation, and this is a trend that will likely increase. It's a real race against time, but hopefully in the future we will have the advantage of two records of the ancient Egyptian past: the careful work of scholars and, with luck, the actual remains themselves.

The Least You Need to Know

◆ The remains of Egypt's past are finite.

◆ It can be difficult to balance the needs of the present and the future with the desire to preserve the past.

◆ Egypt's antiquities are threatened by both human and natural forces.

◆ Egyptians, along with people from around the world, share an interest in saving the monuments.

◆ There are many difficult ethical questions in archaeology and Egyptology, and few clear answers.

Chapter 21

Exploring Egypt Today

In This Chapter

- ◆ Visiting Egypt
- ◆ Going solo or with a group
- ◆ Getting around and getting along
- ◆ Things not to be missed
- ◆ Tasty food and polite phrases!

It's fun to read about ancient Egypt and to view collections of artifacts in museums, but nothing compares to actually visiting Egypt. You might say that Egypt is one of the world's largest outdoor museums. Surviving remnants of the pharaonic age can be found up and down the Nile, along with signs of the subsequent Graeco-Roman, Christian, and Arab civilizations. If you're considering a trip to this fascinating land, this chapter will help you plan it.

Getting There

Egypt isn't hard to get to. Several major international airlines have regular service to Cairo. Egypt's national airline is called Egypt Air, and it flies from several major international airports and also provides air service within Egypt itself. It's also possible to cross the border from Israel or to take a ferry from Jordan or Greece. Whichever way you arrive, you'll be quickly transported to a lively cultural environment that resembles few elsewhere!

Organized or Independent?

One of the big decisions to make before visiting Egypt is whether to go on your own or as part of an organized tour group. Both approaches have their advantages and disadvantages.

> **Pharaoh's Domain**
>
> Don't be fooled by Egypt's reputation as a hot country. Egypt has its seasons. It can get quite chilly in Cairo during the winter, when there can be torrential downpours in Alexandria and snow in the Sinai mountains! On the other hand, the climate can certainly live up to its reputation in the summer—especially in the south.

Get on the Bus!

If you go on a tour, the planning is done for you. You'll probably be picked up at the airport, taken to hotels, and taken via buses to a variety of sites. You probably won't get lost, and guides will explain what you're seeing. If you don't like traveling with a lot of people or having your life planned, group travel may not appeal to you. Also, you probably won't have many opportunities to interact with many of the wonderful Egyptian people, which is unfortunate. Having said that, a well-organized tour will efficiently take you to the main attractions, and if you fall in love with Egypt, as many people do, you can always come back with a little experience under your belt.

Exploring on Your Own

Many people enjoy the challenge of planning and carrying out their own trip. Fortunately, several good guidebooks are available to help you along. If you choose to go on your own, keep in mind that the national language of Egypt is Arabic. Although you will find many people involved in the tourist industry who can speak at least some English, don't expect that most people will be able to do so. You will be surrounded by signs in Arabic script, and you might find that you will have to be very resourceful, especially if you leave the beaten track of the usual tourist itinerary. On the other hand, if you're patient and adventurous, you can have a truly marvelous experience.

My Two Cents' Worth

I am often asked to advise people on whether to visit Egypt as part of a group or solo. Being the independent type, I generally favor the latter option for myself, but I have also participated in some great tours. For a first-timer without a lot of travel experience outside North America or Europe, I suggest the tour—especially for women traveling alone or in a small group. Again, you will get a good look at the most famous stuff and will have an opportunity to see if this is a place you might want to revisit.

Some tours allow free time so that you can explore a bit on your own. Tourists on their own in any foreign land can "get into trouble," so to speak, in dozens of ways, and a tour will help you avoid such things. However, having spent a great deal of time in Egypt, I love traveling on my own, and the only tour you'll ever see me on is the one where I've been invited to lecture!

The average first-time visitor to Egypt usually sees Cairo, Luxor, maybe Aswan, and sometimes Alexandria. I'll note some of the main attractions of these places, along with a few other locations. Perhaps you'll be sufficiently intrigued to take a look for yourself!

> ### Nile Notes
>
> Admission to most of the ancient attractions of Egypt requires the purchase of an admission ticket. This includes most museums, temples, and tombs.

Cairo

Most tourists to Egypt begin their visit in the capital city, Cairo. For the first-timer, it is often a memorable experience. Millions of people of all walks of life go about their business. Donkey carts often share the road with fast-moving cars and buses, all zigzagging through a wild maze of streets. It's very noisy and it appears chaotic, but it is a kind of organized chaos. It's a modern, growing city and can be a delightful place.

A typical street scene in central Cairo.

(David Moyer collection.)

Tourists can find a wide range of available accommodations, from expensive five-star hotels to fleabag flophouses costing only a few dollars a day. The same goes for restaurants. Most people, if they're not on a tour, get around Cairo in taxis. There are also buses, which tend to be jam-packed, and a modern subway, which is actually quite nice. A good guidebook will provide you with the details. You could spend weeks in Cairo examining its many wonders, but here are just a few of the must-see attractions within the city and on its outskirts, for those interested in ancient Egypt.

The Egyptian Museum

This is truly one of the most amazing museums in the world. Located off Cairo's central square, it is a very large building packed with exquisite items from Egypt's pharaonic past. Gallery after gallery will take you through the ages, and many of the original objects on display will be immediately recognizable to anyone who has taken a course in art history. There are sculptures in wood and stone, coffins, furniture, jewelry, and objects from ancient daily life—and, of course, there is the mummy room (perhaps not for the squeamish).

Some of the highlights, of course, are the treasures from the tomb of Tutankhamun, the gold still gleaming over 3,000 years later. The objects fill a very large gallery. Keep this in mind if you ever visit Tut's tiny tomb in the Valley of the Kings—you'll wonder where they put it all! There is so much in this museum that it's overwhelming; if you have enough time, I recommend a repeat visit.

The facade of the magnificent Egyptian Museum in Cairo, home to a virtual warehouse of ancient Egyptian historic and artistic treasures!

(David Moyer collection.)

The Pyramids at Giza

Giza is located southwest of Cairo and across the Nile. Urban sprawl extends all the way to the limestone plateau, where the pyramids sit in somber contrast to the modern development. The ancient quarrying of the smooth outercasing stones will be immediately apparent, but this does not detract from their impressiveness. A walk around the Great Pyramid will give you a good sense of its size. It's possible to go inside the Great Pyramid (Khufu) as well as those of Khafra and Menkaura, although they're not always all open at the same time.

The Giza plateau consists of more than just the three big pyramids, of course; there are also fields of mastabas and other tombs, some of which are open to tourists. There is also the amazing "solar-boat" found sealed in a pit at the base of the Great Pyramid. The boat itself can be seen in a special museum constructed above where it was discovered at the side of the pyramid. And don't forget the Great Sphinx of Khafra!

> ### Nile Notes
>
> A nightly sound and light show takes place at the pyramids. From seats set in front of the Great Sphinx, a dramatic sound-track accompanies lights that illuminate the pyramids. It's quite a visual spectacle, and the narration is offered in different languages as scheduled. A similar show takes place at the temple complex of Karnak in Luxor.

Sakkara

South from Giza, on the west side of the Nile, is another vast necropolis, that of Sakkara. Here you'll find the famous Step Pyramid of Djoser, a number of other pyramids, and many mastabas. You can't enter the Djoser pyramid itself, but the pyramids of Unas or Teti, both inscribed with funerary texts, might be accessible. The beautifully decorated Old Kingdom mastabas of Meruka, Kagemni, and Ptahhotep are other very popular tourist sites. The famous Serapeum, the astounding subterranean cemetery of the sacred Apis bulls, is also one of the many attractions worth visiting.

The important ancient capital of Memphis lies close to Sakkara, and you can visit what's left of the remains, which isn't much. But there is an open-air museum near the site with some interesting things to see, including a massive statue of Ramesses II.

> ### Diggers
>
> Hassan Ragab, a former Egyptian general and diplomat, reintroduced commercial papyrus plantations into Egypt and opened the Dr. Ragab Papyrus Institute for educational purposes and to sell paper made from the plant. You can find the institute as well as an educational Pharaonic Village—an ancient Egyptian theme park, of sorts—along the Nile near Cairo. Among other attractions, the village offers an intriguing replica of King Tut's tomb, as it was found. By the way, Ragab's success spawned a big industry in rival papyrus purveyors, some of whom use banana leaves or other imitation products and pass them off as the real thing. Beware!

Not Only Pharaohs!

For those who are fascinated with Islamic history and monuments, Cairo has enough to keep you busy for a long time! There are also Christian monuments here and there, especially in a section of the city known as "Old Cairo," and a Coptic Museum. The old Ben Ezra synagogue is also in Cairo and is a rare remnant of Jewish life in Egypt.

Consult a guidebook for the details.

Thebes

If you find Cairo a bit too busy for your tastes, a trip to Luxor might provide a refreshing change of pace. Although it's growing, like all cities in Egypt, Thebes has a relatively small-town atmosphere by Egyptian standards. The main road is a corniche that runs along the Nile, where both cruise boats and sailboats dock, and horse-drawn carriages serve as a transportation choice. As in Cairo, there is a great range of accommodation options and other tourist amenities. Luxor is found on the east bank of the Nile, but the majority of its antiquities are found on the west bank. Let's look at both sides of the river.

Temple Time

Temples are two main ancient attractions on the east bank of the Nile. The Luxor Temple is huge. Even during the day, when its once brightly painted walls appear muddy tan and brown, it is a wonder to behold. And when it is illuminated at night, it can be utterly spectacular!

> **Pharaoh's Domain**
>
> Although most people are aware of Egypt's antiquities, many people aren't aware of the country's great physical beauty. With its green fields, palm trees, rugged deserts and mountains, and the Nile, of course, it is a very pretty place.

The Karnak Temple complex is mind-boggling! The accumulated efforts of dozens of pharaohs created this sprawling mass of pylons, pillars, colossal statues, obelisks, and even a sacred lake. Wandering through Karnak, you will feel just as dwarfed as if you are at the pyramids, and you will be utterly impressed at the engineering and construction skills of the ancients. Many of the walls and columns are covered with inscribed texts and scenes, which have kept Egyptologists and epigraphers busy for decades.

The West Bank

Not to be confused with the notorious West Bank in a neighboring region, this bank of the Nile across from Luxor has one of the largest concentrations of important ancient monuments to be found anywhere in the world. You can reach Luxor by ferry or via a new bridge to the south of town. There wouldn't be room in this book to describe the west bank's numerous sites, so I'll list just some of the more famous ones:

◆ The Colossi of Memnon, two huge seated statues of Amenhotep III, the primary leftovers of what was once a huge mortuary temple to that pharaoh. They almost serve informally as the official greeters to the west bank.

◆ Mortuary temples. The Medinet Habu temple of Rameses III is impressive, but so are those of Rameses II ("the Ramesseum") and that of Seti I, likewise found on the west bank. The most spectacular of all is that of Hatshepsut at Deir el-Bahri, with its architectural sophistication and three terraces of decorated reliefs.

◆ Cemeteries. The west bank includes the royal New Kingdom cemeteries of the Valley of the Kings and the Valley of the Queens. Several tombs in each are usually open to the public. There are also hundreds of private tombs of government officials, priests, and other notables; these are usually grouped under the term "Tombs of the Nobles." There is an immense variety of art in these tombs, and you can visit some that are better preserved and nicely decorated.

◆ Deir el-Medineh, the famous workmen's village for the Valley of the Kings. Apart from admiring the layout of this tiny "town," you can visit some of the small private tombs with their colorful paintings.

Before leaving Luxor, don't miss the wonderful Luxor Museum. Although it is quite small compared to its counterpart in Cairo, it features a nicely displayed selection of special objects.

> **Nile Notes**
>
> Despite the old adage that "those who drink of the Nile will return," this is not a good idea today, especially in Cairo. Most foreigners stick to the bottled water.

On to Aswan

Much quieter and smaller than Cairo or Thebes, Aswan lies to the south and is a real favorite for many people who prefer a slower pace of life. But there is still a lot to see. On an island in the Nile known as "Elephantine" you can see a number of interesting sites, and the excellent new Nubia Museum is well worth a visit. You can visit quarries, including one that holds the famous "Broken Obelisk," an absolutely immense piece of stone that would have been the largest obelisk ever, had it not cracked.

> **Glyphs**
>
> If you visit Egypt, you will become very familiar with the word *baksheesh*. It is basically a tip for services rendered, and some Egyptians will ask you for it after they have done something for you. Although the occasional rascal will ask for baksheesh for no apparent reason, a little tip is a nice reward for someone who has done a nice job.

The giant Aswan Dam and Lake Nasser are south of Aswan. You can see the beautiful temple of Philae, which was saved from the flooding waters caused by the damning of the Nile. Even farther south are the temples of Abu Simbel, which were also saved from the dam and reconstructed on higher ground. You can reach these sites by air, land, or water.

A View from the Deck

The presence of the Nile makes visiting Egypt by boat a nice option. Luxurious cruise ships ply the Nile, especially between Luxor and Aswan. Such boats also travel on Lake Nasser, visiting the temples of Abu Simbel and other temples along the way. You can also have a wonderful time renting a local sailboat, called a *felucca*, at Luxor or Aswan. Such cruises can be absolutely delightful with their nice breeze and beautiful views, especially at sunset.

Pharaoh's Domain

A trip on a felucca sailboat can be great fun, but make sure that you negotiate everything clearly with the captain in advance. Food and drinks are generally not provided. Also, make sure that the wind is blowing, or you'll likely require assistance, and you'll have to pay the towboat!

Nile Notes

Don't let your trip be spoiled by the tourist hustlers. They target the most popular areas, and they can be obnoxious. A persistent "No, thank you" is better than getting angry with them. Just remember, that's "their job," and the overwhelming majority of the Egyptian people are not like them.

And Far to the North

Some people say that the old Greek city of Alexandria has lost its charm. Others say that it is experiencing a rebirth. Either way, reminders of this growing city's once cosmopolitan past remain in its midst. For those interested in the latter days of ancient Egypt, the Graeco-Roman Museum is a great place to visit. And the city's location on the Mediterranean automatically makes it different from any other city along the Nile.

Here and There

Egypt has so much to offer! I am rather fond of the Fayyum region myself, with its lake, agricultural land, and Graeco-Roman ruins. Nice beaches and spectacular diving can be found along the Red Sea Coast. The Sinai Peninsula is also beautiful, and you can visit and climb the traditional mountain of Moses, Mt. Sinai. In the Western Desert, more adventurous folks can visit several alluring oases. And there are many interesting sites along the Nile in the center of the country.

Troubled Times

Until just a few years ago, I thought that Egypt was one of the safest places I have ever been. It still is, but a number of radicals wanting to upset the Egyptian government are attempting to wage their own revolution; occasionally, tourists have been their target. In the late 1990s, several tragic attacks on tourists occurred, the most infamous being the one in November 1997, in which dozens of tourists and Egyptians were murdered at Hatshepsut's mortuary temple at Deir el-Bahri.

The attack had the intended effect of scaring away tourists and damaging Egypt's economy. The Egyptian government responded by massively increasing security for tourists. The attacks have diminished, and tourists are returning in droves. Things are not the same, though. You can't go just anywhere anytime, and visiting areas outside the normal tourist routes might require special permission, along with a military escort. This generally includes most of the area between Cairo and Luxor, home to such worthy sights as El-Amarna and Abydos.

A Great and Noble People

I like the people of Egypt. I have found most to be friendly, extremely generous, and resilient in the face of hard times. Some of the poorest people I have met have been in Egypt, but those same people have been some of the most generous I've ever encountered. Most Egyptians also seem to possess a great sense of humor.

The Egyptians are a friendly and hospitable people!

Pharaoh's Domain

Egypt has its own flair and pace. Don't ever forget that *you are the visitor.* You can't expect things to always be the same as they are at home, to work the same way, or to be accomplished as you see fit. That's what traveling is all about, right?

Egypt is an Islamic country with a Christian minority. Mosques of all sizes can be found everywhere, and the call for prayer can be heard throughout the land four times a day. As a tourist, it's important to learn about the local customs of a country before visiting. As an Islamic nation, Egypt is relatively conservative, and they have tolerated some of the regular ignorant excesses of tourists with great patience. For example, you should not dress as if you just came from a beach resort in Greece or Israel. Do your cultural homework, and then experience the country on its own terms. You'll have a much better and enriching experience if you do so.

Hungry?

I could go on for days about various aspects of Egyptian culture. I won't do that, but at least I'll mention one of my favorites: food! Sure, the hotels offer all the hamburgers and spaghetti you can eat, but I find that a big part of visiting any country is enjoying the native cuisine. Try some of the following tasty delights:

♦ **Kofta**—Ground meat with spices.

♦ **Fool**—Fava beans cooked various ways.

♦ **Tameya**—Known as "felafel" in other places. These are fried bean patties eaten on their own or shoved in a sandwich.

♦ **Schwarma**—Thinly sliced meat mixed with tomatoes or other vegetables and served as a sandwich.

♦ **Koshari**—Macaroni and rice topped with lentils, tomato sauce, and grilled onions.

♦ **Vegetable dishes**—There are loads of them, including okra and zucchini stuffed with rice.

Last, but by no means least, I would like to leave you with a few polite phrases that should be in the vocabulary of foreign visitors, wherever they may roam:

♦ **Hello!**—In the morning, the greeting is *sabah il-khair* (to which the response is usually *sabah il-nour*). In the afternoon/evening, you can say *masa il-khair* (or respond to such a greeting with *masa il-nour*).

♦ **Please**—This differs depending on gender of the person to whom you are speaking. Say *minfadlak* to a male and *minfadlik* to a female.

♦ **Thank you!**—*Shukran!*

◆ **My name is …**—*Ismi …*

◆ **Yes**—*Aywa.*

◆ **No**—*La'a*

◆ **Goodbye!**—*Masalam!*

The Least You Need to Know

◆ Visiting Egypt can be a very rewarding experience.

◆ You can visit Egypt alone or in an organized group.

◆ There is plenty to see in Egypt!

◆ Enjoy the land, the people, their culture, and the monuments.

22

Pursuing Your Interest

In This Chapter

- ◆ What it takes to become a professional Egyptologist
- ◆ The jobs available to Egyptologists
- ◆ How to get a piece of the action
- ◆ A few parting words

It seems that not a week goes by that I don't receive some sort of inquiry from an aspiring Egyptologist. Many are young students who have made their minds up that Egyptology is their true love and chosen profession, at least this month. Others are college students who have become hooked on the subject and are seeking guidance on what to do and where to go next. And then there are adults at various stages of life, some of whom want to fulfill a newly found or lifelong dream.

Yes, Egyptology—and archaeology in general—is a profession that seems almost too good to be true. To the average person, it all sounds like intrigue and adventure. Archaeology certainly has long had that reputation, and our fantasy friend Indiana Jones definitely has enhanced it. In this chapter, we're going to explore what it really means to be an Egyptologist and what the opportunities are out there for those aspiring to join the profession.

So You Want to Be an Egyptologist?

Perhaps another name for this chapter could be "Reality Check," and much of it is the same advice I'd give to someone considering an even broader yet nonetheless esoteric field, such as archaeology. I don't want to be discouraging or overly cynical, but because you were kind enough to buy this book, I'm going to be direct with you. And, after you hear the "this" and the "that," the good and the bad, if you still want to be an Egyptologist, go for it! At least you'll have some idea about what might be in store.

The fact of the matter is, there aren't a lot of jobs to be had in Egyptology. It's one of those fun fields that sounds great but has fairly dismal employment opportunities. Although Egyptology is a wonderful and interesting subject of significant humanistic worth, it only occasionally produces anything of practical economic value. Egyptologists don't regularly discover cures for diseases or invent new products for improving our comfort or efficiency. So let's ask the basic questions: What does it take to reach a professional level in this field, and how do you get a job?

Getting the Basics

To have much of a chance at all in being employed professionally in Egyptology, an advanced degree—that is, a *Ph.D.*—in Egyptology or a related field such as archaeology is practically a necessity. The very first step on the long road to that Ph.D. is to achieve the basic, typically four-year, college diploma known as the Bachelor's degree. The process of achieving this is referred to as "undergraduate education" (as opposed to "graduate"). If you're on the Egyptology track from the very beginning, you might choose one of the schools listed later in this chapter that offer undergraduate courses on or related to Egyptology. Although many colleges and universities do not have a specific Egyptology program, they will have classes on history, art, archaeology, and perhaps a dedicated Egypt course or two. A course in beginning hieroglyphs would be a good start.

Glyphs

Ph.D. means Doctor of Philosophy, and it usually involves demonstrating comprehensive knowledge in a given field and doing original research. A Ph.D. allows you to bear the title "Dr.," but it is different from the kind that makes a lot of money and saves lives. Those people have an M.D., the Doctor of Medicine degree.

Those who want to pursue Egyptian archaeology should take classes in archaeology. Such courses are typically found in anthropology programs in North America, while many European universities have separate archaeology departments. If possible, the budding archaeologist should participate in one of the many field schools offered all over the country (and the world, too) to learn how to excavate while gaining college credit.

Graduate school is really where it happens, though. Entrance to some can be very competitive. The first stage of graduate work is a Master's degree, which usually takes about two years to obtain. This typically involves more advanced coursework and the writing of a research paper or thesis. To get to the next stage, a Ph.D. program, a student usually has to pass a rigorous written, and sometimes oral, exam.

After that, there might be more coursework and a major original research project called a dissertation. It can take anywhere from 2 to 10 years or more to finish a dissertation, depending upon the topic, your level of motivation, and your life circumstances. Many graduate students in big universities receive stipends to do research or teach undergraduate classes, and the money provides enough for them to live on. (So, given the miserable job prospects after they graduate, quite a few take their time.)

Houses of Learning

The following list includes the major North American schools where significant curricula in the field of Egyptology are offered. Many professional Egyptologists in America seem to have their degrees from these typically notable institutions. Don't forget that many other schools offer coursework but not necessarily degrees in this subject.

◆ Brown University, Providence, R.I.

◆ Johns Hopkins University, Baltimore, Md.

◆ Memphis State University, Memphis, Tenn.

◆ New York University, New York, N.Y.

◆ Oriental Institute, University of Chicago, Chicago, Ill.

◆ University of California, Berkeley, Calif.

◆ University of California, Los Angeles, Calif.

◆ University of Pennsylvania, Philadelphia, Penn.

◆ University of Toronto, Toronto, Ontario

◆ Yale University, Cambridge, Mass.

Not for the Linguistically Challenged

I hope you like languages, because you're going to have to be competent in several of them if you hope to be a professional Egyptologist! A firm grasp of ancient Egyptian and its hieroglyphic script is mandatory. The student will often begin with Middle Egyptian and then move on to other stages of the language, such as Old and Late Egyptian and Demotic. Many students also study Coptic. Along with the grammar comes the study and translation of lots of texts, and that's where a good deal of the learning takes place. There will also likely be opportunities to study some texts written in the cursive hieratic script. Some students who want to emphasize Egypt's interactions with other cultures in the Near East might choose also to study Akkadian or even Sumerian (languages of Mesopotamia), or Hebrew (a biblical language). Greek is needed if you want to emphasize the Graeco-Roman period.

We're by no means done yet. The literature of Egyptology is written primarily in English, French, and German. I assume that you have some command over the English language (you're reading this book, aren't you?), but if you can't at least read the other two, you'll have very limited access to the scholarly literature written in the field.

There is a silver lining to this: French and German are key languages. With a knowledge of French, you might be able to figure out written Spanish and Italian with the aid of a dictionary. (I studied Spanish in school as a child, and it made it a lot easier to deal with French!) And with a background of German and English, the Scandinavian languages aren't so hard.

Most graduate schools require only that reading proficiency be demonstrated in French and German, usually by a translation exercise of an Egyptological article or a standardized examination. On the other hand, having a speaking (and listening) ability with these languages really helps when attending international conferences, where scholarly papers are typically presented in the speaker's choice of the three languages.

Do you want to be an archaeologist and dig in Egypt? Guess what? The official language of modern Egypt is Arabic, and, as a foreigner, you can't expect everyone to speak your own language. So, for those working there, at least a survival knowledge of Egyptian colloquial Arabic is extremely helpful in going about your business. Learning the written Arabic script will also facilitate the reading of street signs, building and shop names, and even food labels.

Nile Notes

Although there is a Modern Standard form of Arabic that is widely utilized in official media throughout the Arab world, the spoken forms of the Arabic language vary greatly from region to region. The colloquial forms of Arabic of Morocco, Lebanon, and Saudi Arabia are often quite different than what is spoken in Egypt, with sometimes considerable differences in vocabulary and pronunciation. (There are even dialects within Egypt itself!) So, if it's Egypt you're interested in, make sure that you study colloquial Egyptian Arabic. Modern Standard Arabic might also prove to be an asset in the long run.

I should make it clear that obtaining a Ph.D. specifically in Egyptology is not mandatory for participating in the field. Lots of people who are actively involved have advanced degrees in archaeology, anthropology, ancient history, biology, geology, and other fields. The training described previously, nonetheless, is still very relevant to most. Although I'm first and foremost an archaeologist, I was trained in the ancient and modern languages to facilitate my special interest in Egyptian archaeology.

Get a Job!

After the dissertation is approved by a committee (which can be a tricky political game), you've earned your Ph.D. Hooray! Good job, fancy pants! Now what? Maybe you're 35 years old and you know two things really well: You're the world's foremost expert on an obscure Old Egyptian verbal form, and you might know how to teach an introductory freshman survey course on ancient Egypt. Let's find some work!

Professing: Passing the Torch

Universities are one of the few places where Egyptologists get jobs. What do they do? Generally, they teach Egyptology to produce more Egyptologists, or they teach Egyptology as enrichment or specialty courses, and they conduct research. In the United States, that typically is in a department of Near Eastern languages and civilizations or perhaps even in Classics, Middle East Studies, or Art History. The usual minimum requirement for being hired by a university is a Ph.D. in an appropriate field.

There aren't a lot of job openings in the academic world. If you scrutinize the trade papers, you might find one of the few advertisements. It might be a one-year replacement position at Obscure University for someone with a very specialized background or interests. It could be an inside candidate, someone they already intend to hire, yet the university is legally obliged to go through a national search process. Even so, they get a hundred applications, and the choice might be a tough one.

> **Pharaoh's Domain**
>
> Brown University in Providence, R.I., is the only university in North America with a department devoted exclusively to the study of ancient Egypt. (Egyptology is found within broader departments at other schools.) The Department of Egyptology at Brown offers Bachelor's, Master's, and Ph.D. degrees in the subject.

On the Tenure Track

Yes, it's hard to get a position in the academic world. One of the reasons is a thing called tenure, which guarantees that there won't be a lot of job turnover. Tenured faculty essentially have a job for life. Here is how it works: After you're initially hired, there's usually a four- to six-year probation period during which you are scrutinized for productivity, effectiveness, and a pleasing personality. If you pass, you get tenure; if you don't, few others will want to hire you because you were passed up. Meanwhile, Ph.D.'s continue to be produced, making the competition for those rare jobs even more fierce.

Let's say that you get a job as a faculty member. Depending on the university, you might teach anywhere from one to three classes per quarter or semester. Some schools demand that their professors emphasize research, assisted by graduate students who also teach some of the undergraduate courses. It can be a really easy life, or it can be a miserable drudge, but, either way, you're employed.

> **Nile Notes**
>
> This advice has often been given to people pursuing graduate work in such arcane studies as Egyptology: You should either be independently wealthy or not care about money, because there is no guarantee of any sort of employment afterward.

I've met a few professors who check in about twice a week, teach an hour at a time, disappear to who knows where, and make a tremendous salary. Others can be found working faithfully in their offices all day long, at least six days a week. Many professors work hard at writing grants to provide the funds for their research projects. With a limited amount of money available, the competition can be tight, and often when the grant isn't won, the work doesn't get done.

Community Work

Community colleges typically require only a Master's degree for their faculty, although more are hiring from a growing pool of underemployed Ph.D.'s. Many depend on part-time faculty who might teach one course every quarter to supplement their income. The teaching load is pretty heavy for a full-timer and usually involves introductory classes, but there is usually no demand for research.

I taught at community colleges for a few years, and they had me teaching just about everything but Egyptology, although my background and experience in that subject contributed greatly to those things I was asked to teach, including archaeology, cultural anthropology, physical anthropology, geography, ancient history, and history of the Middle East. So, it helps to be flexible, especially, if you've got a degree in archaeology or Egyptology!

Museums: Minding the Warehouse

Another source of employment for Egyptologists is museums, especially those with collections of Egyptian antiquities. Again, not so many jobs are available, but occasionally they have technical or secondary curator jobs that don't require a Ph.D. Such work might involve studying the museum's collection, caring for and restoring artifacts, dealing with the public, and all sorts of other things.

Museums can be wonderful places to work. If you don't mind staying indoors working with databases and old objects, and if libraries are your thing, then a museum might be for you. If you're artistically inclined, there's work designing new exhibits; if you have a knack for public relations, doing promotional work for the museum might prove fun and challenging.

Museums come in all sizes, from massive institutions such as the Metropolitan Museum of Art in New York City or the Smithsonian in Washington, D.C., to local historical societies in small towns. A few universities even offer courses or degrees in "museology," the study of all aspects of museum work, including general administration, collections management, and exhibitions.

Field Work

So you want to specialize in Egyptian archaeology and excavate in the Land of the Pharaohs? First of all, it's not all fun and games. Much of archaeology is tedious work. Expedition life can be tough and strenuous, and, depending on where the site is located, it can be brutally hot, muggy, and buggy. Given the necessity of careful recording, the work needs to be done very meticulously and requires a great deal of patience. Depending on the site, living conditions can be absolutely spartan or relatively luxurious. There are things that can make you quite ill if you're exposed to them, and if you have an impatient streak, you might find yourself frustrated beyond imagination when things don't quite happen how and when you would expect them to back at home.

In Egypt, most of the manual labor is conducted by hired and supervised workmen. The actual digging, however, is only the tip of the iceberg. Most analysis is conducted in the field and can involve months of sorting bones, scrutinizing little flakes of stone, drawing maps, entering data into a computer, and numerous other tedious jobs. Once the information is all compiled, it needs to be studied and conclusions must be

Pharaoh's Domain

Living conditions during some of the author's various archaeological activities in Egypt have ranged from simple tents in an uninhabited part of the desert and in the hot and humid Nile Delta, a close group-living situation in a rented house in a very rural village, a rented apartment in Cairo, and an air-conditioned hotel with a swimming pool in the Luxor area.

Nile Notes

I recommend to my students that if they choose to pursue Egyptology, archaeology, or some other kind of ancient studies, they should also develop a practical skill that will keep them employed while they are looking for an archaeological job. Certification for teaching is a good option, as are other widely useful occupations.

drawn. This usually involves the preparation of scientific articles, conference papers, and a formal publication presenting the findings of the field work.

Before you write a check to help out your local underemployed archaeologist, keep in mind that Ph.D.'s in all fields are often hired by the government or private sector for their intellectual skills and research and writing abilities. One Egyptologist I know makes his living translating books written in German and French into English, and another owns a company that publishes scholarly books. If it doesn't work out, I suppose that Egyptologists are just as qualified as the next person to flip a few burgers, join the Army, or get a regular job.

The author fitting sandals at Pharaoh's Fine Feminine Footwear. Having an advanced academic degree in a field such as archaeology or Egyptology does not guarantee employment in that field.

Getting a Piece of the Action Anyway

Did I scare you? Good. It's better to be informed with a little jolt of reality than to stumble blindly and idealistically into the dark well of disappointment. I've met a good number of Ph.D.'s, some approaching retirement age, who have never been able to achieve a full career in Egyptology, archaeology, or ancient studies, and a few are disappointed and bitter.

On the other hand, far be it from me to be a dream-squelcher! If you're willing to accept the negative employment possibilities, then, by all means, go for it. Just know what you might be getting into. If it works out, great. And if it doesn't, don't worry about it. Be prepared, and make the best of it.

Avocational Egyptologists

Given the limited employment opportunities, you might be able to argue that it's even better to be an amateur Egyptologist than a professional. That way, you can participate to the extent that you like, without having to deal with the economic uncertainties and much of the politics.

Egyptology is one of those subjects where the "amateur" or avocational participants can often be more enthused than the professionals themselves! And I have met several who are just as well informed. Many are genuine experts on various specific subjects, and some have made significant contributions to the field. Attend an Egyptological conference, and you might find that there are as many, if not more, amateurs in attendance as professionals.

Diggers

Dr. Barbara Mertz received her Ph.D. in Egyptology and had a difficult time finding employment. She turned to writing mystery novels and has had a magnificent career doing just that under the *nom de plumes* of Barbara Michaels and Elizabeth Peters. Under the latter name, her academic background plays a vital role in her series of books featuring Victorian Egyptologist Amelia Peabody.

Volunteering Your Services

Do you want to go on a dig? There are numerous opportunities for that in various parts of the world, but, unfortunately, not many in Egypt. I have received numerous offers by people interested in volunteering on digs in Egypt, and this is the advice I have to share: The Egyptian authorities generally don't allow amateurs or volunteers on archaeological projects. They greatly prefer professionals dealing with their cultural treasures. As far as manual labor is concerned, as previously mentioned, it is traditional to use local workmen, many of whom are skilled professionals and very much appreciate the employment.

Your best bet for participating on a dig in Egypt is as a graduate student or professional in archaeology or Egyptology. It helps if you know or have met the project director because many participants are carefully selected for both ability and compatibility. Here's a big tip: If you can develop a special skill that is very useful on an archaeological dig, you might become needed and even sought after. Such skills might include photography, surveying, technical drawing, and artifact conservation. If you're good enough, you might get your expenses paid or even a small salary, which then makes you, in fact, a professional!

Lost and Found

A friend of mine was an attorney in Los Angeles specializing in immigration cases. His real love, though, was archaeology. In his 40s, he decided to pursue his dream and went to London for a year to study artifact conservation. Now he's having the time of his life and is in demand as a paid professional on a variety of digs.

If you can settle for some dig action in places other than Egypt, many field schools are offered by universities, and there are volunteer programs that usually accept applicants of all ages and walks of life. Such programs can be found at a number of sites in North America, Europe, elsewhere in the Middle East, and other places in the world. Typically, the volunteers pay their own expenses and are well supervised by professionals or graduate students, and often an educational program is provided, including field trips. Some amateur archaeologists have become sufficiently competent that they are allowed to supervise some of the field work, and sometimes they are promoted to bona fide staff members.

Have Some Fun!

Here are some things you can do to enjoy Egyptology as a nonprofessional. (See Appendix B, "Exploring on Your Own: A Select Bibliography"; Appendix C, "Resources for Further Exploration"; and Appendix D, "Egypt Abroad: Museums with Egyptian Collections," for some resource details.)

◆ Read Egyptology and archaeology books.

◆ Subscribe to an appropriate magazine, such as *KMT* and *Archaeology*.

◆ Attend Egyptological lectures and museum exhibitions.

◆ Keep an eye out for Egyptological, archaeological, or historical programs found on educational television channels.

◆ Join local or national Egyptological and archaeological societies or museum associations.

◆ Attend annual or special Egyptological conferences.

◆ Participate in an archaeological field school or volunteer program.

◆ Surf the Web for an increasing amount of Egyptological information.

◆ Offer your abilities to your local Egyptologist or archaeologist as a volunteer assistant. They might say no, but, then again, they might appreciate your help.

◆ Support your favorite projects with your money, assistance, or good wishes.

◆ Get out there. Travel and visit Egypt and Egyptological collections in museums worldwide. There's nothing like seeing the real thing!

The author, "walking like an Egyptian."

See You Later

I hope you have enjoyed learning a little about the fascinating world of ancient Egypt. As I explained in the introduction, we can only scratch the surface in a book such as this. In fact, whole books have been written about some of the things we had to cover in a single paragraph. If anything here has caught your interest, check out Appendix B for some suggestions for further reading, and see Appendix C for even more resources. Appendix D lists some of the museums with Egyptian collections.

In terms of the future, there will probably always be a place for Egyptology. We will probably never know all there is to know, and it's unlikely that we will solve all the enduring mysteries. There is a wealth of insight still to be gained. And in a land of so many surprises, we can expect the long stream of surprises to continue for a good many years, if not generations, to come. I hope you're as excited as I am to see what turns up next! Good luck!

The Least You Need to Know

◆ Professional Egyptologists are typically employed at universities and museums, but some find jobs in private or government sectors.

◆ The job prospects for Egyptologists are not great.

◆ There are many excellent resources and opportunities for the nonprofessional to enjoy and participate in Egyptology.

◆ Whether you're an amateur or professional, the study of Egyptology and archaeology is still one of the most interesting fields around!

Glossary

A.D. *Anno Domini*, or "the year of our Lord." The number of years since the birth of Jesus.

akh The "effective" spirit who has successfully passed into the afterlife.

Amarna Period The period within the Egyptian Eighteenth Dynasty of the New Kingdom, characterized by the religious and cultural phenomena of Akhenaten and his immediate successors.

anthropomorphic To have the physical form of a human.

archaeology The interdisciplinary study of the human past.

ba An Egyptian spiritual concept that can be roughly translated as one's soul. The ba was often depicted as a bird with a human head.

baksheesh A word often heard by tourists in Egypt. It is basically a tip for services rendered, usually spoken as a request.

B.C. "Before Christ." Refers to the number of years before the birth of Jesus.

B.C.E. "Before the Common Era." Refers to the same time period as B.C.

B.P. "Before Present." The number of years prior to the present. Essentially, it means "years ago."

canopic jars Four jars, usually made of stone, which held the mummified liver, stomach, intestines, and lungs of the deceased.

cartouche An oval-shaped symbol that contains the hieroglyphs for the names of Egyptian royalty.

C.E. "Common Era"—the equivalent of A.D., or the number of years since the birth of Jesus.

cenotaph A memorial tomb established for an individual who is actually buried elsewhere.

circa "Around that time." Usually abbreviated "ca." or "c."

complex society A society characterized by such features as class, wealth, and status differences; political, economic, and religious elites; craft specialists; relatively large populations; monumental architecture; and usually writing.

Coptic The last vestige of the Ancient Egyptian language, which survives as the liturgical language of the Christian orthodox Coptic church of Egypt. Members of this church are called Copts, and Coptology is the study of that language and the history and theology of the Coptic church.

coregency A practice in which a royal successor is chosen and rules alongside the reigning king to ensure a competent transition from one to the other.

cuneiform A wedge-shaped script typically impressed into clay tablets and characteristic of Mesopotamia and other ancient cultures in the surrounding region.

Duat The Egyptian netherworld or land of the dead.

dynasty A ruling line of related kings.

Egyptology The study of ancient Egypt.

Egyptomania The fascination with the culture of ancient Egypt.

Ennead The first group of nine gods from Egyptian creation, consisting of Atum, Shu and Tefnut, Geb and Nut, Osiris and Isis, and Seth and Nephthys.

epigraphy The art of recording inscriptions. An epigrapher is one who does such.

Exodus The second book in the Old Testament/Hebrew Bible that records the story of the enslavement of the Hebrew people in Egypt and their subsequent divine deliverance.

faience A type of ceramic material made from quartz, which was typically glazed in blue or green in the form of amulets and funerary figurines.

Genesis The first book of the Old Testament/Hebrew Bible that, among other things, contains the story of Joseph in Egypt.

Graeco-Roman Period or Graeco-Roman Egypt The time period during which Greeks and Romans ruled Egypt, beginning in 332 B.C. with the invasion of Alexander the Great through the period of the Roman emperors.

Heb-sed festival A ritual to demonstrate the continuing vitality of the ruler.

Hellenistic   An adjective referring to those things that are Greek.

hieratic   A cursive form of the Egyptian hieroglyphic script.

hieroglyphic   An adjective referring to a script that uses hieroglyphs.

hieroglyphs   The formal Egyptian writing system.

inundation   The annual flooding of the Nile River, which produced a regular renewal of agricultural land.

ka   An Egyptian concept referring to one's life force.

maat   The Egyptian concept of truth, justice, and cosmic order, represented by a goddess, often portrayed with a feather upon her head.

mastaba   An Arabic word meaning "bench," referring to rectangular-shaped tombs.

Mitzraim   The Hebrew word for Egypt.

monotheism   The belief in and worship of one god.

natron   A naturally occurring white chemical substance that was used in the mummification process as a dehydrating agent

necropolis   A cemetery—literally, a "city of the dead."

Neolithic   A period when the hunting and gathering lifestyle gave way to permanent settlements and the tending of plants and animals.

nomarchs   The leaders or governors of nomes.

nomes   The various provinces of Upper and Lower Egypt.

obelisk   A rectangular stone spire with a pyramid top.

ostracon (plural: ostraca)   A piece of broken pottery or a flake of stone that serves as a writing surface.

Paleolithic   The "Old Stone Age," characterized by the use of stone tools and hunting and gathering, extending from about 2 million years ago to 10,000 years ago, roughly corresponding to the Pleistocene geological epoch.

papyriform   A word used to describe wooden boats that are similar in shape to old papyrus vessels, most notably by their upturned bow and stern.

papyrology   The study of (primarily Greek) papyrus documents, typically from Egypt.

papyrus (plural: papyri)   A kind of paper manufactured from the inner pith of the papyrus plant, *Cyperus papyrus*. An individual document written on such paper is known as a papyrus.

Pesach   Also known as Passover, one of the most important of the Jewish holidays and commemorates the Exodus story.

polytheism   The worship of many gods.

prehistory   The course of human events before the time of writing. It is often studied by archaeologists who are referred to as prehistorians.

sarcophagus   A stone box for holding coffins and mummies.

serekh   A rectangular palace façade motif in which was written the names of many of the earlier kings of Egypt.

shabti   A servant figurine placed in tombs to do the bidding of the deceased in the after-life (also called "ushabti" or "shawabti").

stele (plural stelae)   A wooden or stone tablet usually bearing inscriptions.

tell   A mound representing the accumulated debris of past human settlement. Also sometimes called a "kom."

vizier   The highest office in the Egyptian governmental hierarchy below the king. A sort of a prime minister.

Exploring on Your Own: A Select Bibliography

Books, obviously, are an essential resource, especially if you do not have ready access to Egyptological museums or organizations. You should be aware that the scholarly or technical literature on the subject is commonly written not only in English, but in German and French as well. Articles in other languages (particularly Italian, Dutch, Spanish, and Arabic) also can be found. Reading ability in French and German is a basic requirement of students seeking graduate degrees in Egyptology.

Fortunately, though, there are many excellent volumes in English for those without facility in foreign languages, and I am pleased to report that many Egyptologists are not only good scholars, but good writers as well. Following, listed in categories (alphabetically by author's name), are recommended books that people new to the study of ancient Egypt might find useful and enjoyable. You can find them at your local library or order them from your favorite bookstore.

To facilitate its procurement, I have attempted to list the publisher and date of the latest edition for a given title. Note that many of the same titles are published both in the United States and in Britain by publishers with offices in both countries or by affiliated presses (for example, Oxford University Press in New York).

Also be aware of the preponderance of books by E. A. Wallis Budge regularly found in bookshops. Budge (1857–1934) was a talented English scholar who authored more than 130 works on Egyptian and other Near Eastern subjects. Many of his books with attractive titles have been reprinted in recent years after entering the public domain. Although a few of the volumes contain information of current value, many are sadly out-of-date.

Introductions and References

Aldred, Cyril. *The Egyptians.* 3rd ed. New York: Thames & Hudson, 1998. (A nice introduction recently revised by Egyptologist Aidan Dodson.)

Baines, John, and Jaromir Malek. *Cultural Atlas of Ancient Egypt.* New York: Checkmark Books, 2000. (Maps are plentiful, as are concise site descriptions.)

Hayes, William C. *The Scepter of Egypt.* 2 vols. New York: Metropolitan Museum of Art, 1990. (A classic survey of ancient Egyptian history and culture, amply illustrated by artifacts in the collection of the Metropolitan Museum of Art.)

Hobson, Christine. *The World of the Pharaohs.* New York: Thames & Hudson, 1998. (Well-illustrated volume offering immense variety: biographical portraits of Egyptologists, site descriptions, and a little of nearly everything else.)

James, T. G. H. *Ancient Egypt: the Land and Its Legacy.* Chicago: Kazi, 1999. (The former Keeper of Egyptian Antiquities at the British Museum takes a personal view of the ancient sites along the Nile, considered geographically, north to south, rather than chronologically.)

Manley, Bill. *The Penguin Historical Atlas of Ancient Egypt.* New York: Viking Penguin, 1996. (Great maps and short chapters on a variety of subjects.)

Nicholson, Paul, and Ian Shaw. *The Dictionary of Ancient Egypt.* New York: Abrams, 1995.

Redford, Donald, ed. *The Oxford Encyclopedia of Ancient Egypt.* New York: Oxford University, 2001. (Just-published three-volume encyclopedia loaded with articles written by the experts. It is very expensive, but it will probably be available for consultation in many university libraries.)

Quirke, Stephen, and Jeffrey Spencer. *The British Museum Book of Ancient Egypt.* New York: Thames & Hudson, 1996. (History, religious beliefs, arts and crafts, and other topics are nicely summarized in this volume keyed to the Egyptian collection of the British Museum.)

Silverman, David, ed. *Ancient Egypt.* New York: Oxford University, 1997.

Teeter, Emily, and Douglas Brewer. *Egypt and the Egyptians*. New York: Cambridge University, 1999.

Travel Guides

A number of decent travel guides are useful if you are planning a visit to Egypt. Here are a few that serve as detailed and authoritative guides to the antiquities sites:

Lane, Mary Ellen. *A Guide to the Antiquities of the Fayyum*. Cairo: American University in Cairo, 1985.

Murnane, William. *Penguin Guide to Ancient Egypt*. New York: Penguin, 1983. (An excellent guide by the late, great Professor Murnane.)

Seton-Williams, V., and P. Stocks. *Blue Guide: Egypt*. New York: Norton, 1983.

Strudwick, Nigel, and Helen Strudwick. *Thebes in Egypt: A Guide to the Tombs and Temples of Ancient Luxor*. Ithaca: Cornell University, 1999.

Jill Kamil has written several good regionally specific guides to Egypt published by the American University in Cairo and others. Titles include: *Luxor*, *Sakkara*, *Upper Egypt*, *Aswan and Abu Simbel*, *Coptic Egypt*, *Monastery of St. Catherine*, and *Sinai*.

History

Bowman, Alan. *Egypt After the Pharaohs*. Berkeley: University of California, 1996. (Describes the period from Alexander to the Arab Conquest.)

Davies, Vivian, and Renee Friedman. *Egypt Revealed*. New York: Stewart Tabori & Chang, 1998. (Contemporary research and great photos.)

Emery, W. B. *Archaic Egypt*. New York: Penguin, 1984. (A study of Egypt's first two dynasties.)

Gardiner, Alan. *Egypt of the Pharaohs*. New York: Oxford University, 1968. (A classic work by a great scholar.)

Grimal, N. *A History of Ancient Egypt*. Oxford: Blackwell, 1994.

Hoffman, Michael. *Egypt Before the Pharaohs*. Austin: University of Texas, 1990. (A very readable book on the thousands of years of human occupation in Egypt leading up to the establishment of civilization.)

Hornung, Erik. *History of Ancient Egypt: An Introduction.* Translated by David Lorton. Ithaca: Cornell University, 1999. (Short and sweet).

Kemp, Barry. *Egypt: Anatomy of a Civilization.* New York: Routledge, 1992.

Malek, Jaromir, and W. Forman. *In the Shadow of the Pyramids: Egypt During the Old Kingdom.* Norman: University of Oklahoma, 1992. (Excellent text illustrated by superb photography.)

Mertz, Barbara. *Temples, Tombs, and Hieroglyphs: A Popular History of Ancient Egypt.* New York: P. Bedrick Books, 1990.

Mysliwiec, Karol. *The Twilight of Ancient Egypt: First Millennium B.C.E.* Translated by David Lorton. Ithaca: Cornell University Press, 2000.

Shaw, Ian, ed. *The Oxford History of Ancient Egypt.* New York: Oxford University, 2000. (New, and perhaps destined to be a standard reference.)

Spencer, A. J. *Early Egypt: The Rise of Civilization in the Nile Valley.* Norman: University of Oklahoma, 1995.

Steindorff, G., and K. Steele. *When Egypt Ruled the East.* 2nd ed. Chicago: University of Chicago, 1963. (The rise and fall of imperial Egypt.)

Trigger, B., Kemp, B., O'Connor, D., and A. Lloyd. *Ancient Egypt: A Social History.* New York: Cambridge University, 1983. (Four excellent scholars produced an insightful history of Egypt from prehistoric times through the Late Period.)

Historical Characters

Aldred, Cyril. *Akhenaten: King of Egypt.* New York: Thames & Hudson, 1991. (A classic work reprinted.)

Clayton, Peter. *Chronicle of the Pharaohs.* New York: Thames & Hudson, 1994. (All the pharaohs, dynasty by dynasty.)

Fletcher, Joann. *Chronicle of a Pharaoh: The Intimate Life of Amenhotep III.* New York: Oxford University, 2000.

Hornung, Erik. *Akhenaten and the Religion of Light.* Translated by David Lorton. Ithaca: Cornell University Press, 1999.

Kitchen, Kenneth. *Pharaoh Triumphant.* Warminster, U.K.: Aris and Phillips, 1983. (Everything you always wanted to know about Rameses II.)

Quirke, Stephen. *Who Were the Pharaohs?* London: British Museum, 1990. (Names, titles, and cartouches.)

Redford, Donald. *Akhenaten: The Heretic King.* Princeton: Princeton University, 1984. (Akhenaten by a man who knows him well.)

Rice, Michael. *Who's Who in Ancient Egypt.* New York: Routledge, 1999. (Not just the kings, but a lot of other people as well.)

Tyldesley, Joyce. *Hatshepsut: The Female Pharaoh.* New York: Viking Penguin, 1998.

———. *Nefertiti: Egypt's Sun Queen.* New York: Viking Penguin, 2000.

Archaeological Sites

Bierbrier, Morris. *The Tomb Builders of the Pharaohs.* New York: Macmillan, 1985. (Deir el Medina, the village of the tomb builders.)

Edwards, I. E. S. *The Pyramids of Egypt.* New York: Penguin, 1987.

Hawass, Zahi. *Valley of the Golden Mummies.* New York: Abrams, 2000. (A wonderfully illustrated book about one of the latest big discoveries in Egypt.)

Jenkins, Nancy. *The Boat Beneath the Pyramid.* New York: Thames & Hudson, 1980. (Story of the first boat found entombed at the base of the Great Pyramid of Khufu.)

Lauer, Jean-Phillipe. *Saqqara.* New York: Thames & Hudson, 1976. (The Old Kingdom necropolis of Memphis.)

Lehner, Mark. *The Complete Pyramids.* New York: Thames & Hudson, 1997. (An excellent survey by a foremost expert on the subject.)

Manniche, Lise. *City of the Dead.* Chicago: University of Chicago, 1987. (The Theban necropolis revealed.)

Martin, Geoffrey T. *The Hidden Tombs of Memphis.* New York: Thames & Hudson, 1992. (Discoveries of New Kingdom tombs at Sakkara.)

Reeves, C. N. *The Complete Tutankhamun*. New York: Thames & Hudson, 1995. (There are many books about Tut's tomb, but this one is especially recommended.)

Reeves, C. N., and Richard Wilkinson. *The Complete Valley of the Kings*. New York: Thames & Hudson, 1996.

Romer, John. *Valley of the Kings*. New York: H. Holt and Company, 1994.

Strudwick, Nigel, and Helen Strudwick. *Thebes in Egypt: A Guide to the Tombs and Temples of Ancient Luxor*. Ithaca: Cornell University, 1999.

History of Exploration

Adkins, Leslie, and Roy Adkins. *The Keys of Egypt: The Obsession to Decipher Egyptian Hieroglyphs*. New York: HarperCollins, 2000.

Clayton, Peter. *The Rediscovery of Ancient Egypt*. New York: Thames & Hudson, 1982. (The ruins of ancient Egypt, as recorded by artists and writers during the last two centuries.)

Dawson, W., Uphill, E., and Morris Bierbrier. *Who Was Who in Egyptology*. 3rd ed. London: Egypt Exploration Society, 1995. (An excellent reference work containing short biographies and bibliographies of persons involved in the exploration and study of ancient Egypt, from circa 1500–1995 A.D. It does not include individuals still living in 1995.)

Drower, Margaret. *Flinders Petrie: A Life in Archaeology*. Madison: University of Wisconsin, 1995. (An excellent biography of William Matthew Flinders Petrie, a truly unique figure who excavated numerous ancient sites in Egypt and revolutionized archaeological method and theory.)

Forbes, Dennis C. *Tombs, Treasures, Mummies*. Sebastopol, Calif.: KMT Communication, 1998. (Seven magnificent discoveries comprehensively examined in text and photos.)

Greener, Leslie. *The Discovery of Egypt*. New York: Marboro, 1990. (Travelers, adventurers, and scholars in the land of the pharaohs from Roman times through the nineteenth century.)

James, T. G. H., ed. *Excavating in Egypt*. Chicago: University of Chicago, 1997. (The fascinating story of the first 100 years of the Egypt Exploration Society.)

James, T. G. H. *Howard Carter: The Path to Tutankhamun.* New York: Columbia University, 1992. (The true story of the remarkable man who found King Tut's tomb.)

Reeves, C. N. *Ancient Egypt: The Great Discoveries.* New York: Thames & Hudson, 2000. (A large selection of amazing discoveries, well illustrated and arranged chronologically in order of their finding.)

Wilson, John. *Signs and Wonders Upon Pharaoh.* Chicago: University of Chicago, 1964. (A history of the earlier days of American Egyptology.)

Daily Life

Many of the general introductory works listed previously discuss the daily living conditions of the ancient Egyptians. The books noted here specifically deal with daily life or various aspects thereof.

Andreu, Guillemette. *Egypt in the Age of the Pyramids.* Translated by David Lorton. Ithaca: Cornell University Press, 1997.

David, Rosalie. *The Pyramid Builders of Ancient Egypt.* New York: Routledge, 1997.

Decker, Wolfgang. *Sports and Games of Ancient Egypt.* Translated by Allen Guttmann. New Haven: Yale University Press, 1992.

Houlihan, Patrick. *The Animal World of the Pharaohs.* New York: Thames & Hudson, 1997.

James, T. G. H. *Pharaoh's People.* Chicago: University of Chicago, 1994. (An excellent discussion of Egyptian society at different levels during the New Kingdom.)

Janssen, Rosalind, and Jac. Janssen. *Growing Up in Ancient Egypt.* London: Rubicon, 1996.

———. *Getting Old in Ancient Egypt.* London: Rubicon, 1996.

Malek, Jaromir. *The Cat in Ancient Egypt.* Philadelphia: University of Pennsylvania, 1997.

Manniche, Lise. *Music and Musicians in Ancient Egypt.* London: British Museum, 1991.

Mertz, Barbara. *Red Land, Black Land: Daily Life in Ancient Egypt.* New York: P. Bedrick Books, 1990.

Nunn, John. *Ancient Egyptian Medicine.* Norman: University of Oklahoma, 1996.

Partridge, Robert. *Transport in Ancient Egypt.* London: Rubicon, 1996.

Robins, Gay. *Women in Ancient Egypt.* Cambridge: Harvard University, 1993.

Romer, John. *Ancient Lives.* New York: H. Holt and Co., 1990. (The lives and times of the workmen who labored on the royal tombs in the Valley of the Kings, as reconstructed from the remains of their village at modern-day Deir el Medina.)

Steed, Miriam. *Egyptian Life.* Cambridge: Harvard University, 1986. (Well written and illustrated; based upon the British Museum collection of Egyptian antiquities.)

Tyldesley, Joyce. *Daughters of Isis: Women of Ancient Egypt.* New York: Viking Penguin, 1995.

Language and Hieroglyphs

Allen, James. *Middle Egyptian: An Introduction to the Language and Culture of Hieroglyphs.* New York: Cambridge University, 2000. (New, and already highly regarded. The book is more up to date than Gardiner's Grammar, and each lesson ends with an essay on an aspect of Egyptian culture.

Collier Mark, and Bill Manley. *How to Read Egyptian Hieroglyphs.* Berkeley: University of California, 1998. (A best-seller in Britain.)

Davies, W. V. *Egyptian Hieroglyphs.* Berkeley: University of California, 1987. (An excellent short introduction to the ancient Egyptian language from the present Keeper of Egyptian Antiquities at the British Museum. This inexpensive volume is part of the outstanding "Reading the Past" series published by that museum and the University of California.)

Fisher, H. *Ancient Egyptian Calligraphy: A Beginner's Guide to Writing Hieroglyphs.* New York: Metropolitan Museum of Art, 1983. (Learn how to draw those 'glyphs!)

Gardiner, Alan. *Egyptian Grammar.* 3rd ed. Warminster, U.K.: Aris and Phillips, 1978. (For decades, this volume has been the standard textbook and reference grammar for serious students of Egyptology. Though not particularly casual reading, beginners might especially find useful the introduction and the essays on royal titles and numbers, and the list of hieroglyphic signs.)

Malek, Jaromir. *ABC of Egyptian Hieroglyphs.* Oxford: Ashmolean Museum, 1994. (A great little book—and it's not just for kids!)

Parkinson, Richard, and Stephen Quirke. *Papyrus*. Austin: University of Texas, 1995. (Paper and writing.)

Zauzich, Karl-Theodor. *Hieroglyphs Without Mystery: An Introduction to Ancient Egyptian Writing*. Translated by Ann Roth. Austin: University of Texas, 1992.

One more recommendation: If you decide to get serious about studying hieroglyphs, it's good to have a dictionary. A standard volume used by most students (and professionals) is Raymond Faulkner's *Concise Dictionary of Middle Egyptian* (Warminster, U.K.: Aris and Phillips, 1976).

Literature

Foster, John L. *Love Songs of the New Kingdom*. Austin: University of Texas, 1992. (Modern translations of ancient romantic poetry.)

Lichtheim, Miriam, ed. *Ancient Egyptian Literature*. 3 vols. Berkeley: University of California, 1980-1996. (Each of the volumes deals with a chronological period and offers a wide range of texts in translation: volume 1: the Old and Middle Kingdoms; volume 2: the New Kingdom; volume 3: the Late Period.)

Parkinson, R. B. *Voices from Ancient Egypt: An Anthology of Middle Kingdom Writings*. London: British Museum, 1991. (A truly diverse collection of texts from various contexts.)

Simpson, W. K., ed. *The Literature of Ancient Egypt An Anthology of Stories, Instructions, and Poetry*. New Haven: Yale University, 1973. (A handy one-volume assemblage of some of ancient Egypt's best-known and most important literary works.)

Wente, Edward. *Letters from Ancient Egypt*. Atlanta: Scholars Press, 1990. (A fine collection of surviving letters from the Old Kingdom through the Twenty-first Dynasty.)

Religion

Assmann, Jan. *The Search for God in Ancient Egypt*. Translated by David Lorton. Ithaca: Cornell University Press, 2001.

Lesko, Barbara. *The Great Goddesses of Egypt*. Norman: University of Oklahoma, 1999.

Forman, Werner, and Stephen Quirke. *Hieroglyphs and the Afterlife in Ancient Egypt*. Norman: University of Oklahoma, 1996.

Hornung, Erik. *Conceptions of God in Ancient Egypt: The One and the Many.* Translated by John Baines. Ithaca: Cornell University, 1996. (An examination of the nature of ancient Egyptian deities.)

———. *The Ancient Egyptian Books of the Afterlife.* Translated by David Lorton. Ithaca: Cornell University, 1999.

———. *Idea into Image: Essays on Ancient Egyptian Thought.* Translated by Elizabeth Bredeck. New York: Timken, 1992.

Meeks, Dimitri and Christine Favard-Meeks. *Daily Life of the Egyptian Gods.* Translated by G. M. Goshgarian. Ithaca: Cornell University Press, 1996.

Pinch, Geraldine. *Magic in Ancient Egypt.* Austin: University of Texas, 1995.

Morenz, Siegfried. *Egyptian Religion.* Translated by Ann Keep. Ithaca: Cornell University, 1992.

Quirke, Stephen. *Ancient Egyptian Religion.* London: British Museum Press, 1992.

Sauneron, Serge. *The Priests of Ancient Egypt.* Translated by David Lorton. Ithaca: Cornell University Press, 2000.

Shafer, Byron E., ed. *Religion in Ancient Egypt: Gods, Myths, and Personal Practice.* Ithaca: Cornell University Press, 1991.

———. *Temples of Ancient Egypt.* Ithaca: Cornell University Press, 1997.

Taylor, John. *Death and the Afterlife in Ancient Egypt.* Chicago: University of Chicago, 2001.

Traunecker, Claude. *The Gods of Egypt.* Translated by David Lorton. Ithaca: Cornell University Press, 2001.

Wilkinson, Richard. *The Complete Temples of Ancient Egypt.* New York: Thames & Hudson, 2000.

Mummies

And for those of you fascinated by ancient Egyptian mummies:

Andrews, Carol. *Egyptian Mummies.* London: British Museum, 1998.

Brier, Bob. *Egyptian Mummies: Unraveling the Secrets of an Ancient Art*. London: Brockhampton, 1996.

David, Rosalie, and Rich Archbold. *Conversations with Mummies*. New York: HarperCollins, 2000.

Ikram, Salima, and Aidan Dodson. *The Mummy in Ancient Egypt*. New York: Thames & Hudson, 1998. (A well-illustrated and fascinating book.)

Spencer, A. J. *Death in Ancient Egypt*. New York: Penguin, 1983.

Art and Architecture

Aldred, Cyril. *Egyptian Art*. New York: Thames & Hudson, 1985.

Andrews, Carol. *Ancient Egyptian Jewelry*. New York: Abrams, 1997.

Curl, James. *Egyptomania: The Egyptian Revival*. Manchester, U.K.: Manchester University, 1994. (The influence of ancient Egyptian art and architecture during recent centuries.)

James, T. G. H., and W. V. Davies. *Egyptian Sculpture*. Cambridge: Harvard University, 1983.

James, T. G. H. *Egyptian Painting*. Cambridge: Harvard University, 1986.

Malek, Jaromir. *Egyptian Art*. London: Phaidon, 1999.

Robins, Gay. *The Art of Ancient Egypt*. Cambridge: Harvard University, 2000.

Smith, W. S., and W. K. Simpson. *Art and Architecture of Ancient Egypt*. New Haven: Yale University, 1998.

Wilkinson, Richard. *Reading Egyptian Art*. New York: Thames & Hudson, 1994.

——. *Symbol and Magic in Egyptian Art*. New York: Thames & Hudson, 2000.

Of General Interest

Shire Publications (Princes Risborough, U.K.) publishes a series of little, inexpensive, and typically well-written volumes on a variety of topics in its "Shire Egyptology Series," including: *Predynastic Egypt, Protodynastic Egypt, Rock-cut Tombs, Graeco-Roman Egypt, Textiles, Pottery, Household Animals, Metalworking and Tools, Woodworking and Furniture, Medicine, Warfare and Weapons, Coffins, Models and Scenes, Boats and Ships, Gods and Myths, Akhenaten's Egypt, Towns and Cities, Tutankhamun's Egypt,* and *Food and Drink.* More information is available on the Shire Publications Web site, www.shirebooks.co.uk/ Egyptology/egyptology-bl.htm.

Gerald Duckworth and Company, in London, has begun reprinting some classic Egyptological volumes, including G. Elliot Smith's *Royal Mummies* (1912) and Howard Carter's *Tomb of Tut-ankh-amen* (1923–33). The publisher's address and Web site are: 61 Frith St., London W1V 5TA, U.K., www.ducknet.co.uk.

For A Good Time ...

In Chapter 18, "Egyptomania!" I mentioned some of the Egyptological fiction. The Amelia Peabody mystery tales authored by Elizabeth Peters are especially charming and well researched. Peters is a pen name of Egyptologist Barbara Mertz (author of *Red Land, Black Land* and *Temples, Tombs, and Hieroglyphs,* mentioned previously). Peters/Mertz has many fans and even some Web pages dedicated to her work—for example, see www.mpm-books.com.

Illustrated Books

And for your coffee table, here are some big and beautiful books:

Arnold, Dorothea, et al. *Egyptian Art in the Age of Pyramids.* New Haven: Yale University, 1999. (Superb photos and excellent articles.)

James, T. G. H. *Tutankhamun.* Vercelli, It.: White Star, 2000. (Absolutely stunning! Magnificent photos accompanied by authoritative text.)

Schulz, Regine, and Matthias Seidel, eds. *Egypt: The World of the Pharaohs.* Küln, Ger.: Koünemann, 1998.

Siliotti, Alberto. *Egypt Lost and Found: Explorers and Travelers on the Nile.* New York: Stewart, Tabori & Chang, 1999.

Teradritti, Francesco, ed. *Egyptian Treasures from the Egyptian Museum in Cairo.* Vercelli, It.: White Star, 2000. (An outstanding sample of the Egyptian Museum's wonderful collection.)

Resources for Further Exploration

Apart from books, a number of other resources are available to help you pursue your Egyptological interests. There are magazines and organizations, and the Internet has an ever-growing number of sites devoted to Egypt and archaeology. In this appendix, you'll find some of the better resources. Keep in mind that the information is skewed mostly toward North America, but I can assure you that Egyptology is very big in Britain and many other places around the world!

Magazines

KMT Magazine debuted in 1990 and offers an outstanding variety of interesting articles and news for the ancient Egypt enthusiast. The magazine is available at select newsstands and museum bookshops, or by writing to KMT Communications, P.O. Box 1475, Sebastopol, CA 95473-1475. You can visit the magazine's Web site at www.egyptology.com/kmt.

Egypt Revealed is quite new and offers colorfully illustrated articles. Find it at a newsstand, visit the Web site www.egyptrevealed.com. You also can order a subscription by calling 1-800-870-9364.

Other subscription or newsstand periodicals that carry occasional articles on ancient Egypt include: *Archaeology, Archaeology Odyssey, Discovering Archaeology, Near Eastern Archaeology* (formerly *Biblical Archaeologist*), *Biblical Archaeology Review*, and *Minerva*.

The American Research Center in Egypt, the Egypt Exploration Society, and the Society for the Study of Egyptian Antiquities all publish scholarly journals and other materials as well.

Organizations

The following organizations cater to people with a special interest in Egypt. Membership includes newsletters and journals, and attending organization functions is a great way to hear the latest research news and to meet others with an interest in Egypt.

The American Research Center in Egypt supports scholarly work dealing with both ancient and modern Egypt. The organization maintains a research facility in Cairo that assists individual scholars and expeditions with their projects. Membership in ARCE includes a subscription to the quarterly newsletter, *NARCE*, and the annual journal, *JARCE*. The annual meeting of the Center is *the* function in North America to attend the latest Egyptological research. Contact ARCE at:

American Research Center in Egypt
Emory University West Campus
1256 Briarcliff Road, NE, Building A, Suite 423W
Atlanta, GA 30306
www.arce.org

Regional ARCE chapters sponsor local lectures and often invite professional Egyptologists to speak. Currently there are active chapters in Southern California, Northern California (hometown.aol.com/hebsed/index.htm), Arizona (www.arizona.edu/~egypt/ARCE_AZ.htm), North Texas (www.arce-ntexas.org), and Washington, D.C. (www.arcedc.org).

The Egypt Exploration Society was begun in 1882. This London-based organization sponsors archaeological exploration in Egypt and publishes the annual *Journal of Egyptian Archaeology* and a color bulletin, *Egyptian Archaeology*, which appears twice a year. The society also offers a variety of other excellent scholarly publications. Even though those living outside Great Britain might not be able to attend the regular lectures and other society activities, the journal, bulletin, and book discounts that are a benefit of membership, make joining the EES quite worthwhile. Besides, you'll be supporting a lot of great work! The society's address is:

Egypt Exploration Society
3 Doughty Mews
London WC1N 2PG
United Kingdom
britac3.britac.ac.uk/institutes/egypt/index.html

The Society for the Study of Egyptian Antiquities is a Canadian organization that publishes a newsletter and journal. The SSEA holds Egyptological lectures and an annual symposium (in November). For more information, write to:

Society for the Study of Egyptian Antiquities
Box 578, Postal Station P
Toronto, Ontario M5S 2T1
Canada
www.geocities.com/ssea.geo

Although based in Toronto, the society maintains regional chapters in Calgary (www.geocities.com/ssea.geo/calgary.html) and Montreal (go.to/ssea_mtl), Canada.

The Ancient Egypt Study Association is located in the Pacific Northwest and hosts lectures, study groups, and other activities. The association is quite active: It holds meetings in both the Portland and Seattle areas and publishes a quarterly newsletter, *The Scroll*. Contact the association at:

Ancient Egypt Study Association
927 NE 175th Ave.
Portland, OR 97230
www.aesa-nw.org

The energetic Egyptian Study Society is associated with the Denver Museum of Nature and Science. The society sponsors an interesting array of lectures and study groups. It also produces a monthly newsletter, *The Scribes Palette*, and a research journal, *The Ostracon*, that appears three times a year. Information is available at the Web site www.egyptstudy.org.

Internet Web Sites

An increasing amount of Egyptological information is available on the Internet. As is the case with the Internet in general, the quality of the information can range from inspirational to mediocre and everything in between. Web sites can also be ephemeral, appearing and disappearing unpredictably. The sites listed here were active as of summer 2001, but I can offer no guarantee as to their survival or changing content. Needless to say, I am not responsible for their content, except, of course, for my own material on my own site.

My best suggestion is to choose some of these good sites and do a little "surfing," especially if they have associated links to other sites. Keep in mind that this is a mere sample. Try using your favorite search engine to locate specific topics of interest.

Institutions

Ägyptische Museum, Berlin, Germany
www.smb.spk-berlin.de/amp/s.html

Egypt at the British Museum
www.thebritishmuseum.ac.uk/world/egypt/egypt.html

Centre for Computer-aided Egyptological Research
www.ccer.ggl.ruu.nl/ccer/default.html

Egyptian Museum, Cairo
www.tourism.egnet.net/Attractions_Detail.asp?code=6

Griffith Institute, Oxford (The notes of Howard Carter, Sir Alan Gardiner, and others are housed in this wonderful Institute.)
www.ashmol.ox.ac.uk/Griffith.html

Museo Egizio, Torino (One of the world's great Egyptian collections.)
www.multix.it/museoegizio_to

Oriental Institute, University of Chicago (A prestigious institute specializing in Egypt and the rest of the ancient Near East.)
www-oi.uchicago.edu/OI/default.html

Supreme Council of Antiquities, Egypt (The Egyptian government agency with the awesome responsibility of supervising Egypt's ancient monuments.)
www.guardians.net/sca

Research Resources

Regional Index: Ancient Egypt (Lots of online sources.)
www.oi.uchicago.edu/OI/DEPT/RA/ABZU/ABZU_REGINDX_EGYPT.HTML

Egyptology Resources—Cambridge (The first, and certainly one of the best, Egyptological sites on the Net.)
www.newton.cam.ac.uk/egypt/index.html

Tutankhamun Data Base, Griffith Institute (Notes from the tomb.)
www.ashmol.ox.ac.uk/gri/4tut.html

Other Good Sites

Ancient Egyptian Language Discussion List (This site is aimed at those of all abilities interested in studying ancient Egyptian language and texts on their own. Beginners are welcome.)
www.rostau.demon.co.uk/AEgyptian-L/index.html

Animal Mummies
www.animalmummies.com

Australian Egyptology
www.zeta.org.au/~ptahotep

Egyptian Ministry of Tourism
touregypt.net

Egyptologists' Electronic Forum (A useful reference site and serious discussion list.)

showcase.netins.net/web/ankh/eefmain.html

Guardian's Egypt
www.guardians.net/egypt/egyptreg.htm

George Hart's Egyptology Page
www.homeusers.prestel.co.uk/hatbat

Zahi Hawass (Home page of one of Egypt's foremost archaeologists.)
guardians.net/hawass/index.htm

National Geographic: At the Tomb of Tutankhamun
www.nationalgeographic.com/features/98/egypt/

Reeder's Egypt Page
www.egyptology.com/reeder

Don Ryan's Home Page (Egyptological research in the Valley of the Kings and other topics by the author of this book.)
www.plu.edu/~ryandp

The Theban Mapping Project (Loads of information on the Valley of the Kings and the Theban Necropolis.)
www.kv5.com

Scottish Egyptology
www.akhet.co.uk/scotland.htm

Theban Royal Mummy Project
home.talkcity.com/CurioCt/thebanmummies/mummypages1/intro.htm

Fun Stuff

Ancient Egypt Films
www.wepwawet.nl/films/

Mousey, the famous Mouse-Egyptologist (This mouse really gets around … squeek!)
members.aol.com/Egyptmouse

Tomb of the Chihuahua Pharaohs! (Enter if you dare!)
www.neferchichi.com

Trumpet of Tutankhamun (Hear the honk of one the actual trumpets found in Tut's tomb … before it shattered during a 1939 performance.)
www.ccer.ggl.ruu.nl/ccer/trumpet.html

Appendix D

Egypt Abroad: Museums with Egyptian Collections

It's great to read about ancient Egypt, but there's nothing like seeing the actual physical remnants of that remarkable civilization to bring life to your studies. Short of traveling to Egypt itself, a visit to a museum holding Egyptian antiquities will prove a very fascinating and educational experience. Many museums in North America have varying quantities of Egyptian antiquities in their collections. Special traveling Egyptian exhibitions are held occasionally, and many museums with Egyptian collections provide lecture series on topics of Egyptological interest. In an effort to be concise, only a few museums, generally with large Egyptian collections, are listed alphabetically. Some of the Web sites offer excellent peeks.

Art Museum of the University of Memphis
University of Memphis
Memphis, TN
www.memst.edu/egypt/main.html

Brooklyn Museum of Art
200 Eastern Parkway
Brooklyn, NY
www.brooklynart.org

Carnegie Museum of Natural History
4400 Forbes Ave.
Pittsburgh, PA
www.clpgh.org/cmnh

Cincinnati Art Museum
Eden Park
Cincinnati, OH
www.cincinnatiartmuseum.com

Cleveland Museum of Art
11150 East Blvd.
Cleveland, OH
www.clemusart.com

Detroit Institute of Arts
5200 Woodward Ave.
Detroit, MI
www.dia.org

Michael C. Carlos Museum
Emory University
Atlanta, GA
www.emory.edu/CARLOS

Field Museum of Natural History
Roosevelt Road and Lake Shore Drive
Chicago, IL
www.fmnh.org

Kelsey Museum of Archaeology
University of Michigan
Ann Arbor, MI
www.umich.edu/~kelseydb

Los Angeles County Museum of Art
5905 Wilshire Blvd.
Los Angeles, CA
www.lacma.org

Phoebe A. Hearst Museum of Anthropology
University of California, Berkeley
Berkeley, CA
www.qal.berkeley.edu/~hearst

The Metropolitan Museum of Art
5th Avenue at 82nd Street
New York, NY
www.metmuseum.org

Museum of Fine Arts, Boston
465 Huntington Ave.
Boston, MA
www.mfa.org

Nelson-Atkins Museum of Art
4525 Oak Street
Kansas City, MO
www.nelson-atkins.org

Oriental Institute Museum
1155 East 58th St.
Chicago, IL
www-oi.uchicago.edu/OI/MUS/OI_Museum.html

Rosicrucian Egyptian Museum
Rosicrucian Park
San Jose, CA
www.rosicrucian.org/mus-plan/0-museum.html

Royal Ontario Museum
100 Queen's Park
Toronto, ON, Canada
www.rom.on.ca

Museum of Archaeology and Anthropology
University of Pennsylvania
33rd and Spruce Streets
Philadelphia, PA
www.upenn.edu/museum

Virginia Museum of Fine Arts
2800 Grove Ave.
Richmond, VA
www.vmfa.state.va.us

Walters Art Gallery
600 North Charles St.
Baltimore, MD
www.thewalters.org

Egypt, Europe, and Elsewhere

Collections of Egyptian antiquities can be found all over the world. Here are some of the bigger ones.

Egypt

Egyptian Museum, Cairo
www.tourism.egnet.net/Attractions_Detail.asp?code=6

Graeco-Roman Museum, Alexandria

Luxor Museum, Luxor

Nubia Museum, Aswan
www.sis.gov.eg/egyptinf/culture/html/nubia000.htm

Numerous smaller museums also can be found throughout Egypt.

Europe

Many museums in Europe display Egyptian antiquities. Four of the largest collections are as follows:

British Museum, London, United Kingdom
www.thebritishmuseum.ac.uk/world/egypt/egypt.html

Musée du Louvre, Paris, France
www.louvre.fr/louvrea.htm

Museo Egizio, Turin, Italy
www.multix.it/museoegizio_to

Ägyptische Museum, Berlin, Germany
www.smb.spk-berlin.de/amp/s.html

Index

B

Y–Z